PREDATOR HUNTING
PROVEN STRATEGIES THAT WORK FROM EAST TO WEST

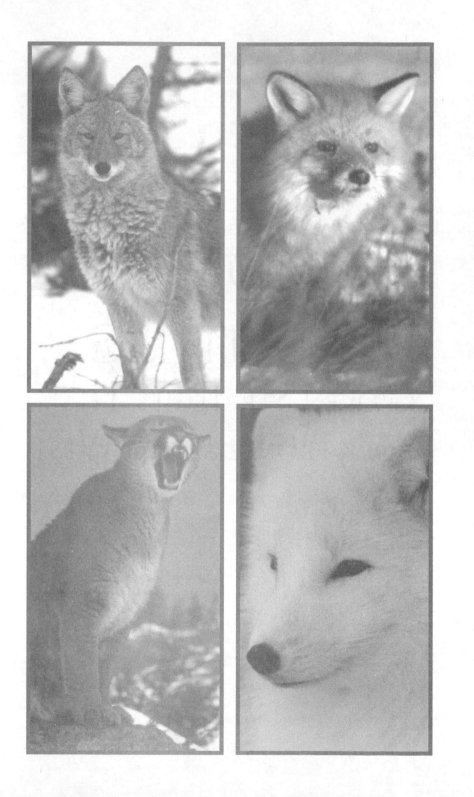

PREDATOR HUNTING
PROVEN STRATEGIES THAT WORK FROM EAST TO WEST

Ron Spomer

SKYHORSE PUBLISHING

Skyhorse Publishing books may be purchased in bulk at special discounts for sales promotion, corporate gifts, fund-raising, or educational purposes. Special editions can also be created to specifications. For details, contact the Special Sales Department, Skyhorse Publishing, 307 West 36th Street, 11th Floor, New York, NY 10018 or info@skyhorsepublishing.com.

Skyhorse® and Skyhorse Publishing® are registered trademarks of Skyhorse Publishing, Inc.®, a Delaware corporation.

Visit our website at www.skyhorsepublishing.com

10 9 8 7 6 5 4 3

Library of Congress Cataloging-in-Publication Data is available on file.

ISBN 978-1-61608-709-8

Printed in the United States of America

Dedication
To Allen, Mike, and Richard, who set me on the hunter's path.

Table of Contents

Introduction

Competition created the first predator hunter. Jackals stealing freshly killed meat would not have endeared themselves to hungry hominids. Wolves that ravaged flocks along the Euphrates needed to be killed or driven away. And so it went throughout history. Fox in the henhouse. Lion in the cow byre. Coyote among the flock. The competition had to go. And so predators were despised and systematically eliminated from much of Europe, the Eastern United States, the Plains, and the Rockies. It was a dog-eat-man, man-eat-dog kind of world.

These days, few of us are directly affected by marauding meat-eaters. Our poultry and beef are safely stored in supermarket coolers. But still, we hunt predators—no longer with enmity, but with respect—respect for their cunning and persistence, respect for the roles they play in nature, respect for balance in the remnants of the natural world we have tipped askew with our roads, farms, cities, and ranches. By draining wetlands, flooding rivers, claiming the most fertile lands, and harvesting the best vegetation, we shortchange prey species like quail, waterfowl, deer, and antelope. By mowing, trimming, burning, and spraying, we deplete nesting and escape cover for songbirds, grouse, and rabbits. At the same time, we provide new habitat to feed and sustain predators.

On the glaciated plains of the Dakotas, we've planted trees and shrubs that provide winter shelter for fox, skunks, and raccoons that couldn't survive there in the past. Come spring, they are fat and ready to raid duck nests. Across the nation, we've provided culverts, junkyards, old barns, cellars, haystacks, and rock piles where predators breed and hide, ready to pounce on quail, grouse, rabbits, pheasants, and deer. There are table scraps and bowls of pet food at our back doors and road-killed birds, deer, and rabbits on our highways for fox and coyotes that could not catch them themselves.

With the natural system out of whack, it seems only reasonable that we assume our responsibilities to manage predator populations—for their own good as well as the good of prey species. Since the decline of the fur market in the late 1980s, rabies and mange epidemics have killed hundreds of thousands of overly abundant predators—a particularly gruesome form of population control. Hunters can do better, while sparking the economy through the purchase of tools and supplies, funding wildlife research through purchase of hunting licenses, and easing pressure on prey species by controlling their predators. A report released by the International Association of Fish and Wildlife Agencies noted that the coyote population in the southeast United States alone could increase by 210 percent if hunting and trapping were outlawed.

If you believe in working within nature's system of organic renewal and limiting the impact of humans on the environment, why wouldn't you use biodegradable fur? Rodents, rabbits, and birds died so that predators could grow that fur. Why waste it? It seems particularly disrespectful and wasteful to permit a fox pelt to rot on the ground while we pollute the planet with petrochemicals to manufacture faux fur.

None of this is to suggest that predators are evil and should be extirpated. Such was the mistaken philosophy of the past. We now know that carnivores are essential cogs in the gears of life. They eat overachieving rodents, mold deer into the alert, swift beasts they are, and force quail to fly fast and strong. At the same time, we must acknowledge that farmers and ranchers lose millions of dollars to predators each year and that government animal damage control specialists remove thousands of problem predators annually, costing taxpayers more millions. We must also recognize that, in certain situations, coyotes can and do nearly wipe out isolated populations of antelope or deer; that mountain lions have exterminated populations of endangered bighorn sheep; and that black bears in some areas are the number one killer of elk calves.

One of the major differences between humans and other predators is that four-legged meat-eaters do not comprehend the ramifications of their actions. A coyote would eat the last whooping crane on earth and wish only that he could eat another. A red fox would gobble the last mountain plover without flinching. A bobcat would happily eat the last masked bobwhite. We cannot condemn them for this. They are only doing what nature has programmed them to do for millions of years. It is not their fault that humans have pushed so many species to the edge of existence. Nor is it their responsibility. But it *is* ours. Ideally we should strive to protect and restore wild habitats for all species. When that proves impossible and our activities favor predators over prey species, we should accept our responsibility to control predator populations.

So get out and enjoy a predator hunt from time to time, especially in places where predator populations are high and prey populations are dwindling. Contact private landowners and offer to help control predators that are killing livestock. If you don't, a government control officer will probably have to, consuming your tax dollars in the process. Assisting farmers and ranchers in this manner cements relationships and opens doors to other outdoor opportunities.

Predator hunters may never alleviate the imbalances in nature, but we can at least try.

—Ron Spomer

1

Sons of the Pioneers

A Brief History of Predator Hunting

There is no Columbus of Predator Hunting; no father of Fox Hunters. No historical record exists of the first human to stalk or lure a toothy competitor to its demise, so we can speculate freely. Given how close early humans lived to the land, it isn't hard to believe that they saw predators running to the cries of rabbits and quickly learned to imitate them. Ah, but it's even more likely that they first saw predators running to the cries of human babies. Gruesome though that now sounds, it must have once been a common natural event—and it explains the shiver down your spine when you hear your first "dying rabbit" cries.

Using your own voice to mimic a crying baby isn't difficult. This was probably the manner in which predators were lured to spear, bow, and gun for thousands of years. But somewhere along the line, hunters discovered how to hold a tough blade of grass between their thumbs and blow over it to raise a realistic scream. Much later, someone fooling around with a duck or crow call probably recognized how similar it sounded to a rabbit in distress, modified it, and invented the reed predator call.

However often primitive humans mimicked the sounds of prey to lure predators, it

With no historical record of the first predator hunter, it is easy to speculate predator hunting has been around since early humans.

1

was not known or widely reported as a hunting tactic until halfway through the last century. That's when men like Murray Burnham, Adam Lindsey, and Dwight Thomas began building and selling rabbit squallers made of wood, plastic, or cow horn. Johnny Stewart, of Waco, Texas, gave predator calling a big boost in the early 1960s when he began selling not only calls but also 45-rpm phonograph recordings of animals in distress. These proved to many skeptics that wild animals did scream—and suggested they could imitate them.

For many years predator calling was a mere sideshow in the panoply of American hunting. Few folks could afford to waste time and money shooting "worthless" predators when there were tasty birds, bunnies, and big game to pursue. However, increasing leisure time and a booming economy after World War II made it possible for more average people to hunt more often. Many picked up one of the new predator calls on the market and, while hunting other game, tried them. Of course, each time a call brought a fox or coyote into shooting range, the caller's heart skipped a beat and the news spread down to the local feed store or gun shop.

The lid blew completely off in the 1970s, when fox and coyote pelts began selling for $30, $50, even as much as $100, and bobcat pelts bounced as high as $300. A good caller could make a living hunting four months a year. Even a mediocre caller could pay for a new rifle or shotgun with a few weekend hunts. Predator calling quickly came of age.

Since the mid-eighties, fur prices have fluctuated, but predator calling is more popular than ever. Rifle makers offer special "coyote" and "predator" rifles. Camouflage designers sell grassland, woodland, and snow patterns. There are closed-reed calls, open-reed calls, diaphragm calls, digital electronic calls, coyote howlers, rabbit decoys, scents, scent removers, scent-proof clothing, bipods, scopes, enough varieties of predator ammunition to confuse a ballistician, instructional videos on DVDs and YouTube, and even predator-hunting books— like this one.

Predator hunting is popular for all the obvious reasons. Seasons are long. Bag limits are generous or nonexistent. Licenses are inexpensive and available over the counter. Most public and private land is open to predator hunters. A fur-bearing carnivore of some species lives in every state and every type of habitat in North America.

Competition is still relatively light. There are no antler points to count, no trophy scores to tally. Mostly, though, there is the indescribable pleasure of going afield to interact with some of the slyest, wariest, most beautiful, most exciting animals on earth—critters that jump start the most jaded heart. The best reason to hunt predators is because you love it.

Why Do They Do the Things They Do?

Come and Get It—The Call to Dinner

Most of us understand the basic premise of predator calling. The eaters hear the eatees calling, "Come and get it!" So they do. But why cry wolf in the first place? What compels every bird, bunny, fawn, and frightened pup to wail in distress? Some have suggested that the sudden, sharp sounds are an attempt at distraction. Shock your uninvited dinner guest into dropping you and you might be able to hastily excuse yourself from the table. But this doesn't quite explain why rabbits bawl when caught in a fence.

Another theory holds that calling attention to your plight invites competition. At first this sounds like a really stupid idea. More gluttons lusting after your flesh? Ah, but gluttons being gluttons, they are likely to squabble over the choicest morsels, giving said morsel a chance to escape. I can see possibilities in this approach. Let's say an inexperienced hawk sinks its claws into your hind leg instead of your lungs. You scream, you flop, you wail, and Hi-Yo Silver, your friendly neighborhood coyote comes to the rescue. Dog sees bird, dog attacks

A predator's ears are always alert to the sounds of prey.

Normally secretive and nocturnal, bobcats will hunt in broad daylight, especially if they hear the wailing of prey in distress.

bird. Bird sees dog, bird drops bunny and tries to fly away. Dog chases bird, trying to catch it. Rabbit crawls into hole to lick its puncture wounds. Cry me a river—this could work.

Yet another hypothesis suggests that a form of altruism is at work: the cry warns other animals away. We're not implying conscious choice here, but an instinctive, self-perpetuating genetic adaptation bred over millennia. Let us suppose that some ancient cottontails involuntarily screamed when attacked. Neighbors and friends heard and hid to live another day. They remembered the screams and hid again when they heard similar cries. Slowly, ever so slowly over generations, the rabbit populations that screamed when attacked were the ones that flourished. The populations that didn't scream languished because their numbers were more quickly reduced. Bingo. Survival of the fittest.

I don't know. Sounds like a stretch to me, particularly when you consider that many species that shriek are loners and most predators that eat them are loners. There are limited chances to learn and limited benefits in flight once an attack is underway. If a bobcat already has a bunny in its clutches, it isn't likely to attack another bunny. Now among colonial animals such as prairie dogs, this theory makes sense. When one shouts in alarm, dozens around it see what the fuss is about. Thus, prairie dogs bark warnings and dive underground when coyotes stroll through town.

My favorite explanation for why prey animals scream hinges on observation and common sense: terror. They scream because they're surprised, frightened and just plain terrorized. And maybe because it hurts. What does a baby do when a stranger picks it up? Cries. What does a nonsocialized puppy do when a human grabs it? Cries. What does a fawn, lamb, or calf do when cornered against a fence? You

By the time it's three months old, a red fox pup has already learned to keep those satellite dish ears up and tuned to the wails of prey animals in trouble.

4

guessed it. It makes sense to keep quiet when you're trying to avoid detection, but once you're in the clutches, why not give voice to your hopelessness and despair. *Terror.*

Call Me Anything but Late to Supper

We may never know exactly why prey animals cry, but I think we understand what motivates predators to respond. A free lunch. Duh.

Some response to panic cries may be genetic. Any species that's been around as long as coyotes or bobcats would have to have benefited from an inbred curiosity to investigate the sounds of prey. The critter that moves toward the sound gets extra fuel and survives lean times, passing its traits to subsequent generations. The critter that ignores distress cries goes hungry and dies—no descendants to ignore the next distress cry.

But education and experience, I believe, play a much larger role in how eagerly and quickly a meat eater answers the call. This explains why jackrabbit calls might elicit just a few responses in eastern forests but eager responses in Wyoming sagebrush. Eastern coyotes should have a genetic curiosity to check out the alto wails of a big jack, but western coyotes have personal experiences to drive them forward.

Most predators learn to associate prey screams with food when dear old mom brings home a crippled but very much alive rabbit, bird, or fawn. Set down before the den of tumbling kits, the hapless victim tries to run, is bowled over, screams in terror, and attempts again to run. The pups play with it, swat it, worry it, and eventually taste blood. They tear it apart. A couple of classes like this and they're all ears when they hear that familiar hullabaloo. Later, when mom guides them on their first training hunts, they hear more wailing prey. Last one there gets table scraps. Within weeks, like Pavlov's dogs, they're programmed to race to the dinner bell.

Not So Fast, Shorty

In puppyhood, the early responders get the worm, so to speak, but eventually complications modify behavior. Suppose the runt of the coyote litter one day gets left behind by its more energetic siblings and mother? Its sharp little ears detect that happy cry—"fresh meat"—and it rushes to be first in line for once. But when it rounds the corner, it stumbles onto a big, dark stranger that chases it off, growling and snapping at its heels. Thus is born the cautious responder.

Similar scenarios may account for the slow approach of most bobcats. If they're living in coyote country—and most are—they quickly learn that a screaming rabbit could be the centerpiece at a coyote picnic. Not even a sharp-clawed, fully grown tom bobcat wants to crash a party of nearly grown, late-summer coyote pups and their hard-bitten bitch. So, discretion being the better part of valor, cats creep, stalk, and watch—they take their time.

Then there are the nervous fox, both red and gray. As pups, they learn pretty much the way coyotes do. Mom brings dinner on the hoof, they finish it off and remember the sound effects. If they range where bobcats and coyotes are scarce to nonexistent, they learn about first-come, first-served. Sometimes they catch a small hawk or owl in the bargain. But the first time they crash a party of bigger predators, they're lucky to escape with their lives. A sudden attack from what should have been "dinner on the house" can ruin a little fox's appetite for months. Thus educated, any carnivore comes more cautiously to the call.

Competition

While Disney and Hollywood have systematically brainwashed generations with the happy myth of Nature as Harmony, predators have been living a grittier reality. Instead of singing and dancing together, they compete, squabble, and fight for limited resources. This leads to repeated, identifiable behaviors. Hunters who know them can turn them to advantage.

Territoriality

Unlike grazing animals, predators are aggressively territorial. They must be in order to survive. Grazers live amid a veritable ocean of helpless forage. Bite to the right, bite to the left—there's enough for everyone, and it isn't running away. Grazers can afford to amass in huge herds that provide protection from predators. Extra eyes and noses on alert; extra bodies to surround and defend the young; slower associates to deflect attention from you. Sharing the grass is an acceptable trade-off for that kind of security.

Predators, on the other hand, would soon lick the platter clean and find the cupboard bare if they all congregated where food was abundant. Wolves and lions will join in cooperative packs or prides in order to take down large beasts, but they don't share their hunting territories with other packs. Coyotes will sometimes hunt in family groups when deer are the main course.

A mature whitetail may be tough to pull down, but coyotes quickly learn to heed the cries of weak or injured deer, especially fawns.

Mated pairs of many species hunt together for a short season. Otherwise, predators are loners. Every cat for himself. To improve their odds of success, they stake
out their living spaces based on relative prey abundance and actively defend
them. Woe to the wolf that trespasses into the heart of another wolf pack's territory. It'll be torn apart.

Territorial defense is why wolves, coyotes, and fox urinate on rocks and posts
and why cats squirt against trees and scratch dirt piles over their dung. A need to
protect the home turf sets coyotes and wolves to howling and mountain lions to
prowling. They've got to show the colors, rattle the sabers, and intimidate the
neighbors. Male mountain lions attack any other males they come across in order
to maintain breeding rights to all females within their vast territories. While
females might find enough prey to live comfortably within twenty to fifty square
miles, males often defend three hundred square miles in order to have access to
additional females.

Fox, being smaller and placing lighter demands on local resources, can live in
smaller territories—perhaps three to five square miles. Bobcats, too. Adaptable
coyotes might make do with a few square miles in rich country but might range
over one hundred square miles where food is scarce. Wolves require even larger
home ranges.

This need to spread out inspires pioneering among predators, which in turn
fills new or recently emptied habitats. Young animals, especially, wander widely
in late fall either because of an innate yearning or a shortage of prey or as a
response to pressure from established adults. When the resident "top dog" starts
kicking your butt every time you come within view, you soon develop a taste for
travel. Red fox and coyote pups may move a hundred, even two hundred miles
during this period, following predictable travel routes like ridge tops, cattle trails,
and stream valleys. En route, they are set upon by established locals, so they keep
moving until the harassment stops. If the hunting is good, they hang out their
shingle: Wile E. Coyote, Proprietor. No Trespassing. Day by day they extend or
retract their territorial bounda-
ries as necessary, marking scent
posts and noting the No Trespassing signs of neighbors until
an uneasy, fluctuating status quo
is established. Where territories

Predators that don't compete for the
same resources tolerate one another in
close proximity. Red fox routinely
scavenge tidbits from grizzly kills.

Arctic fox are attacked and killed by wolves in far north Canada, but usually not eaten.

are overpopulated, constant conflict wastes energy. Excessive harvest depletes resources until everyone goes to bed hungry. Disease afflicts weakened animals and spreads through frequent contact. Misery and death follow until a shortage of predators enables rodents, rabbits, birds, deer, and other prey to flourish. The few surviving predators—or pioneers from far away—can again earn a decent living and raise families. And the cycle repeats.

There is some evidence that wandering may be genetic. The biggest, strongest, healthiest pups in any litter seem to disperse sooner and farther, as if some internal mechanism were pushing them. Humans should be able to relate to this. Children who are bright, strong, energetic, and creative seem to strike out on their own early and boldly, while the less secure, less successful kids stick close to home, becoming fodder for late-night comedians.

Racist Troubles

While we expect species to squabble among themselves, many of us are surprised to learn that some predators are, well, racists. Perhaps species-ists would be a more accurate term. This flies in the face of conventional wisdom. In Hollywood's reality, wolves and fox frolic together—or at least ignore one another. In northern Canada, researchers have documented wolves regularly killing arctic foxes and playing with their corpses. They don't eat them, just toss them about and chase one another like Afghanis playing their version of polo with the body of a dead calf.

Mountain lion researchers have come upon bobcats freshly killed by cougars. Wolves have been documented killing cougars. Bobcats will surprise and kill young fox. Wolves will drive off coyotes and kill them if they get the chance. Biologists call this interspecific competition. Whether the critters understand that their resources are coveted by their neighbors or they're merely being bullies, the result is the same. The smaller animals get marginalized.

It's telling that widely disparate predators don't seem to exhibit interspecific animosity, while more closely competitive species do. The grizzly, for instance, will ignore the fox scavenging about its kill, but not the wolves. Wolves and grizzlies compete for moose and caribou. Similarly, grizzlies catch and kill black

Colonial prey species such as prairie dogs benefit from bold displays and alarm barks when predators are sighted.

bears. Thus you don't find black bears in grizzly country unless there are trees large enough to climb. Lewis & Clark found silvertips far out on the plains but black bears only in or near forests.

The interspecific competitors of most interest to human hunters are fox and coyotes. To a large degree, the bigger canine hunts the same prey as the smaller—mice, voles, kangaroo rats, cottontails, and small birds. Neither probably appreciates the competition, but only the coyote is in a position to do anything about it. It harries, chases, and kills every red or gray fox in its territory. Death to the fox. What option does its little cousin have but to flee? Even if it stays and manages to keep one jump ahead of its persecutors, a fox in a coyote neighborhood will spend so much time looking over its shoulder it won't find enough to eat.

Two hundred years ago, coyotes found themselves in the fox's boots— er, paws—when wolves ruled most of North America. In the West, where there was room to see trouble coming and run before it got close, coyotes eked out a living, staying one jump ahead of their bullying cousins. In fact, much of coyote's daily bread came in the form of bison carcasses left behind by sated wolves. In the East, however, vast forests limited the availability of small prey species and enabled wolves to surprise coyotes at close range.

Once wolves were extirpated from the East and forests were broken into a patchwork of fields and pastures where smaller, more easily caught prey could thrive, coyotes pioneered eastward. Today they live in virtually every state, to the detriment of red and gray fox. Where wolves are again proliferating in the Rocky Mountains and Great Lakes states, coyotes are either declining or at least becoming much more cautious.

Red fox are call shy and approach cautiously, usually circling to get your wind.

9

Open, rolling grasslands are tailored for coyotes and long-range rifles.

When I was a boy, red fox were the biggest, baddest canine predators in eastern South Dakota. By the early 1970s, coyote populations began expanding east from the Missouri River hills, and fox melted before them. Today I'm shocked to see a red fox where, in the 1960s, they were common. Research in North Dakota revealed that fox learn to live where coyotes fear to tread. The bigger dogs, for instance, prefer large, relatively undisturbed chunks of rugged grasslands and pastures. Fox, therefore, settle close to farms, towns, and disturbed agricultural fields. I've observed this same relationship in Idaho and Texas. Out on the sage and grass, I find coyotes. Around barns, in roadside culverts, and on the edges of towns, I find red fox. I stopped for gasoline late one winter night in McCall, Idaho, and suspected I'd been driving too long when I saw a red fox sitting between two pumps. But it was a red fox. The proprietor came out and fed it a hot dog.

Normally, when I go to Texas I see, hear, and often hunt coyotes, but one year I hunted the Pecos River country and never saw so much as a track. Turned out it was sheep country, and local ranchers had worked long and hard to eliminate every coyote within earshot. As a result, I saw more gray fox, raccoons, and skunks than I ever had before. Last February I called predators on several Texas ranches for three days and saw dozens of coyotes and two bobcats, but nary a fox. Two years ago in west Texas we hunted at night, bringing in numerous swift fox, gray fox, and bobcats, but no coyotes.

Bobcats are aloof to most of these internecine wars because, despite eating many of the same critters as coyotes and fox, they are not dogs. Certainly they'll kill small fox and even coyotes when it's easy—and coyotes will take out bobcats when they think they can get away with it unscathed, but mostly each avoids the other. Cats hang in heavy cover, using stealth to ambush prey. Fox and coyotes roam more open habitats, eat a more varied diet, and do more chasing. Thus, you can expect to find bobcats living among canines in areas with considerable brush, trees, riparian habitat, dense weeds, and jagged, rocky cliffs. Here they can hide, hunt, and escape the clutches of their enemies.

Knowing these things can improve your success afield. If you hunt big, open, isolated country, expect coyotes rather than fox. In wolf country, expect coyotes to be less abundant or at least shy. As you near more settled areas with crops, anticipate fox. If you see little or no coyote sign, watch for fox. Where you find considerable close cover, assume that a bobcat could be slowly stalking in for a look. Remember, too, that the presence of coyotes will inhibit a fox's response to a call. Depending on their experiences, fox may run from, rather than to, the cries of a wounded rabbit. You may have more luck calling with a mouse squeaker. You may need to work nearer escape cover—get closer to your subjects—before they'll respond. It may take them a bit longer to come in when set up near escape cover. Many predators will almost certainly try to circle downwind.

You don't have to be a world-class naturalist to hunt predators, but it helps. Study behavior both in the field and in the library, and you could become a better predator hunter.

3

Biography and Biology

The Natural History of Predators

Our government spends millions on investigative agencies like the FBI because criminals are easier to catch when you know something about them. The same applies to hunting predators. When are they most active? Where do they hunt and sleep? What routes do they travel? What evidence do they leave behind? Know your adversary and you're halfway to catching him.

Coyote

We can thank or curse farmers and ranchers for today's abundance of coyotes. Until farming and animal husbandry came along, coyotes were restricted to wide-open western habitat and oppressed by wolves. But wolves, because they ate

Most coyotes weigh between twenty and forty pounds.

sheep, cattle, and Old Bess the milk cow, were shot and poisoned into oblivion. Coyotes sat up and cheered. The little thirty-pound prairie wolves had been promoted to Chief Canine Predator, and they threw themselves into their new assignment with vigor, if not wild abandon.

Chickens, lambs, house cats, calves, foo-foo dogs, and even watermelons— there isn't much organic that a coyote won't eat. They've even carried off infants. None of these gastronomic choices has endeared the wild canines to humans, who, for well over a hundred years, have trapped, shot, poisoned, and cursed coyotes to no avail. Instead of shrinking under our onslaught, the durned dogs have thrived, increased, and spread to every state save Hawaii—and they're probably plotting to hijack a boat to get there.

Size and Color

Western coyotes range between twenty and forty pounds, males slightly larger than females. Northern specimens are larger than southern varieties. While migrating east around the Great Lakes, coyotes hybridized to some degree with wolves and domestic dogs (coydogs). Specimens as heavy as sixty pounds have been recorded in the Northeast. Overall, coyotes appear thin, sharp-nosed, sharp-eared, and relatively dainty compared to gray wolves, which are four times larger. Coyotes stand roughly two feet high at the shoulder and stretch three and a half to five feet from tail tip to nose.

Coyote coats vary from salt-and-pepper gray over the back and sides to buff—almost white—on neck, chest, and belly. Long, coarse guard hairs over the shoulders stand taller than elsewhere, giving the appearance of a ruff on older specimens. Sometimes these guard hairs trace a dark, almost black line down the spine and top of the bushy, fourteen-inch-long tail, which is carried below the back line most of the time. Lower legs, face, and back of ears are usually reddish brown. Eyes are yellow or amber.

Senses

The nose knows. A coyote sees well enough, but smell is its main defense. Much of its communication is also done through the nose. Its hearing is so sharp and accurate that from four hundred yards away, it can pinpoint a caller to within a few feet. On a calm day a hungry coyote sometimes responds to a call from two miles away. Like all dogs, coyotes are nearly color-blind. So long as you don't move or stand in the open, you can dress like a crazed NFL fan and call a coyote practically into your lap. Just don't let it smell you.

Voice and Communication

They howl, they yip, they bark, they growl. Coyotes may be our most vocal predator. High-pitched yipping and yowling—the classic coyote howl—is used for pack cohesion, territorial defense, and staying in touch. Single, clear howls are used to locate mates and announce territorial boundaries. Barking denotes alarm, suspicion, or dominance. If a coyote starts barking at you, your cover's blown. Coyotes mark territories and identify individuals with urine as well as dung scented with anal glands .

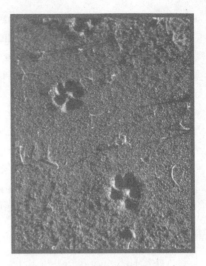

Coyote tracks look just like those of a medium-sized dog.

Tracks and Sign

Look for medium-sized dog prints along trails, dry washes, and field edges. Footprints will show four toes in an arc ahead of a triangular-shaped pad. Claws usually show ahead of toes. Prints measure 2 to 2 1/2 inches long and 11/2 to 2 inches wide. The stride— the distance between front and back feet—is around fourteen inches. When running,

Coyote scat frequently has lots of hair.

back feet strike ahead of front, and all are closely bunched, with several feet between the clusters.

Coyote scat is commonly left on roads and trails. It's cylindrical, usually half an inch in diameter and three to five inches long, black turning to gray with age, often with lots of hair that indicates what's been on the menu. Seasonally there may be berries, insects, and so on in the dung.

Mating and Young

Coyotes usually pair up in their first winter, breed in February, and stay together to raise the two to eighteen pups born sixty days after conception. The more abundant the forage and lower the coyote population, the higher the number of pups in a litter. Dens are usually enlarged badger or rockchuck holes on slopes, knolls, and banks. They're often partly concealed by brush or weeds. The male alone brings food the first few days after the pups are born. Then both

The wide-ranging and adaptable coyote can survive nearly anywhere, but is most abundant where prey is abundant and easy to catch.

adults hunt for the family. Within three weeks, the pups are venturing out of the den and eating solid food. If disturbed, the female may move the pups. They are weaned after a couple of months and begin traveling with ma and pa, learning how to hunt. Families may break up in early winter or stay together and hunt big game as a pack. Pups often stick together until late winter. Rarely youngsters from a previous litter will assist with their dam's new batch of pups.

Habitat

Coyotes remind me of a line from Frank Sinatra's hit song "New York New York," and I paraphrase: "If they can make it there, they'll make it anywhere." I've heard there are coyotes in Central Park. So there you go. Obviously coyotes do better in some habitats than others. On the Plains, it's wide-open grasslands. In the mountains, they like tundra ridges and meadows. In the desert, everything from brushy river bottoms to cactus flats suffices. Nowhere do they prefer deep woods except possibly in the East, where they are noted to avoid big, open fields. This, I assume, is a trait learned due to harassment. An abundance of prey, more than anything, seems to influence where coyotes live. Oh—they love to hang around cattle. Must remind them of great-great-great-great-Grandpa's bison.

Distribution

From Alaska through Mexico. Extreme northeast Canada doesn't support coyotes, but they are now widespread across eastern states. Just recently I hunted and bagged my first Florida coyote near Tampa Bay, of all places. The times they are a-changing.

Spomer proves that coyotes are now living under palm trees in Florida, a strange land for this predatory icon of the West.

Coyotes are opportunistic scavengers ready to feast on road-killed deer, winter-starved elk or anything else fortune throws in their path.

Daily Movement

In their five to one hundred-square mile territories coyotes generally hunt at dusk and dawn, sometimes deep into the night, and lay up by day, though this is no fast rule. You'll find coyotes in open pastures at noon sometimes. Mornings are usually most productive for calling. They like to howl at dawn and dusk, probably to round up their families or let the neighbors know they're home and defending the turf. In drought, they'll go to water daily. They like to bed at the heads of draws, in deep grass or brush, and near the crests of ridges.

Prey

Anything they can catch or scavenge—whatever is most abundant. When necessary they'll eat berries, fruits, insects, even cow dung.

Wolf

North American pioneers and settlers had no use for the world's largest wild dogs because they were direct and potentially dangerous competition for the same resources. The voracious predators ran in gangs and ate anything they could tear down—which was everything. Once wild bison and elk had been cleared to make room for farms and gardens, wolves were cleared to make room for sheep and cows. By the mid 1930s, government trappers had pretty much killed off wolves across North America to the south of Canada, leaving an uneasy peace. The huge dogs still thrived in the

Most wolves weigh between 100 and 150 pounds.

northern wilderness where moose, bison and vast herds of caribou could sustain them.

Now that has changed. Wolves are again roaming in the northern Great Lakes states and from northern California to central Montana where they find no caribou and precious few bison. So they're eating mule deer, moose, elk, and domestic livestock in what many consider excessive numbers. Elk herds in some areas have declined 90 percent since wolves were introduced in 1995. Hunting seasons are opening and the wolf is becoming the hot new commodity.

Here's how it happened: Wolf lovers, dissatisfied with a shattered North American landscape that didn't have all of its original denizens, insisted wolves be brought back to the Northern Rockies, forgetting or ignoring the absence of 30 million bison that historically fed them. An experimental population of Canadian gray wolves was turned loose in Montana, Idaho, and Wyoming with an agreement between the Federal Government and those states that, if and when the wolves increased to three hundred individuals and ten breeding pairs (packs), management would return to the states. The wolves did their part within about five years, but (surprise!) animal rights activists screamed, sued, and got judges to overrule biologists and block the states from taking over management. This went on year after year until more than 1,800 wolves were scouring the region for prey. U.S. Fish and Wildlife Service agents were trapping or shooting dozens of wolves each year that were killing cattle and sheep. USFWS biologists said the new wolves were thriving far above population goals and the states should take over management. Moose numbers nosedived. Wolf packs even killed off other wolf packs as they fought for territories. Congress finally agreed with USFWS biologists and removed these wolves from the Endangered Species Act protection. Eventually even President Obama agreed with the biologists. Yet the antis insisted they knew better. They filed lawsuits and requested court injunctions and prevented returning wolf management to the individual states. Year after year.

As this is written in early 2012, Montana and Idaho have been allowed to again manage their wolves. Wyoming probably soon will. Hunting seasons have been conducted and a few hundred wolves taken. Meanwhile, wolves have pioneered into Washington and Oregon. One made it into Northern California where it was given a hero's welcome—by urban humans, if not rural deer, elk, and Angus herds. Inevitably, more and more wolf seasons and hunts will have to be conducted as these top predators proliferate and again compete for many of the same things people want—more mule deer, whitetails, blacktails, elk, moose, and other wildlife squeezed into ever smaller areas of suitable habitat. Someday hunts will become legal in Minnesota, Wisconsin, and Michigan where wolves are also thriving. Given the toughness, resilience, cunning, and ability of these social animals to survive nearly anywhere, they'll undoubtedly continue to spread across the West and probably the Midwest, Southwest, and even the Southeast. Expect annual hunts to continue in an effort to control the packs and permit their prey a chance to reproduce and grow. States will establish annual seasons and

Northern wolves usually have white, gray, brown, and black fur.

harvest a few wolves, but hunters will never jeopardize the species. At best they can hope to hold their numbers at levels that permit large ungulates to recover and again thrive. You'll want to do your part by making a wolf hunt of your own some day.

Size and Color

If you think a coyote looks big, wait until you see your first wolf. A big male will stand as high at the shoulders as a small whitetail and stretch six feet from nose to tail tip. Long hairs make them look even larger in winter. These are coyotes supersized. Some folks claim they'll weigh 200 pounds, but 175 pounds is probably the record. Figure 100 to 150 pounds as a good average for adults.

Wolves vary from pure white to jet black and every shade between. The southern wolf is quite reddish-brown, thus called "red wolf," but they are endangered and rare, although introductions have been planned or undertaken. A pack of northern wolves can and usually does contain white, gray, brown, and black specimens. The eyes are yellow or amber.

Senses

Like coyotes, wolves use their sense of smell as an unfailing defense. Just as trained golden retrievers can smell drugs or bombs hidden deep in luggage, wolves can smell things we'd never imagine. They track one another and their prey for miles just by smelling footprints, often hours old. Those sharp wolf ears aren't far behind the black nose. Wolves communicate by howling, and they're always alert for the slightest audio disturbance in their world. They'll also stare across vast, open spaces watching for moving game, but they aren't particularly effective at picking out a human standing or sitting motionless in just a bit of cover. They do not see a full range of colors, having sacrificed cone cells in their eyes in exchange for additional rod cells, which give them superior night vision.

Voice and Communication

Everyone knows the howl of a wolf. It's the baritone version of the coyote. Lone wolves call to find others. Packs howl to summon one another for a hunt. But these dogs do a lot more growling, whining, snarling, and moaning than howling—everyday communication that settles quarrels, establishes dominance, and otherwise manages pack life. Like coyotes, wolves do a lot of scent marking with both urine and droppings. They also scratch after defecating to enhance the smell from anus glands or to add a visual marker. The bulk of their day-to-day communication is probably through body language—how the tail is carried, ears are laid back, teeth are bared. Dominant wolves carry the highest tails, subdominant the lowest tails. But for hunters, it's the howls that are most useful, for they identify a pack's whereabouts and, one hopes, call them in.

Tracks and Signs

You won't mistake a wolf track for anything else. The paw prints are huge. Figure four to five inches front to back, and about four inches wide. The front feet are larger than the hind feet. You'd need a Great Dane to match these, and Great Danes rarely travel in packs. Wolves follow trails, roads, beaches, riverbanks—wherever the going is easy. I've seen their tracks running for miles down Idaho back roads.

Wolf scat is classic dog poo. Think elongated cylinders, but full of hair, bone, and other prey parts that couldn't be digested. Wolf teeth and jaws are strong enough to crush nearly every bone on an elk and most on a bison. Watch for swarms of ravens, crows, and magpies feasting on the remains of wolf kills, but don't expect to find a lot of remaining edibles. I've seen a pack polish off a full-grown caribou bull in an hour. In Jackson Hole I followed wolf tracks to what remained of a bull bison, and it wasn't much. Some wooly winter hide, the skull, a few vertebrae, and leg bones.

Wolf tracks are easy to distinguish, as they are about five inches long and the front feet are larger than the hind feet.

Even the cartilage in the hooves had been cleaned out right down to the black keratin of the external hoof itself.

Mating and Young

Wolves are unique in that an alpha male and female mate while the rest of the pack plays a support role. Funny how the subdominant ones will tolerate this, given what we know about domestic dogs around a bitch in heat. But that's the program worked out by Nature to enable the pack to find enough food to fuel itself and bring new recruits into the group. The alpha female will carry her growing litter (four to as many as eighteen pups) for about three months before whelping in a den, usually a burrow on a slope or bank. A month after birth, pups will be venturing out of the den and eating regurgitated meat. At just six to eight weeks they'll be weaned. If danger threatens, the female will move the pups. If not, the entire pack will abandon the den site when the pups are about ninety days old and capable of trotting along for considerable distances.

Habitat

For now, mountain forests and meadows, some vast sagebrush, and grassland deserts. But as wolves pioneer ever deeper into their historic homeland, which is virtually everywhere on the continent, expect to start seeing them wherever humans tolerate their presence. Unlike genuine endangered species, the wolf finds no shortage of suitable habitat to support its lifestyle. Despite the massive changes we've made to this planet, we have not removed much of anything a wolf needs for survival except huge numbers of large prey, i.e. bison. Those we've replaced with domestic cattle, and no rancher is going to voluntarily donate those to marauding wolves. Expect wolves to "hide out" in deep forests and isolated mountains. When wilderness ungulates grow scarce, expect wolves to stage raids on lowland pastures where sheep and cattle provide easy pickings. Catching them while it is still daylight will be the challenge.

Distribution

Common to abundant across Alaska and northern Canada, from tundra to the southern edge of the boreal forests, down through the Rockies to the edge of the prairies. Expanding packs in the northern Rockies center around Yellowstone and Glacier National parks and western Montana mountain ranges into the central Idaho wilderness mountains. Packs have moved into various Washington and Oregon mountains and are showing up in Utah and Colorado. They will continue to pioneer, expand, and spread as long as humans tolerate their depredations.

Daily Movements

Extensive. A wolf pack of two to as many as two dozen members requires huge quantities of meat, and they'll travel vast distances to find it. Here today, sixty miles away tomorrow morning. A long-legged, deep-chested wolf trots along at about ten miles per hour and can maintain that better than a human marathon master. They've been timed running 40 mph for at least four miles. I once watched one trot across a highway in Jasper National Park, cross the Athabasca River

Wolves travel far and wide to satisfy their ravenous appetites.

valley, and continue more than 2,000 feet up and over a steep mountain covered in deep snow without stopping. This extensive trekking makes it difficult to pinpoint a pack's whereabouts from day to day. When you find fresh sign or hear a howl, jump right on it or your chance may trot out of your life.

Prey

Anything made of meat. Unlike coyotes, wolves rarely eat berries, fruits, or vegetation of any kind. They'll gobble up carrion, and crush bones to get at the marrow, but they prefer fresh, bloody victims and need them to fuel their massive bodies. Packs have been filmed tormenting, harassing, nipping, and biting moose and bison for hours, sometimes days before weakening them to the point they could be eaten alive. Wolves will even successfully kill and eat mountain lions and grizzly bears. Historically, Siberian wolves have killed and eaten humans by the dozens. Old Russian paintings depicting wolves chasing horse-drawn sleighs weren't invented from whole cloth. North American wolves do not have that history, but in recent years they have killed and eaten at least two people, one in Saskatchewan, and one in Alaska. Experts say that wolves, when not harassed and taught to fear humans, will begin targeting them. The new packs in the Northern Rockies have killed many dogs in the twenty-first century.

Bobcat

Somewhat rare thirty years ago, bobcats have bounced back in the past two decades, becoming common in most parts of the country where brushy valleys, rocky canyons, badlands, ravines, swamps, and brushy forests provide cover and forage in the form of small mammals and birds. Only in Iowa, Illinois, Indiana,

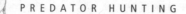

Bobcats are North America's most common and attractive wild feline.

and Ohio are they extremely rare or absent. Bob is our most common and abundant wild cat, and a real caller's trophy.

Size and Color

Figure fifteen to thirty-five pounds, body size roughly two to three times that of an average house cat. Being somewhat more compact and muscular than coyotes, they'll stand slightly shorter, about twenty inches at the shoulder, and stretch thirty to thirty-five inches. The black-tipped tail is a stubby afterthought. Bobcat pelts are uniformly short, thick, and soft, but not deep or particularly luxurious. It's the spotting that makes them striking, though this is usually limited to the white underbody and legs. Some cats are heavily spotted, even over the back; others show hardly any spots. Back and sides are uniformly tawny, sometimes gray-brown, often shading to orange. Stiff, black hairs at the tips of the pointed ears accent their long, sharp look. An enlarged ruff along both sides of the face frames it handsomely.

Senses

Leave odor detection to the dog clan. Bobcats will trust their eyesight, hearing, and caution to find prey and avoid danger, thank you. It isn't unusual to watch a cat stalk directly up your scent trail, paying no more heed than a human would. But twitch or wiggle a feather and the cat will focus on it instantly. Because they are so effective at stealth and camouflage, bobcats tolerate hunter mistakes, often watching when any self-respecting fox or coyote would be long gone. More than one hunter has turned to leave a calling site only to see a bobcat sitting a few yards away, watching curiously.

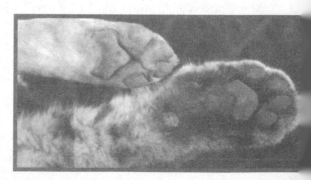

A coyote's paw is more pointed and elongated than a bobcat's, especially its central pad.

Bobcat kittens start learning to hunt when they are about two months old.

Voice and Communication

The antisocial cat has no need for nightly communications with its own kind or any other kind. Stealth and silence, please. Kittens meow, hiss, and spit, but mature cats keep conversation to a minimum except during altercations over breeding rites and during courtship and consummation—lots of cater-wauling then. (That's why they call it "cat"erwauling.) Oddly, cats share information among themselves through scents. Both sexes scrape visual mounds over droppings perfumed with anal gland scents. Males squirt redolent urine against trees, logs, boulders, and ledges.

Tracks and Sign

Befitting its quiet, nocturnal nature, bobcats leave little sign compared to coyotes. Snow, dust, or sand are required to take and hold their paw prints, but since they usually prowl thick cover, we don't often find their spoor. Water holes are as good a place as any for finding tracks. You won't find many piles of dark scat littering the roadsides, either. Look instead for scratched-up mounds of dirt where Miss Kitty has covered her toilet.

A cat track looks surprisingly like a fox or small coyote track. It's about two inches long and wide. Claws don't show, but then neither do coyote claws all the time. Overall, bobcat tracks look more circular or rounded than dog tracks. A real clear print will show an indentation—a scoop or scallop— at the apex of the pad, just behind the two middle toes. A coyote's track here is pointed forward toward the toes.

Mating and Young

Unlike wild dogs, cats may breed and raise young in any season. I've seen kittens in December small enough to be mistaken for half-grown house cats. Mature cats live and hunt alone but tolerate members of the opposite sex for a few days when the female is ready to mate. This is accomplished with considerable yowling and screaming. Then the lover-combatants go their separate ways for another year. If the male has anything to do with kittens, it's eating them.

Females den in caves and tree hollows, under ledges and old barns, and in old holes, cellars, etc. Two to five kittens are born a couple of months after conception, blind and helpless. Within a month, they are exploring outside the den and learning to eat flesh. Within two months they are weaned and following mother to learn the ins and outs of the stealth lifestyle.

When not sleeping, a bobcat spends most of its time quietly prowling, waiting, and watching for dinner.

Habitat

Brush. Woods. Swamps. Forests. This cat needs cover for stalking and escaping wild canines. Trees are almost mandatory. Rocky ledges, canyons and deep ravines are good. Don't expect bobcats out on the Plains like coyotes, though they'll occasionally cross wide fields and grasslands while traveling or hunting. Since cottontails are their number one prey, think cottontail habitat.

Distribution

Central British Columbia deep into Mexico, Maine to Florida. Bobcats find only the central Midwest, centering on Illinois, poorly suited for habitation.

Daily Movements

While cats may claim territories at large as twenty-five square miles, they don't roam them as widely and freely as coyotes do theirs. Bobcats spend more time watching, waiting, and sneaking than loping and traveling. Radiotelemetry studies indicate that females center much of their activity around a favored den, ledge or other safe resting site, moving two miles or fewer per night. Males double that mileage and divide their time more evenly within their territories.

A bobcat's favorite dinner guests include rabbits, rats, mice, voles, squirrels, and game birds.

Prey

Meat, preferably fresh, preferably rabbit. Don't bother Robert with carrion, certainly not fruits and vegetables. He wants his meat alive. Cottontails, rats, mice, voles, squirrels, quail, pheasants, grouse, ducks, turkeys, and songbirds are all on the menu. From time to time an ambitious, cocky old cat will tackle a deer. Some become quite effective at it, biting into the spinal cord at the base of the head. Bobcats are never common enough to be considered serious threats to local deer herds, though.

NO CAUTIOUS CAT

The sun was setting, and I was making the last stand of the afternoon, sitting on the shadowed side of a grassy hill. A coyote had responded to my cries, but hung up at three hundred yards. I couldn't understand why it had stopped so soon. Surely it couldn't have seen me. I switched to a squeaker to break the spell, and that's when a bobcat leaped out of a nearby draw and raced down the ranch trail toward me. I almost dropped my rifle. Forget everything you've heard about sneaking and stalking. This kitty was hell-bent for dinner, long front legs reaching forward, hind legs bunching and pushing. I've seen precious few coyotes come as fast. The instant I lifted the rifle, that cat had me made. Yellow eyes glared. Bobbed tail twitched.

Don't assume every cat is going to tiptoe in.

Red Fox

Famous in legend and song, the sly fox is a challenge for any hunter. Alert, secretive, quick, and cautious, red fox have persevered and even prospered in the face of persecution. They are capable of sharing the world with grizzly bears north of the Arctic circle and housewives in suburban Atlanta. Long after man leaves the scene, red fox will continue to trot jauntily over the earth.

Size and Color

"Red" says it all. The rusty red coat with white throat and underbelly are instantly recognizable. Legs and the backs of the large, sharp-tipped ears are black, as are the tips of long guard hairs covering that famous brush tail with its white tip. A black color phase, the silver fox, sports black guard hairs with white tips. Cross-fox sport a black cross over the shoulders and down the upper back.

The big ears and tail project more mass than exists under all that covering. Stripped to its skin, Red might stand fifteen inches at the shoulder, stretch three feet nose to tail tip, and weigh fifteen pounds after a good meal. Twelve pounds is average.

Senses

Sometimes it seems the red fox is a walking radar. Ears, nose and eyes are on full alert, and each is tuned to perfection by a few million years of honing. Of the three, the eyes are weakest. Hearing is so good that you can call a fox from several hundred yards with the tiniest squeak. They are sensitive to sound and can be spooked with loud blasts of a predator call. Most will circle to confirm with their noses what they think they've identified with their ears, so be ready.

Voice and Communication

Red fox do howl, but never as loudly or frequently as coyotes. They do quite a bit of barking some nights—it sounds like a lap dog yapping. They have a funny yowl or scream, too, most often heard during mating and pup rearing. They scream at one another during battles for status. Scent marking is done with urine in the usual dog fashion, with feces perfumed by anal scent glands, and by rubbing anal scent glands against brush.

Tracks and Sign

Because fox live near humans and travel a lot while hunting, their tracks and scat are commonly seen along roads, paths, and fencelines. Paw prints are about 2 to 2 1/2 inches long and two inches wide, easily confused with coyote or small dog prints. A fox spoor is usually straight-lined with minimal spread between left and right feet. Dog trails usually wander, looking less purposeful. Winter fox paws are so hairy they leave fuzzy, indistinct prints. Droppings are black, cylindrical, two to four inches long and half an inch in diameter, often with hair mixed in.

Mating and Young

Reds, usually solitary animals, pair up in December and January, breed from January to March, and whelp litters of four to ten pups in a self-dug hole or enlarged badger or

Red fox's keenest sense is its hearing. A fox can be called in from several hundred yards with the tiniest squeak.

woodchuck hole. Dens are usually on elevated ground in or near some sort of cover such as weeds, brush, or a rock pile. Multiple entrances are common. One pair of fox may construct several dens in its territory, moving pups from den to den when danger threatens. Four to six weeks after birth, pups crawl above ground and begin eating meat. The den entrance becomes progressively littered with bones, feathers, and droppings. By the time the family is ready to leave, the entrance looks like the punch line of a redneck joke. Males usually help raise the young, which begin roaming away from the den when they're just two months old. By three months, they've largely abandoned the dens and begun living above-ground like all self-respecting fox.

In early fall the family unit dissolves, but pups often travel and hunt together into winter. Males may disperse as far as two hundred miles to find open territories. Females have been known to raise pups of their own their first summer or remain with their mother to help raise her next brood.

Habitat

Red fox don't subscribe to *Architectural Digest.* They'll live happily in nearly any habitat. Short-grass plains. Tundra. Brush. Cropland. Pastures. Woodlots. Even open forests. As long as there are plenty of smaller critters on hand to serve as dinner guests, a fox is satisfied. When pressed by coyotes, they'll set up shop in suburban fringes, active farmsteads (without dogs), and even city cemeteries.

Distribution

Northwest Alaska to Florida. Only the extreme Southwest seems unsuitable for red fox. There the smaller swift fox takes over.

Daily Movements

Like most mammalian predators, red fox are primarily nocturnal, waking from their daybeds to begin hunting late in the day, and retiring by mid-morning. Home ranges vary from one to eight square miles. Within this territory each fox will follow paths to and from favored hunting areas such as grassy meadows, brushy woodpiles, and weedy thickets. Obviously they hunt longer and range more widely when hunting for pups and in winter when pickin's are slim. In some areas fox are highly territorial. In others they share habitat.

Prey

What the cottontail is to bobcats, the mouse and vole are to red fox. These little dogs are expert mousers, listening for small mammals in the grass, then leaping high to pounce nose and feet first, tail corkscrewing overhead. Fox also hunt with their noses, sniffing out bird nests and eggs, snakes, rabbits, game birds, and—of course—barnyard chickens, though these are in short supply in today's America. Fox also eat fruit and carrion. Many become experts at gleaning road kill.

Gray Fox

You might call the gray a woodland version of the red. Its stronghold is in the South. Grays are not as famous as their flashy cousins, being harder to see in the dense habitats they prefer. These little dogs are perhaps best known for their undoglike ability to climb trees.

Size and Color

Grays are slightly smaller than reds, but a bit more solidly built. Weight varies from seven to twelve pounds. You'll notice a bit of classic red fox color around a gray's neck and lower sides, but the bulk of its body is covered in salt-and-pepper guard hairs that give a grizzled look. I'm surprised no one's nicknamed it the "grizzly" fox. Face and muzzle become quite black in most specimens. Throat, breast patch, and belly are white. The top of the fourteen-inch, bushy tail is usually lined in deep black that can continue well up the back. The tail tip is black. Grays often flatten their tail hairs on either side, giving the tails a paddle-like appearance.

Senses

Like the red fox. Excellent eyes, ears, and nose. These guys don't miss much. Because they live in close cover, they probably depend on their noses to give them the final word.

Voice and Communication

See red fox above. Yapping, screaming, minor howling.

Tracks and Sign

Tracks are much like red fox, but less often seen due to brushy habitat and leaf litter on forest floor. Scats similar: doglike, black, tapered at ends, filled with hair, fruit pits, insect exoskeletons, and so on.

The seven- to twelve-pound gray fox is surprisingly adept at climbing trees and vertical rock walls in search of prey or security.

Mating and Young

Again, like the red fox. December pairing; January through March breeding; two-month gestation; one to seven young; dens in hollow trees, under ledges, rock piles, old buildings, occasionally in burrows. Dens are often near water and usually in brush, thickets, or woods. Kits are weaned between two and three months and taken hunting from then until late fall, when the family breaks up. The young are killed and eaten by anything that can catch them—bobcats, coyotes, owls, and hawks. The young probably do not disperse as far as red fox, but have been known to move thirty miles.

Habitat

Eastern woodlands, Midwest riparian zones, desert scrub and chaparral, and brush of all types. This is a fox of cover.

Daily Movements

Mostly nocturnal. The home range may cover five square miles—less in productive habitat, more in poor habitat. It ranges farther in winter to find scarce food and beds in dense cover, often near a den. It may have several dens within its territory.

Distribution

Maine to Florida, eastern North Dakota to Arizona and California. Gray fox have been expanding and do well wherever there is brush, woods, and thickets except on the northern Plains, northern Rockies, and Northwest.

Prey

Grays will climb trees to access bird nests and squirrel dens. They eat nearly anything they can catch. In summer up to a third of their diet may be plant material, mostly fruits, nuts, and berries. They eat insects and grubs, too, but small mammals and birds are the main ingredients of the gray fox diet.

QUICK, TOUGH, AND PERSISTENT

My first gray fox was one tough customer. And fast. He streaked in to Gary Roberson's calls moments after they'd started. I'd barely settled my buns into the Texas winter dust before I had to throw up the borrowed Savage over/under rifle/shotgun combination and shoot. By the time I did, the front half of the fox had already disappeared behind a protective wall of prickly pear pads. The few pellets that stung the critter's butt caused it to leap back, growling and thrashing. I figured it was expiring, but it quickly leaped up and resumed running to the call. I heard more growling and barking, and then the fox dashed back the way it had come. I missed with the .22 Hornet barrel, and the show was over.

Gary explained that the fox had stuck its head out of a thicket less than ten yards away. "What was all the growling about?" I asked.

"I don't know. I think it saw me and was displeased that I wasn't the rabbit it expected."

"Why didn't you shoot?"

"Couldn't get my gun up fast enough."

You've got to be prepared and quick as a fox at this game.

Mountain Lion

North America's biggest cat remains an enigma to many. Rustics have always told tales of catamounts, panthers, painters, pumas, and cougars that were part animal, part spirit. Even decades after they were extirpated from much of their range, locals told of strange cries in the night and livestock disappearing without a trace. Today we know our lion is just a secretive, nocturnal stealth hunter. No magic. No ghosts. But extremely powerful and currently expanding and reclaiming much of its range. A South Dakota lion was killed on a highway in Connecticut recently. Lions are rarely called in, but it can be done. Odds of it happening improve every year. Chip Beiner, an Arizona hunting guide, calls in a lion or two every year.

Size and Color

Average males weigh 130 to 250 pounds, but record specimens have reportedly pushed the scales to three hundred pounds. Females vary from seventy to 150 pounds, stand about three feet at the shoulder and stretch six to seven feet, tail to snout. Males may measure nine feet long and stand a bit over three feet.

Most tom mountain lions weigh 130 to 250 pounds. Females average 70 to 150 pounds. The sexes tolerate one another only when mating.

Mature males' heads are much broader than females'.

The lion's scientific name, *Felis concolor,* references their uniformly tawny color, which seems to camouflage them in any habitat. Kittens are beautifully spotted, but the only spots on adults are a black tip on the tail, a black spot on each side of the muzzle, and black backsides of ears. Hairs are dense and uniformly short, presenting a sleek appearance.

A mountain lion print is usually three to four inches in diameter and about as wide as long.

Senses

This is a cat, so it's primarily a sight hunter. Canines will sniff out prey, but cats invariably have to see before they attack. Hearing is acute, and these secretive predators will slink away upon hearing danger.

Voice and Communication

Although they don't trust their noses for finding prey, they use them for communicating among themselves. Like bobcats and house cats, lions scrape dirt and debris over their dung and urinate on objects to mark their territories. They also claw trees as a possible visual signpost. Kittens mew, and adults chirp, purr, whistle, growl, and scream during the mating season. Most of the time, however, they're silent.

Tracks and Sign

Mountain lions (also called cougars) might be able to pad silently over their terrain, but a one hundred-pound animal can't help but press a print into dirt, sand, mud, or snow. Look for rounded cat tracks roughly three to four inches in diameter along trails and roads, in dry washes, and at water holes. A walking lion strides twelve to sixteen inches and trots with about twenty-four inches between paw prints. Sometimes their long tail will drag in snow.

Like most cats, lions hunt by sighting, then stalking or ambushing, their prey, usually from atop a tree or ledge.

Scat, uncovered some of the time, looks like large dog droppings with tapered ends, and is usually full of deer hair.

Mating and Young

Lions mate at any time, but most often in winter. One male will patrol a huge territory encompassing as many females as possible. Whenever he finds a receptive one, he stays with her, mating repeatedly until she goes out of estrus. Then each resumes its solitary existence. Three months later, the female whelps two to six kittens (average four) under a ledge, root mass, or brush pile or in a cave. Pops does nothing to rear the brood, but if he stumbles upon it he might eat the lot. Mama must nurse and protect the kits and hunt for food. Tough assignment. After three months, she weans her spotted spit-ters, and then lets them tag along as she hunts. Six-month-old kittens have been documented killing deer, but most must practice stalking, pouncing, and killing again and again on everything from wood rats to bighorn sheep until they become proficient enough to make it on their own. Since mom kicks them out of the house when she's ready for her next family, young lions begin roaming and struggling to survive at fifteen to eighteen months old. These are the cats most likely to attack humans and livestock. They are forced to travel because resident adults chase them from territory to territory, and many end up near humans for this reason. In saturated habitats, old, established lions must be removed before young males can establish themselves. Removal of old males actually increases total population numbers.

Habitat

Cougars inhabit the widest range of any predator in the New World, living coast-to-coast from central Canada nearly to the tip of South America. They adapt to a wide variety of habitats including eastern hardwood forests, mountain pine forests, desert scrub, rocky canyons, even sage deserts. As long as prey is abundant and there is cover for stalking, hiding, ambushing, and protecting young, they will thrive.

Stealth incarnate. A light-footed lion can tiptoe within pouncing distance of an elk and break its neck within seconds.

Daily Movement

Males roam as many as twenty-five miles each night across territories as large as 350 square miles. Within this vast territory may live several females on their own territories of twenty to fifty square miles. Females will tolerate other females to a large degree, but males attempt to keep all other males out of their stomping grounds. They scent-spray liberally to enforce boundaries. Males that smell other males tend to shift away from that area, avoiding confrontation. Toms that do meet face-to-face often fight to the death. Cougars may "camp" near a kill for several days until it is consumed. On average, they kill the equivalent of one deer per week. Most lions seem to patrol their territories on fairly predictable routes over fairly predictable time frames. For example, an old tom might pass through a certain mountain saddle every three weeks, give or take a few days.

Prey

Deer are to cougars what cottontails are to bobcats. Sure, lions will kill anything they can get their claws on, but they're adapted to springing upon deer-sized animals, hanging on with long claws, and biting into the spine with big canines or wrenching the head back to snap the neck. Bighorn sheep are also appropriate subjects for such attacks, but being quite rare, they can't support a huge population of cats. No, credit this continent's large deer population with fueling the recent upsurge in mountain lion numbers. You might think a six hundred-pound bull elk a bit much for a cougar to handle, but you'd think wrong. Little ninety-pound female cougars have been documented dropping onto mature, six-point bull elk and breaking their necks within seconds. One powerful gal killed a healthy nine hundred-pound horse and dragged it nearly a hundred yards. These are not small predators. They've killed several humans in the past two decades.

HAVE YOU CALLED A MOUNTAIN LION YET?

The challenge of talking a mountain lion into rifle range intrigues most predator hunters. Everyone has an opinion on how to do it. Few have done it. I almost did. Twice.

My Mexico lion episode is related in Chapter 11. My Texas lion story starts right here. We were hunting free-roaming aoudad sheep in the mountains of west Texas and testing the then-new .270 Winchester Short Magnum rifles and 140-grain Fail Safe bullets. Beautiful country. Hills, draws, rocks, canyons, and peaks as high as 7,700 feet. Grass, cacti, yucca, mesquite, junipers. Desert mule deer, Coues whitetails, javelina, coyotes, bobcats, and mountain lions. The place looked like a setting for a Zane Grey novel.

I got lucky and shot a splendid ram the first morning. My old hunting compadres Kevin Howard and Marty Malin weren't so fortunate, so I tagged along to help them glass. Aoudad, transplanted from North Africa, where they evolved in desert mountain habitat quite similar to west Texas, are colored like the desert landscape and roam in amazingly large herds. Kevin saw one bunch of two hundred head. Find one and you find them all, but this leaves a lot of empty country. During our search we found more mountain lion tracks than any of us had seen in the previous ten years. We even found a half-eaten sheep covered with debris. I began enter-

Marty Malin with his west Texas mountain lion.

taining notions of trying a few calls, but no one wanted to stop sheep hunting to placate me. At mid-afternoon on our second day, we split up to search more efficiently. Big mistake. Within thirty minutes, Marty spotted a band of aoudad, shot at and missed a long-range ram, and just about swallowed his mustache when a cougar dashed out of a draw in hot pursuit of the fleeing sheep. "It must have been stalking the herd when I shot," Marty later explained. "She chased them over a hill, then gave up and stood there twitching that long tail."

Never one to look a gift horse in the mouth, Marty turned to his young guide and asked, "You got your predator call? Blow it and see what she'll do." The kid blew. The lion spun and stared. "Blow it again." He did. And here she came. According to Marty, there was no skulking, no sneaking, no stealthy cat behavior—and no time to hide. He was standing on a bare hillside with nowhere to go. Within seconds, the lithe cat had closed to within 175 yards. Then she stopped to consider just what form of prey she was responding to. That's when Marty decided to shoot. His .270 slug caught her in front of the shoulder and angled back to exit behind the far shoulder, nicking the spine for an instant kill.

I don't suppose every cat is going to behave like that. That one was obviously in hunting mode, fully aroused and perhaps even frustrated at having missed her first attack. But it does prove you can attract the big lions with a little distressed cottontail wail. Now all you have to do is get into cougar habitat and give it a try.

Black Bear

Our most common bear is a big game animal with strict hunting seasons and harvest restrictions limiting its take, but it can be called in, so what the heck, let's include it. Let me assure you, sitting alone on a mountain and imitating dinner for a three hundred-pound bear takes some nerve. I've never heard of a predator caller being abused by a black bear, but the potential is there. For this reason, most bear callers work with a partner to watch the back door. The rest are nuts.

In the East black bears are just that, but they can be brown, blonde, silver and almost white. Color variations are more common in the West.

Size and Color

Everybody knows what a black bear looks like, but not everyone knows they can be brown, blonde, silver, or almost white. Most odd color phases live in the West, where it is possible to confuse them with grizzlies. Know your bears before you shoot! Blacks can pig out to seven hundred pounds, but most fall within the 150- to 300-pound range, stand forty inches at the shoulder, and stretch five to six feet. Females are about twenty percent smaller than males. First-year cubs are half the size of adult sows. Second-year cubs are roughly adult female size. Short, rounded ears are good indicators of a mature bear. Large, pointed ears top off smaller bears.

Voice and Communication

Bears are mostly silent, but become quite vocal when interacting. They bawl, roar, cough, and woof. If you hear them popping their teeth, you're probably agitating them. Most bear communication centers around visual and olfactory

A bear might look fat and lumbering, but it can pad silently on broad feet. You won't mistake a bear track for anything else.

Black bear cubs climb trees at mom's command to escape predators. They retain these climbing skills throughout life.

marking. They reach as high as possible and claw trees as if to say, "If you can't reach this, don't mess with me." Males straddle saplings and "walk" them down, rubbing scent on them from belly, penis, and anus. Males deposit obvious heaps of dung on trails and road edges. The bigger the pile, the bigger the bear. I only assume that other bears recognize this.

Tracks and Sign

A bear's hind foot lays an imprint quite similar to a human foot. It shows five toes, a long pad, and an instep. If you see claw marks beyond the toe prints, it's probably not a human footprint. Yogi's front foot is similar, but the pad behind the toes is only about half as long as that of the back foot. Front pad width in inches plus one inch correlates to body length, nose to tail. A five-inch-wide front pad, then, would indicate a six-foot-long bear. Close, anyway.

Bear scat is unmistakable whether cylindrical or in a loose mass. Nothing else can match it for sheer volume. It's usually filled with yesterday's dinner—berries, deer hair, seeds, grass, and now and then, a running shoe.

When scouting bears, watch also for torn-up logs and flipped boulders where they were hunting grubs. During breeding season, watch for broken and chewed saplings.

Mating and Young

Bears are summer breeders—May through July. Females delay implanting of the fertilized eggs until late fall. A sow in poor condition may absorb the eggs then to increase her chances of surviving winter hibernation. Fat sows go to bed and bear two or three naked, blind eight-ounce cubs in January or February. They'll weigh five pounds when she emerges with them in May, follow as she roams and forages all summer, and den with her again in the winter. Only in their second summer does she chase them off so she can breed and prepare for her next cubs. Sows are fiercely protective of their cubs because boars kill and eat them. In prime habitat with lots of food, a female may breed at three and one-half years, but doesn't breed until six and one-half years in poor habitat. Males are capable of breeding when two or three years old, but rarely get the chance, because older, bigger males beat them to the punch.

Habitat

Trees. Black bears need trees, which provide visual cover, escape habitat for cubs, and often food like nuts and berries. Secondly, they need brush—again for cover and berries. Lots of lush grass and flowering plants add salad greens to the diet. An abundance of small and large

Omnivorous black bears thrive on grass, flowering plants and berries, but seldom turn down a meat dinner.

mammals adds protein. You'll find black bears in southern swamps, eastern hardwoods, northern conifers, southwest oaks and chaparral, and western mountain forests of all types.

Daily Movement

Instead of defending sharply defined territories, bears roam widely searching for food. They'll tolerate their own kind when and where food is abundant. Territorial defense seems to be practiced only by boars during breeding season, but even then they'll sometimes share a female or at least tolerate competition hanging around. Nevertheless, bears do spend a considerable portion of their lives following routines, returning to the same areas again and again seasonally to access known food sources such as berry patches, ground squirrel colonies, oak mast, calving areas, etc. They may roam from fifty to as many as two hundred square miles, but also might remain within a few square miles for weeks on end.

Bears forage at dawn and dusk, but also midday in early spring and late fall when feeding heavily. They'll bed near food sources and walk the same trails to and from water and forage. Drought will set them wandering for food.

Prey

Depending on availability, black bears may eat more vegetable matter than meat. It's easier to catch. Still, bears can be deadly predators on fawns and elk calves. They're opportunists and eat nearly anything. Where small mammals are abundant, they may respond to cottontail cries, but fawn and elk calf calls may work better in some areas. In parts of the country you'll need to sound like a blueberry in order to call in a black bear.

BEAR TRACKS

Tom and I were seeing plenty of bear sign around our north Idaho elk camp, but our impromptu calling sessions had yielded nothing. "Let's give it a real try tomorrow," Tom suggested. "Sit for an hour at each spot; cover an entire basin."

We hiked out on fresh snow, cut bear tracks, called with enthusiasm. No response. Not even a coyote came in. Blown out, we trudged back to camp, and there in our morning boot prints were fresh bear tracks. They had to have heard us, yet they showed no interest. Either those bears had never heard a bawling rabbit or they were dialed in to autumn berries. Fish and Game Department studies in the area had revealed significant black bear predation on elk calves. Perhaps calling would work in spring. You have to think creatively and be ready to try something different in this game.

CAMERA BEAR

We were trying to call a black bear while taping an episode of *Winchester Legends* in British Columbia when a bear cooperated, but the camera did not. Our guide directed us to a clear cut in which he'd been seeing a large, chocolate-phase boar feeding. We set up at the edge of an old logging road looking down into the clear-cut slash and into the wind. Conditions were perfect. I began blowing an open reed Dakota Howler, trying to sound like a bear cub in distress. After my second series, the big brown bruin loped out of the standing forest, coming as if late for dinner.

"That's him," our guide said.

I leveled the Winchester M70. "Wait! Wait!" my cameraman hissed. Videographers often say that, buying time to roll more tape or perhaps fine-tune focus. I waited. The bear kept coming.

"You ready?" I hissed back.

"No."

I wondered how much more footage this kid needed. He'd gotten me calling, and the bear was bouncing out of the trees and now climbing the hill practically to our feet. Was he hoping for personal contact?

"Now?"

"Don't shoot! The camera's not working."

The bear finally got our scent and humped back into the pines. The camera was dead. Not only did we not get that bear, we never got a show. But the action was hot for a few seconds. Black bears do respond to calls.

Raccoon

The masked bandit is an omnivore, but will occasionally respond to a rabbit call. Imitating the squall of young 'coons may lure mature animals in summer and early fall, but can also spook them.

Size and Color

The raccoon has a grizzled coat of long guard hairs and dense gray underfur. Pelage may be almost black to yellow, but usually appears gray with more black on the head and the top of the back. The gray-to-brown tail is ringed with five or six black bands. General body shape is hunchbacked, with large hindquarters tapering to a low, narrow front. Weight varies widely from eight to thirty-five pounds, and length is twenty to forty inches, nose to tail tip.

The humped-back, ring-tailed, masked bandit lays down a distinctive track with those long, fingerlike toes.

Voice and Communication

Raccoons can be noisy and squabbling as they forage in family groups. The standard call is a rolling, Scottish burr with a background tone rising or falling in inflection. You'll also hear snarls, growls, and squalls. They have no obvious scent marking behavior, but feces are regularly deposited in "bathrooms"—often on large, horizontal tree trunks or in abandoned buildings—and may have associated glandular secretions.

Tracks and Sign

Toes. That's what's striking about a 'coon track. Five long toes ahead of a long, human-like pad marks the hind foot. The front foot looks like a human handprint. They're common around muddy streams and ponds. Droppings are like miniature bear piles: grainy cylinders, half an inch in diameter, broken sharply at the ends, not tapered. They're often on trees and boulders and have lots of company. Look for huge piles of piled up piles.

Mating and Young

Males begin to wander—in December in the South and February in the North—up to ten miles per night to locate receptive females in their winter dens. Two months after mating, the female births three to seven young in a hollow tree, rock den, or old building. Kits are surprisingly vocal in the den, twittering and

Agile and adaptable raccoons prefer life near water, woods and agricultural fields, but get by in rocky western canyons, too.

churring. They begin crawling and exploring around the den when five to six weeks old. At ten weeks they're weaned and begin traveling with mom. Breeding is the last of Pop's family duties. After sixteen weeks the young begin going off by themselves more and more, the males eventually dispersing up to twenty miles.

Habitat

The water's edge. Littoral zones. Riparian habitat. But also woods and thickets far from water. In the prairie states, raccoons have adapted to rock piles, culverts, and cattail thickets so as to prowl the prairies and grain fields by night, raiding chicken coops and duck nests, and taking a terrible toll on nesting birds.

Daily Movements

They're working on their night moves. Hole up by day, hunt by night. That's the raccoon's life. So if you want to tease one into range, hunt the first and last hours of the day or hunt by night. I've seen plenty of 'coons in daylight, but I never count on this. They aren't big wanderers anyway, sticking inside home ranges as small as twenty acres and as large as several square miles. When they do travel, they use traditional corridors such as stream courses.

Prey

Frogs, fish, crayfish, mice, voles, fruits, nuts, honey, eggs, sweet corn. Like bears, they eat darned near anything. That's why they're difficult to call in most places. Where legal, spotlighting cornfields bordering riparian brush can be quite productive. The most successful calls imitate raccoons fighting or young squalling for help.

Sleep all day, hunt all night. That's a raccoon's life.

Play a tape of these near a raccoon den (hollow tree, old building, etc.) and coons will emerge even in daylight to see what the fuss is about.

TEXAS COON FIGHT

I was watching a Texan's crop field for marauding hogs one evening. The hogs never showed up, but two coons did. At full dark they began screaming and growling and caterwauling as if someone had slammed their ringed tails in a door. I clicked on the big SureFire flashlight clamped atop my scope and illuminated a dark pair of coons rolling and fighting in a compact ball about 240 yards away. It appeared they'd rip each other's hides to tatters if I didn't interfere. So I leveled the reticle just atop them and touched off the .260 Remington. As luck would have it, the bullet passed through one and then the other, earning me my first raccoon "double."

4

When I'm Calling You

All About the Sounds and Tools That Make Them

There are days when you swear predators have never responded to a call and never will. So to heck with it. Then there are days when you could play "Yankee Doodle Dandy" on a kazoo and bring a pack of drooling canines into your lap. If you blow it, they will come. So why? Why are they all over you one day, seemingly extinct the next? I don't know. But I do know this. It's not the melody.

When I joined this calling club, I listened hard and often to a flimsy 45-rpm recording of a dying rabbit captured by Johnny Stewart of Waco, Texas. In the dim recesses of my memory I can still hear that tinny, monaural voice, the hum of the amplifier, and the shivering wails of that lost bunny. With a brown plastic, square-sided Burnham Brothers fox call, I practiced imitating those screams, their cadence, and duration. Then I mixed in a bit of real rabbit squalls I'd heard over the years while catching young cottontails and jackrabbits in the hay fields. Figured I had nature duplicated. Knew it when my first coyote came a-runnin'. Then another and another. Soon I was a self-proclaimed expert, laughing at the ridiculous sounds my young hunting partner, Tom Lowin, blasted from his call. "You'll scare 'em right out of the county," I said. "Blow like this." But Tom, for all his talents, had a wooden ear. It didn't matter. He still called in a pack of coyotes. A whole pack. All at the same time.

It was late October in Montana. The Gravelly Range. Doug firs, ponderosa pines, sagebrush, and grass meadows. Local coyotes were running in packs, chasing mule deer. Early in the month we saw six of them bring down a doe and tear her limb from limb, polishing her to bone by dawn. I called a single one evening, shot it, and called a pair one morning, but missed my chance when they got my scent. Tom heard their evening chorus in a narrow side canyon dark with pine. He stuck his call to his lips and blew his sorry impersonation of a rabbit in trouble. The coyotes shut up. Seconds later six of them poured from the woods in an all-out charge. "I shot the closest one, and by the time I reloaded, they were gone," Tom told us later. "But I could hear them running all around me." Tom hustled back to the cabin, whistling past the graveyard, half expecting a mass attack. It had been an eerie encounter, but it proved there was nothing wrong with his calling.

At that time, 1976, my idea of a proper rabbit squall was a series of quavering cries lasting a second or two each with a split-second pause between them. I'd carry on in this manner for roughly a minute, then shut up for a few minutes to watch and listen. I'd blow the next series louder, the third at maximum volume, adding a dramatic crescendo and decrescendo as I imagined the bunny slowly expiring. Some of my performances were Oscar contenders, I tell you.

Then Tom came along with that silly, long, choking scream that sounded like two Buicks mating in a wrecking yard and called more coyotes in a minute than I had the previous month, proving two things: I didn't know as much as I thought, and coyotes are the best judges of what calls sound correct.

In the years since, I've shot predators that responded to a cacophony of calls blown by various virtuosos who played a variety of instruments pitched from bass to soprano, blown fast and slow with short pauses, long pauses, and no pauses. Some sounded perfect, some horrible, some weird. All I can tell you is there's no accounting for a predator's taste in music. The blamed things will come to durned near any sound. Heck, buddy Brad and I once called two in a row with a canoe.

We hadn't planned to "blow" the canoe when we set out for a bear hunt along north Idaho's Dworshak Reservoir. The idea was to paddle along the shoreline, watching spring meadows for grazing bears. Upon seeing one, we would stash the canoe, hike up and shoot it (the bear, not the canoe). Well, we located a bear eventually, high in a lush meadow, so we carried the canoe far up the bank in order to hide it deep in the woods. As we shoved it over a fallen fir, a number of sticks and staubs screeched across the fiberglass bottom like fingernails over a chalkboard. "Hey, here comes a coyote!" my partner Brad Deffenbaugh hissed. I turned in time to see the crazy dog running up from the shore, hot on our trail. When it recognized us, it bounded into the brush. "That was weird. You suppose it had rabies or something?" We chalked the event off to coincidence.

After studying our hiding spot, we decided it was too open, so we hauled the canoe back to the lake and paddled to a brushier takeout. Again we slid the boat into the woods. Again it screeched. But this time we had our rifles out when a second coyote ran up from the beach. One shot from my .30-06 proved adequate. The coyote looked healthy enough (other than the fact it was dead). "Hey wait a minute!" I said. "Did you notice how he acted just like all our coyotes do when they're coming to a call?" "Yeah."

"I think he was coming to the screech of the canoe. I think they both were." Brad agreed, and we're sticking to our story.

Two Schools of Calling

The Tom and canoe incidents suggest that anything can work, but most callers try to stick with more natural sounds and cadences. The most popular approach seems to be similar to what I do, as described above. Call a little, wait a lot. We'll label this call-and-wait. The other style involves calling a lot and barely waiting at all. We'll label this continuous calling. They both work.

The theory behind call-and-wait is "That's what rabbits do." They don't wail nonstop. But they usually don't start up again after a three- to five-minute rest, either.

The theory behind continuous calling is "Once you've got 'em coming, keep 'em coming." Don't give them a chance to slow down, get suspicious, or circle. With that helpless bunny crying for attention, they can't resist racing straight in, even though no rabbit ever wailed for ten minutes nonstop. Let's examine these methods in depth.

Call-and-Wait

The typical call-and-wait performer starts with a low-volume series of plaintive cries, each lasting a second or two with just enough interlude for a breath if needed. Some folks blow for only fifteen seconds; some go for a minute. Then they wait and watch for as long as five minutes before playing their second verse, slightly louder. Another wait, verse three, more volume to reach distant ears. Wait again, verse four louder yet. Coyote callers usually give it fifteen to twenty minutes before moving. Cat callers hang in there for thirty minutes to an hour.

The main advantages to this style of calling are improved ability to spot and hear approaching game. When your ears are full of the sound of your own blowing, you aren't likely to hear drumming paws behind you. In brushy habitat this'll cost you a few shots—maybe get you bit. It's also easier to spot distant game if you're not concentrating on the call. Lastly, you'll shoot better if you aren't gasping and heaving from all that blowing.

The downside to pausing is that it gives critters a chance to lose interest. I've seen this many times, most recently in Texas, when a bobcat ran out of the brush in response to my partner's calls. Because my buddy was covering one alleyway through the brush and I another, he couldn't see the cat or me. When he stopped calling, Miss Kitty stopped and sat down. I eased my own call up and got her restarted with three good cries, but as soon as I dropped the call to grip my shotgun, she stopped again. Then she saw a mouse or vole or something in the grass. Chased it into the brush. End of story. No amount of calling could coax her out.

Calls and ammo boxes. Open reed call (left) and bite-reed call (right) are two of the most -used mouth calls for luring predators. The ammunition represents the "bigger is better" school of thought. A bit more powerful than needed for coyotes, but preferred by some.

Similarly, I've had coyotes come on a dead run, but when the calling stopped, so did they. Some looked the situation over and began circling to catch my wind. Some just sat and watched, hoping to see something encouraging. Some just lost interest and trotted away. This is when a moving decoy earns its keep. Restarting the calls in these situations usually restarts the coyotes, but not always. Switching to a higher-pitched squeaker call sometimes turns them back on. Just purse your lips and suck air or kiss the back of your hand. Many callers keep a bulb squeaker taped to their gunstock.

Continuous Calling

This approach also starts out softly, so as not to spook nearby listeners, but instead of pausing, the caller merely gulps air when necessary and gradually cranks up the volume. If you're alone, swing your head slowly back and forth, always watching. When a subject appears, you may change volume, but keep the sound rolling. Move your gun into position early, pick the animal up, and either shoot as it lopes in or stop it with a bark and then shoot.

The downside here is the possibility of a sneak attack. More than one preoc-cupied caller has been scratched or bitten, unaware that an animal has come into range. Continuous calling may not be ideal in heavy cover where the sound of thumping feet is often your first clue that you have a customer. Oxygen depriva-tion is another real possibility when continuously blowing. You probably won't faint, but all that huffing and puffing will make it harder to hold steady for a

precise shot. This is the major reason I employ the call-and-wait style. It gives my heart a few seconds to slow down for the shot. Electronic callers, however, really change that dynamic. Not only can they play continuously without making you out of breath, but you can control their volume, dialing back to better hear those approaching feet. By placing the speaker or entire unit ten to thirty yards away, you also reduce the noise you hear and direct the animal's attention away from yourself. Electronic calls are the best option for continuous calling.

Alternate Sounds

The old dying rabbit is the hands-down favorite call nationwide, but not always the most productive. Depending on habitat and local species composition, the distress cries of other critters can be more effective.

The first alternative I ever tried was the staccato cry of a yellow-shafted flicker. Tom Berger was with me at the time. We were standing in a big Kansas shelterbelt, so it seemed only natural to work the bird call. Besides, attempts at calling with a rabbit cry had netted nothing at several sites earlier that morning. This time, however, we knew a coyote was close enough to hear us, because we had seen one about four hundred yards out in a pasture climbing in and out of a dead Hereford carcass. "It's pigging out on beef. Why would it come to a call?" Tom whispered.

"I don't know, but let's find out." Each of us stood against a tree trunk for cover, and I blew while Tom watched through binoculars.

"He's lookin'. Blow it again."

I blew.

"Here he comes!" Belly distended, coat reeking of putrid flesh, that glutton loped right up to us. He stunk so bad we had to tie him from a long pole to carry him back to the truck.

The jackrabbit call is probably the second most used sound in the predator caller's repertoire. It's much like the cottontail's call, only lower-pitched. The jack squall has never produced as well for me as the cottontail squeal, even in good jack habitat. I think the higher-pitched call simply reaches farther.

Pork chops for dinner? Most big predators will come running if you squeal like a pig in javelina or feral hog country.

Where deer are common prey, fawn bleats and low-pitched doe calls blown frantically work pretty well. In the Southwest, the squeals of baby javelina can really bring the dogs and cats a-runnin', but beware mama javelina. I've found myself surrounded by popping tusks on more than one occasion. As long as they don't threaten me too closely, I don't scare them off. Real pig snorts and scents just add to the attraction.

Feral pig distress sounds can be hot where those animals are common, and that includes most of the southern states from coast to coast. Again, anticipate a visit from an upset mama. If a thirty-pound javelina makes you nervous, wait until a two hundred-pound ticked-off sow tries to run you off.

In forested habitats where tree squirrels are common, the high-pitched whistle of a frightened young squirrel can be an effective draw. These calls are designed to attract adult squirrels during the early season when they're still pro-grammed to protect their young, but they'll lure predators, too. The call is a flat disc with a hole in the middle through which you suck air to make the distress whistle.

Many songbird screams and cries also turn the trick if you can mimic them. You won't find mouth calls geared to play these tunes, but they're available on tapes and computer chips for play in electronic callers. These work best during the spring nesting season when fledglings are falling from nests.

Not all calls must mimic animals in distress. Turkey hunters regularly call bobcats and coyotes with normal turkey yelps. These can be especially effective in areas where predators have become educated to the usual rabbit calls. If you want to increase the tension and urgency, go with the kee-kee run of a poult. This starts out something like the squeal of a bull elk, then breaks into an excited yelping.

Crows are so common across the country that most predators know them intimately. Try a fighting crow call sometime and see what happens. You'll prob-ably bring in a passel of crows, but their cawing and flapping will only add to the effect.

Last but not least are the puppy-in-distress calls. Oh my, are they effective in late summer when pups are wandering but still being guarded by mom and pop! I don't hunt predators in that season because the pelts aren't prime, but those who must control predators around livestock report that the crying puppy call is deadly. I use it in fall as a backup sound immediately after shooting a coyote that has come to a regular call. I start yipping frantically like a hurt pup. This often brings a second coyote that may have been traveling with the first but was hesitant to come in. Sometimes it even brings a third. This call sounds like a domestic puppy yipping or crying.

Calling Devices

Virtually one hundred percent of all predators are called with three types of calls: mouth-blown, hand-operated and electronic. Mouth calls can be divided into two categories: those that imitate prey and those that imitate the predators themselves.

Prey Calls

Mouth-blown prey calls are far and away the most popular because they are compact, versatile, inexpensive, effective, and never run out of batteries. Anyone who can exhale can blow one effectively, and entice visitors. No fancy hand controls are necessary. Tone and cadence are not critical. Just make it go waaa waaa waaa and you're in business. These common calls come in seven flavors.

Closed-Reed

The closed-reed variety consists of a wooden or plastic mouthpiece and barrel with a metal reed inside. In many cases this reed is the same as found in toddlers' squeaky toys. These calls are as common as mushrooms after a spring shower and virtually foolproof, but the sound is fixed. They are deadly effective until too many locals start using them. Then the local critters wise up, and it's time to switch to a different sound.

One exception to the nonvariable sound rule is the Mini-Blaster from Burnham Brothers. It's a tiny call consisting of a long metal reed inside a flexible plastic tube stuck into a small walnut barrel. By biting on the plastic tube, you can change the pitch. The volume from this call is enough to hurt your ears. Another closed-reed call you can modify in mid-blow is the Johnny Stewart PC-1, which has its metal reed beneath a rubber button you bite down on to touch the reed and change its pitch. Knight & Hale has a variation featuring twin reeds for a different sound. There are other twin reeds on the market, too. It's smart to carry a variety of calls and mix them up while in the field. For whatever reason, predators sometimes

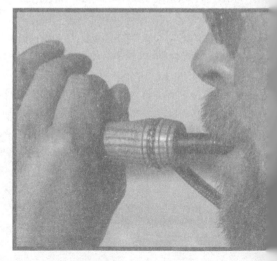

Semi-closed-reed calls can be manipulated to produce a variety of low or higher pitched cries.

respond to one better than the others on certain days, rather like turkeys do. In fact, carrying a turkey call or two isn't a bad idea. The "kee kee" run turkey call can bring coyotes on the run.

Semi-Closed Reed

These are based on the crow-call style, which is a reed sandwiched between two long lips of plastic that can be squeezed with the teeth to vary the pitch. These are a bit tougher to master than metal squeaker reed models, but can produce a wider variety of calls—from low-pitched jackrabbit to high-squeal cottontail. If you already have a crow call, just use it. The Primos cow elk call and antelope call with bite-down lips also work nicely. Steve Thompson's Dakota Jack Bite Reed is specially designed for predator calling. Many others can be found.

Open-Reed

Here's one of the most versatile mouth calls. It features a barrel with a plastic reed riding above a curved platform or sounding board at the blowing end. The reed is held in place by a wedge of cork or plastic or sometimes a fat rubber band. By pressing this exposed reed with teeth or lips while blowing, you change tone from the low bawl of a fawn or lamb to a squeal high enough to shatter glass. If you're good, you can make it quack and bugle like an elk. More importantly, you can make it howl like a coyote—thus the open-reed performs double duty. Growl into the call while blowing to make it raspy.

Diaphragm Calls

You guessed it. This is the standard turkey or elk diaphragm caller. Just a bit of tape and latex held in the mouth. Variable tongue pressure against the palate mixed with variable air pressure changes the notes of this device to nearly anything. Make it cry like a cottontail, bawl like a fawn, howl like a big dog, yipe like a puppy, yelp like a turkey, or bugle like an elk. Since it's contained completely within your mouth, both hands are motionless and free for shooting. You get maximum volume with minimum air pressure, too, so you don't wear out so fast or breathe so hard.

One spring Ken Sandquist and I were scouting turkeys from rimrock above a big, deep Idaho canyon. It was mid-morning and nothing was happening, so when two giant Canadas flew over honking, I did my best to mimic them with my diaphragm call. No cigar, but close. Then Ken pointed out a pair of coyotes climbing onto an overlook about a quarter-mile up canyon. "Think you can call them?'" he asked. Without missing a beat I howled, and both animals spun to

Plastic funnels or megaphones add resonance to coyote howls and project the sound in specific directions.

look right at us. I howled again, and here they came. Neither of us wanted to shoot a spring coyote, so we backed out of there, but we'd proven the versatility of the diaphragm call.

Many hunters who can't seem to get the hang of operating traditional diaphragm calls or gag on them should try either the Primos Hyper Plate models with a raised metal "roof" over the latex or the H.S. Tone Trough with a plastic roof over the latex. Both are much easier to blow than standard diaphragms and can be held farther toward the front of the mouth. Some manufacturers are now marketing special "predator" diaphragms, but nearly any turkey or elk caller will work. Heavier reeds are usually pitched lower, lighter reeds higher. You may need one of each to mimic old dogs and females or pups.

Rubber Band Squeakers

These are high-pitched, close-range calls with low volume. Two slender strips of plastic hold a strip of rubber band between them under slight tension. A caller can change the tension and raise the pitch by biting down on the plastic. Good for calling bobcats and fox and coaxing coyotes.

Bellows

Rubber air reservoirs are squeezed to activate internal reeds. Small versions are known as mouse squeakers, and they're good for fox and bobcats or coaxing coyotes those last few steps for a shot. Scotch used to make a large bellows call you operated like an accordion to activate the internal reed, but all that hand motion can work against you.

Voice

Some might not consider the human voice a predator call, but it sure can be. I took my brother out to one of my favorite calling sites in South Dakota one evening and blew through four series with no response. Being the joker he is, Bob began teasing me by "showing how it was done" using his voice. You guessed it—a coyote popped over the horizon and trotted right in.

Since then, I've used my voice to call several coyotes. Voice calling is wonderful because there are no devices to lose or forget and no hand movement. Sadly, few of us can call very long without getting sore or ineffective. My throat gets raw in a matter of minutes.

We Never Talk Anymore—Coyote Language

Howling to locate coyotes began long, long ago. Anyone living outdoors with coyotes is inevitably tempted to imitate their howls. Doing so often elicits a reply. Bingo! You've located a coyote. Just as domestic dogs howl at sirens, so do coyotes. By the mid-twentieth century, numerous Westerners had learned to stop every mile or two along county roads and sound a police siren to inspire coyotes to howl. Then they'd move in, set up, and call them with rabbit cries. Such sirens still work and are used by many callers to scout for animals. In fact, several of these "locator" sirens are sold just for finding coyotes. They should also work on wolves.

In recent years a number of manufacturers have begun selling specialized coyote howlers that are usually nothing more than open-reed prey calls. Just blow through them with the typical coyote howl cadence. Most howlers come with a plastic funnel or megaphone resonator, but these aren't critical to success. Diaphragms produce wonderful howls, too, and can be used with megaphones or an old kitchen funnel for a bit more resonance. Wolfer hunters are getting responses from our biggest wild dogs by imitating their low-pitched, mournful howls by voice. Often this is the only and best call you need to bring in wolves. If you're in their territory and sound like another wolf, they tend to take exception to your presence. Be ready to defend yourself against a whole pack. An Idaho hunter recently called in a pack and shot two before they split. Outfitter Coke Wallace in Alaska uses a tape of wolf howls to bring packs in during late summer/early Fall. But he only gets one, perhaps two cracks at this before the surviving wolves are too wise and wary to fall for the ruse again.

Most naturalists recognize a complex variety of coyote calls and attempt to interpret them. They've identified as many as thirty-three calls, including pair-bonding calls, puppy-feeding whines, yelps of submission and so on. Most are seldom heard and difficult to differentiate, but a few are fairly obvious and of value to the hunter. The following descriptions should serve to introduce you to conversational coyote, but don't cling hard and fast to these descriptions. Combine them with your own interpretations and experience to detect nuances and meanings. A written description of any animal sound is rough at best. Try to "feel" the call as much as hear it. Some calls sound lighthearted and friendly, others angry, others nervous or edgy. Such tones should help you interpret meaning. Mimic them and use them when you deem appropriate.

Territorial or Dominance Call: Can be given by male or female. Males are typically lower pitched. The dominance call is a no-fooling-around, aggressive-sounding collection of choppy barks and abbreviated howls. It's saying, "Keep out." Use it in late winter after most coyotes have paired and established distinct territories in which they'll soon raise pups. Expect a quick and angry response. This call can spook young coyotes.

Warning or Alarm Call: Similar to the territorial call, alarm calls are a series of barks that warn other coyotes of danger. Alarm barks are usually higher pitched than territorial barks, with a rapid, almost frantic delivery. You'll hear it when a suspicious coyote coming to your call spots you or otherwise determines something is amiss. Once this happens, it's virtually impossible to call anything in, but it is possible to sneak around and get a shot at the barker.

Distress Call or Puppy Whines: The yipping and crying of a frightened puppy. Mature dogs will yipe and cry too, so blowing this call after a shot may pull in a nearby mate.

Greeting, Welcome, or Pack Communication: High-pitched short barks, yaps, and happy howls. Two or more coyotes together sound like a choir of sopranos warming up before a concert. Packs may use this to tell other packs of their location. You hear these wild pack singing parties more often than any other calls. They're useful for locating subjects.

Location Howl: A lone, long, classic howl used to locate others. Can be used to call in coyotes, especially territorial males in winter. The howl starts low and immediately rises two octaves or more, where it is held for three to as many as ten seconds before tapering in volume and dropping smoothly in pitch over the course of a few seconds. Like a Hollywood wolf howl but higher-pitched.

Turn Me On—Electronic Callers

Battery-operated mechanical callers began as turntables playing 45-rpm records. The speaker was attached to the player or, more often, set several yards away using a long extension wire. The records played actual recorded animal-in-distress cries or an expert's mouth calls until the phonograph needle spun through the record's grooves. The hunter then had to reset the needle to restart the sequence. Obviously this rather delicate mechanism was subject to malfunction due to debris, dust, wind blowing the needle off track, rain, and snow.

Western Rivers callers are remotely controlled and contain all sounds plus speaker in one handy, easily carried unit. Add shooting sticks, binocular, rifle, and scope and you're ready for action.

Cassette tape players improved things dramatically. One tape could play continuously for thirty minutes, and most of the moving parts were protected inside the box, though debris still got inside the tape opening and created problems. An operator could fairly easily change tapes to play different sounds, and since the tapes were compact and lightweight, it was easy to carry a number of them.

Today, cassette tape players are still marketed but machines that play CDs and MP3 digital files are the big deal. Some of these are becoming quite compact and durable. The all-in-one, self-contained units seem to be the most popular. They look like a large flashlight. Most can be controlled wirelessly via a remote. Some are integral with a decoy, the sound coming right from the fake bunny. A handy feature on digital machines is the ability to select tracks instantly without rewinding. Some will play two sounds at once, like rabbit squealing and coyote howling. When testing various units, determine how easily you can find the various controls and manipulate them. Some use fine gradations in sound control while others jump from super quiet to extra loud a bit too abruptly. Some handheld control units seem too sensitive—barely touch them and they change sounds or volume. Good tactile control is important when you're excited, your hands are cold, or your fingers are handicapped inside gloves. You don't want to have to hammer a button to change things, but neither do you want it activated by a mere glance.

Listen to volume levels and compare them when shopping, too. A few units don't seem to crank out the sound levels or quality of others. While you're listening for this, check out how many actual critter sounds are available and whether they come built in or on plug-in memory cards. For a time, electronic

An electronic caller's remote speaker concentrates a predator's attention away from the shooter.

callers required different cards for each sound. Then they started putting several on a card. These days, with iPods and even smartphones able to store and play thousands of complicated songs and symphonies, you should be able to get a predator caller with every known animal sound in the world.

By the way, many of these sounds can be found on the Internet and down-loaded for free. Build your own MP3 sound library, load it into your caller, and you're ready for everything. And while calling, don't be afraid to mix and match sounds in one setup. We've started with cottontail cries, switched to lower-pitched jackrabbits, then flickers and squawking chickens and howling coyotes and who knows what all before pulling in coyotes. Once we even brought in a bobcat using a mix of jackrabbit cries and coyote howls. Don't be afraid to experiment. I think predators approach out of curiosity as much as hunger.

While dedicated electronic game callers are handy and ready to rumble (be sure to keep spare batteries in your truck), ordinary tape, CD, and MP3 players can be modified to handle the same job. All you need to do is add an external speaker and perhaps an amplifier to a portable player such as a smartphone or iPod. Technicians at electronics stores (or your thirteen-year-old nephew) should be able to advise you on building such a rig.

Being old-school, I've always been a mouth caller, but in recent years my buddies and I are relying more and more on the machines. Their advantages include 1) the ability to play odd critter distress calls not easily imitated with a mouth call (various bird calls come to mind); 2) long, continuous playing—extremely useful when trying to call cats for thirty to sixty minutes. Cats, more than canines, seem to prefer a continuous call without interruption, and an electronic caller can give it to them; 3) infinite volume control. By merely turning a dial, you can drop an electronic call to a whisper; 4) minimum hand movement. Other than adjusting volume and punching in a new sound, you just sit and watch. Keep the machine between your legs and they'll block virtually all hand movement; 5) a remote sound source. This may be the absolute best reason to hire a machine to do your calling. Stick the speaker fifty to seventy-five feet away, and incoming clients will not be focused on you. Place the speaker next to a decoy for ultimate realism.

Because machines can malfunction, batteries die, and tapes break, always carry a backup mouth call or two. Or six.

LIST OF CALL MANUFACTURERS

Buck Expert, Inc. www.buckexpert.com
Buck Gardner Calls www.buckgardner.com
Burnham Brothers www.burnhambrothers.com
Cabela's www.cabelas.com
Carver www.carverpredatorcalls.com
Circe (see Flambeau Outdoors)
Dakota Predator Calls (Steve Thompson) www.sdsnake.com/coyote
Dan Thompson www.danthompsongamecalls.com
Extreme Dimension Wildlife Calls, LLC (see Phantom Calls)
Faulk's Game Call Company, Inc. www.faulkcalls.com
Flambeau Outdoors www.flambeau.com
Flextone www.flextonegamecalls.com
Foxpro Systems www.gofoxpro.com
Haydel's Game Calls, Inc. www.haydels.com
Hunter's Specialties www.hunterspec.com
Johnny Stewart www.hunterspec.com
Knight & Hale www.knightandhale.com
MAD (see Flambeau Outdoors)
MossBack Game Calls www.mossbackgamecalls.com
Sceery Outdoors www.sceeryoutdoors.com

Phantom Pro (Extreme Dimension Wildlife Calls) www.phantomcalls.com
Primos Hunting Calls www.primos.com
Predator Quest (Les Johnson) www.predatorquest.com
Verminator Predator Calls www.verminatorpredatorcalls.com
Weems (Replica) www.danthompsongamecalls.com
Wild Game Innovations (see Flextone)
Western Rivers www.western-rivers.com
Woods Wise Products www.woodswise.com
Zepp's Predator Calls www.markzepp.com

CHANCES ARE YOUR CHANCES ARE PRETTY GOOD

New callers usually wonder just what the odds of calling a critter are. Some seem to think they're poor, having heard of hunters who've tried calling for an entire season without luck. The answer depends on what you're calling, where you're calling, and how you approach the site and set up to cover it. Don't fret about the sound of the call itself. Location is the key.

If you're working coyotes in high-density areas like parts of Texas, Oklahoma, Arizona, and Kansas and play your cards right, you should average one response for every four or five setups. You could easily call a dozen stands in a row and see nothing, but the next day you might be swarmed at every stand. One morning last February in Texas, we called at six places and pulled coyotes from five of them. Saw six at one stand, killed two at another. It balances out.

For some reason, probably frequent human disturbance, eastern coyotes are more reluctant to chase down every whisper of bunny-in-distress. A realistic average for good callers who know their territory might be one taker in ten tries.

Odds for bobcats are much lower simply because they don't live in the densities coyotes do, nor do they usually come as far and aggressively to calls, although I have had them race right in. However, if you set up in known bobcat territory, you should expect a response eventually. The nice thing about cats is they're quite tolerant of human scent and even motion. While a coyote will usually turn and flee when it sees you, or at least stop approaching, a cat will usually sit and watch, sometimes for fifteen minutes. If a coyote catches a whiff of human odor, it's gone. Cats will stay. But those sneaky kitties are hard to detect. Look long and hard and often. And then look again before you leave. A hard scan with a binocular is wise.

Gray fox generally come eagerly if you call within a few hundred yards of them. Red fox can be equally aggressive if they aren't harried by coyotes. Where they are, expect them to take 30 to 45 minutes to arrive. Raccoons are not good candidates for calling with prey sounds in most places, but they're suckers for coon squalls. These are the sounds coons make when fighting. Lions and bears are real trophies for a predator caller. I've never called a lion, but have called four black bears. You'll need to prospect long and hard to find just the right location and conditions to entice one of these into range. With them, it's not so much the sound, as the location.

5

Please Select Your Shootin' Iron

Firearms for Effect

I hate to be the bearer of sad tidings, but somebody has to break the news: You can't buy the perfect predator rifle. It doesn't exist. Habitat, terrain, weather, and the critters themselves demand not just one but a diversity of harvesting tools. The dense oak forests that make a shotgun deadly in Kentucky render a long-barreled, medium-caliber, heavyweight, precision target rifle virtually useless. Yet such a rifle might be just the ticket on the wide-open shortgrass plains of eastern Montana. The explosive speed and energy that make a .22-250 Remington ideal for coyotes can destroy fox pelts. Ah, but the .22 long rifle rimfire is easy on fox hides—but too anemic to stop big coyotes. Sometimes a .22 Winchester Rimfire Magnum is just what the bobcat ordered. But the .17 HMR might do even less pelt damage.

The upshot of all this is that your perfect predator rifle may actually be several rifles plus a scatter-gun. It all depends on what and where you hunt. So before rushing out to buy, assess your needs carefully. And be prepared to change. Most serious predator hunters experiment with numerous firearms, cartridges, bullets, shot sizes, and sights as they try to uncover the consummate tools for the game and habitat they hunt.

Most veteran predator hunters started with whatever went bang, usually the deer rifle or shotgun they were carrying when serendipity placed them within range of their first fox, bobcat, or coyote. I tossed lead (harmlessly) at the first red fox I ever jumped with a Winchester Model 190 autoloader chambered for the venerable .22 long rifle. At the time, 1967 or so, this was the only rifle I owned. Every winter Saturday and most Sunday afternoons, I'd carry it over plowed fields and corn stubble where my buddies and I harried big, white-tailed jackrabbits that fetched a dollar each at the local mink farm. The hides were tanned for glove liners, and the meat was fed to the mink. Mixed with the maze of hare tracks we followed through the snow was the occasional spoor of a red fox. To fourteen-year-old boys in farm country, the clean, straight-line trail of a fox could just as well have been laid by a polar bear. Major predator. Big game. Top of the local food chain if you didn't count the farmers down at the local Bowling Alley Cafe, and we didn't.

Sadly, a continental glacier some ten thousand years earlier had scraped the local topography so flat that every fox within a mile of an upright Homo sapiens could see him and slip away unseen—except when the wind was blowing snow. On those days, Old Red might hide under his tail in the lee of a weedy fence line. Covered by the howling wind, a determined boy might awaken such sleeping beauties at slingshot range, shocking himself as much as the little carnivores that shot like flames through the swirling white. Alas, the very wind that permitted the close encounter usually buffeted the shooter so badly that aiming was impossible. Even when it wasn't, wind drift usually pushed the little 40-grain hollow point bullets well off course. Despite all this, my brother once swung his .22 past a running fox, doubled his lead, added plenty of elevation, and made a perfect double-lung shot at a heroic 150 yards.

I didn't topple my first red fox until my sixteen-year-old hunting partner, Gary Lowin, and I flushed one from dense cattails while hunting pheasants. Although the range was long, we both fired three times, the chance at a fox worth this prodigal expenditure of 12 gauge shells. Despite our extravagant efforts, the fox just kept running, but just before it disappeared behind a weedy fence line, it stopped, looked back, and fell over. We found one 6-shot-sized hole in one side of its chest, one 4-shot-sized hole in the other, and shared the ten-dollar fur check.

In my late teens, following local tradition, I bought a Winchester M94 for hunting whitetails in the famed Black Hills of South Dakota. That proved adequate, but when I tried the .30-30 on January fox, its limited range and buck horn open sights proved wholly inadequate. I couldn't even see red fur behind that big gold bead. Within a year I traded that classic deer rifle for a Remington Model 788 bolt action chambered for the 6 mm Remington. A Bushnell scope—a 3-9X variable if I remember—improved my sighting abilities. With that little rig, I was soon rolling sleeping foxes off snowbanks at 250 yards and picking up coyotes running to my calls at less than thirty yards. Impact energy kept me up nights sewing fox pelts, but coyote hides held together quite well unless hit around the edges.

Eight years later I traded up to a .270 Winchester in a Ruger M77 mostly because I wanted to hunt elk and could only afford one rifle. By then I was hand-loading, and figured I could concoct some 90-grain Sierra hollow point loads that would suffice for predators. The .270 shot virtually as flat as the 6 mm but blew even larger holes in everything. That's when I determined that one center-fire rifle was not going to meet all of my hunting needs. Fortunately, I was by then making enough money to afford a second. I ordered a .22-250 Ruger M77 and had a matched pair of rugged, dependable bolt rifles that carried me for many years.

Since then, I've hunted predators with everything from a .22 Long Rifle to a .300 Weatherby Magnum (not always intentionally), and I've formed some educated (and some mostly prejudicial) opinions on which calibers, actions, barrels, stocks, and sights work best. Let's consider them, starting with cartridges.

.17 Hornady Magnum Rimfire

Released in 2002, this new bottlenecked rimfire, created by necking down a .22 Winchester Magnum case, shows potential to be a mild-shooting, hard-hitting varmint round that should be more than adequate to take small predators inside 150 yards. Beyond that, remaining energy dwindles fast (72 foot-pounds at two hundred yards) and wind drift becomes excessive (15 inches at two hundred yards in 10-mph crosswind.) Muzzle velocity with Hornady's 17-grain V-Max bullet is rated 2,550 feet per second. This poison pill could prove ideal for minimizing pelt damage. Penetration through bone remains to be seen. Many consider this a fine fur cartridge for calling set ups if quarry can be sucked inside of 100 yards. I think it's too light for coyotes in general, but a careful shooter can make it work.

.17 Remington Fireball

Long a wildcat based on the .221 Fireball, which was itself made from a shortened .222 Remington case, the .17 Fireball was finally legitimized by Remington in 2007. This could be the ultimate fur-harvester's cartridge. It drives a 20-grain bullet more than 4,000 feet per second, a 30-grain almost 3,600 feet per second—fast enough to shoot delightfully flat. MPBR is three hundred yards with a two hundred-yard zero using the 20-grain V-Max. There's not much remaining energy at that range, but should be enough to ruin a coyote's day without ruining his fur. Wind deflection can be big, since B.C. of the 20-grain V-Max is just .185. Recoil is so mild that you should be able to watch impact with an 8-pound rifle. Barrel fouling is less with this than the Fireball's big cousin. I'd consider the .17 Fireball a candidate for ultimate fur-getter inside two hundred yards, but this is just conjecture because I've never tried it. But I'd sure like to.

.17 Remington

I'll give this fastest commercial centerfire cartridge a thumbs down for extreme-range open-country coyotes but a thumbs up for foxes and bobcats. I say this even though I've never fired a .17 Rem at game. Those who have tell me it absolutely flattens coyotes. So what's my beef? Reputation and basic physics. By most reports the tiny .17 bore, which burns 4 grains more powder than the Fireball to get 250 feet per second more speed, fouls quickly and must be cleaned frequently to maintain accuracy. I do know that cleaning a .17 bore is a bit of a pain. You need special, narrow cleaning rods and tips that bend and break easily. Most .17 bullets are rather delicate things, and at 4,300 feet per second liable to blow apart upon striking even minimum vegetation. Handloaders claim slight variations in powder charge weight result in dramatic velocity/pressure changes. There are few choices in .17 bullets and even fewer in factory-loaded ammunition, but I'm not sure you need many. The 25-grain V-Max starts life at 4,000 feet per second and deflects 9 inches at 300 yards in 10-mph crosswind, 1.5 inches more than a .22-250 Rem. Its .230 B.C. means slightly less wind deflection than the 20-grain version. Like its shorter cousin, this biggest .17 has a mild report and mild recoil. Its tiny bullets should make it easy on pelts and safe in heavily settled farm country. Handloaders can load down to match .17 Fireball ballistics, yet have the option to grab the extra speed for those longer shots. Hmmm. This might not be a bad option after all.

.204 Ruger

One of the more exciting, useful cartridges to come along recently is this .20 caliber treat from Ruger. Made by slightly modifying and necking down the old .222 Remington Magnum, the .204 Ruger falls between the .22-250 Rem and .17 Rem in performance. Some think it's the ideal, all-round predator round. It shoots as flat as a .22-250 but punches little holes about like the .17s. A 32-grain Nosler Ballistic Tip can be driven 4,100 feet per second. It usually enters, but doesn't come out. Perfect. Some have found that fringe hits can result in wounding loss, but that can happen with .220 Swift and even .243 Win. fringe hits. The 32-grain bullet's B.C. is slightly higher than the 20-grain .17's B.C., so wind deflection is slightly less. I consider the .204 Ruger the perfect compromise for coyote hunters who plan to call them in close and minimize fur damage, yet still want to punch 'em out to 350 yards if they have to. Recoil is nearly zilch, so with fairly heavy rifles you can hang on target and see your hits. As with any tiny cartridge, powder and bullet expenses are minimal.

.22 Long Rifle

Over its lengthy career, this ubiquitous rimfire has sent thousands— perhaps millions—of predators to that big rabbit warren in the sky, but it certainly can't be considered ideal for the job. The little 32- to 40-grain slugs usually loaded atop this tiny brass powder reservoir generate a mere 140 foot-pounds of energy at the muzzle. This dwindles to ninety at one hundred yards and eighty at 150 yards. Slipped through a coyote's ribs, it'll usually extinguish the life force, but some-times even hard-hit predators escape into cover or run hundreds of yards before succumbing. The trajectory of the bullets pretty much limits effectiveness to one hundred yards anyway. They fall nearly seven inches at one hundred yards if sighted dead-on at fifty yards. At 150 yards they're twenty-one inches low. Some hypervelocity .22 long rifle loads use lighter, hollow point slugs to increase velocity and improve trajectory, but they lose downrange energy as a trade-off. I consider the .22 long rifle adequate only for fox, raccoons, and small bobcats called to within fifty yards. You might stretch that to seventy-five yards, but no more. Low-cost ammo, minimum noise, and virtually no recoil make this rimfire a delight to shoot and inconspicuous in settled areas. An extremely accurate one might suffice for head-shots on coyotes to 75 yards.

.22 Winchester Magnum Rimfire

By driving a 50-grain hollow point at 1,525 feet per second or a 40-grain hollow point at 1,900, the .22 Mag fills the power gap between the .22 long rifle and the .22 Hornet. It's adequate for coyotes to one hundred yards and fox to 150 yards. Sighted dead-on at one hundred yards, a 30-grain hollow point spit from a muzzle at 2,200 feet per second will be six inches low at 150 yards. The 10-mph wind drift at one hundred yards will be seven inches. At 150 yards it'll stretch to a ruinous seventeen inches. Retained energy at 150 yards will have fallen to eighty foot-pounds.

Popular coyote cartridges include .223, .22-250, .220 Swift, .243, 6mm, and .25-06.

These ballistics are matched with a 40-grain bullet launched at 1,910 feet per second, but at 150 yards retained energy will be about thirty footpounds higher. I rate the .22 WMR only slightly behind the .17 HMR. Consider it a 150-yard tool.

.22 Hornet

The old Hornet, around since the "Dirty Thirties," is a great little cartridge for predators as large as coyotes out to about two hundred yards. Because the case holds only enough powder to propel a 50-grain slug to about 2,600 feet per second, energy drops rapidly and wind drift increases dramatically as the ballistically inefficient 45- and 50-grain bullets are slowed by air drag. That 50-grain bullet will be packing 750 foot-pounds of energy when it leaves the barrel, but this drops to 533 at one hundred yards, 368 at two hundred yards and a paltry 250 at three hundred yards. In comparison, the same bullet launched from a .22-250 Rem at 3,800 feet per second will still be hauling 621 foot-pounds at three hundred yards.

The trajectory news is even worse. At three hundred yards a 50-grain Hornet slug sighted for one hundred yards will drop twenty inches. A two hundred-yard sighting will improve that to twelve inches, but mid-range trajectory becomes a bit high.

Ten grains of powder in a Hornet doesn't generate much recoil or noise, so it's a pleasure to shoot and less obtrusive than the bigger .22s in settled farmland. I consider the Hornet an outstanding calling cartridge, but it can leave you frustrated when a coyote hangs up at three hundred yards.

.218 Bee

This 1938 creation is rarely chambered in today's rifles, but occasionally you'll find it in a single-shot or a revival of an old model. When first released, it was supposed to out-sting the Hornet, but because it was initially chambered only in a Winchester M65 lever action with tubular magazine, bullets had to be flat-tipped, costing downrange performance. Loaded with spire-point bullets in a modern stacked-magazine rifle or single-shot, the Bee will generate nearly 2,750 feet per second with a 50-grain pill. Like the Hornet, it's a mild shooter, easy on pelts, and effective to 250 yards.

.221 Fireball

Remington resurrected this shortened version of the .222 Remington in 2002 when it again began chambering rifles for it. Originally it was brought out as a handgun cartridge for the XP-100 pistol in 1963. This is another good cartridge for close work. Obviously, at 3,100 feet per second with a 50-grain bullet, it won't keep pace with its larger kin, but neither will it damage pelts to such a degree. I took a Texas bobcat with a .221 Fireball inside 40 yards once and found but one entrance hole. Unfortunately, I almost didn't find the cat. At the shot, right on the point of the shoulder, it leaped and ran, expiring in an oak thicket. No blood trail. The bullet had passed through both lungs, but didn't exhibit the expected shock one usually gets from a faster bullet. You can load 45-, 40- and even 35-grain bullets for increased frangibility and shock, but less resistance against wind deflection. Oddly, this same cartridge and 50-grain varmint bullet took down a feral hog from about 120 yards, passing through both lungs and lodging against the far side hide. Velocity had dropped enough for the frangible bullet to mushroom like a classic deer bullet. Call this a good two hundred and fifty-yard option.

.222 Remington, .222 Remington Magnum, and .223 Remington

The .222 Remington was a benchrest accuracy champ and proven varmint cartridge fourteen years before the .223 came along in 1964, but since the latter became an official military round (5.56 mm Ball cartridge) with slightly longer case and higher operating pressures, it generated one hundred to three hundred feet per second more speed than the old Triple Deuce and has all but run it out of town. The .222 Rem Mag also started as an experimental military round, but when it was not officially adopted by Uncle Sam, Remington released it as a commercial cartridge in 1958. It and the .223 are nearly dimensional and performance twins, so of course no one chambers rifles for the .222 Rem Mag anymore. Any of these cartridges makes a fine predator puncher out to three hundred yards with 50- to 55-grain bullets, but at the 3,100- to 3,400-feet-per-second velocities they generate, pelt damage becomes a factor. The .223 Rem is hugely popular since it's the original chambered for the AR-15 style rifles, and those are gaining fans in the predator hunting world.

.22 PPC

This is one of the new short, fat, efficiency cartridges. It was designed in 1975 to win benchrest accuracy matches, and that it does. But by tossing 50- to 55-grain .224 slugs at 3,400 to 3,500 feet per second, it also qualifies as a superb long-range predator getter. With a mere one hundred feet per second speed advantage over the .223 Rem, the PPC offers no major ballistic advantage. In field rifles it probably offers little or no accuracy advantage, either. And the fat cases reduce magazine capacity, arguing for the .223. Availability of ammunition is much higher for the .223 as well. However, if you crave something different, this is it. I've seen rifles from Dakota, Sako, and Ruger chambered for the PPC.

.22-250 Remington

Make way for the king. Maybe. There is no official confirmation, but I have a strong hunch backed by decades of experience that this hot .22 center-fire is the hands down favorite of coyote hunters. It will drive a 55-grain bullet to 3,650 feet per second, a mere 150 slower than the .220 Swift. That means it will have as much wallop at three hundred yards as the .22 Hornet does at its muzzle. Sight

Today's factory ammunition performs as well as custom reloads in many rifles. Winchester's Ballistic Silvertip loads in .223 and .22-250 are great for long-range coyotes.

the .22-250 to strike dead-on at two hundred yards, and it will land only five inches below line of sight at three hundred yards. In the hands of a great shooter, it's effective to four hundred yards. Of course, these speeds come at a price. Out to about 250 yards, pelt damage can be excessive. Almost every rifle maker chambers for the .22-250.

.220 Swift

In one respect, this is the king—the velocity king. When released by Winchester in 1935, the Swift was reportedly pushing a 48-grain pill over 4,100 feet per second. Factory horsepower has been throttled back slightly since then, but this war-horse is still good for 3,800 feet per second with a 55-grain bullet. The heavier slug provides a higher B.C. than the lighter ones, so it drifts less in the wind and retains more energy downrange. Sight this baby to hit point of aim at two hundred yards and it's only 4.4 inches low at three hundred. Set it up for maximum point-blank range with a 5-inch target zone, and it will shoot no higher than 2.5 inches at 157 yards and will not drop 2.5 inches below line of sight until 312 yards. With this setup, you could aim dead center on a coyote's chest and hit it at any distance out to 312 yards without worrying about precise distance or holdover. Just aim carefully and shoot. That should cover about ninety percent of all shooting opportunities.

.223 Winchester Super Short Magnum

For a time it seemed this stubby chubby would become the new darling of the long-range varminting world, but rumors of barrel burning plus a legal mess with royalties has sent it into a tailspin. I don't know if anyone chambers rifles for it anymore. Too bad. With fast-twist barrels, it is capable of driving highly efficient, wind-resistant, 60- to 75-grain bullets 3,500 to 3,800 feet per second. Zeroed at 250 yards, the 75-grain pill would rise just 2 inches above line-of-sight and drop just 4 inches at 325 yards. That's a dead on hold for the vast majority of all shots a predator hunter will ever take. The .223 WSSM burns about 3 grains more powder than the .22-250 Rem, so barrel burning shouldn't be that big of a problem, particularly if you don't shoot it with a hot barrel. I wouldn't want to use if for high-volume ground squirrel eradication, but for long-range coyotes, it's a winner. If you handload and find a used .223 WSSM for sale cheap, buy it. Or have a custom rifle built with a 1-8 inch twist, 26-inch barrel for maximum velocity and long-range performance. It's excessive for fox and bobcats, but coyotes waaaay out there aren't going to like it.

.243 Winchester

Here we finally step up in caliber from .224-inch to .243-inch slugs which, given adequate weight and sleek profile, resist wind drift slightly better than the .224 pills. Of all .243 cartridges, none is more popular worldwide than the .243

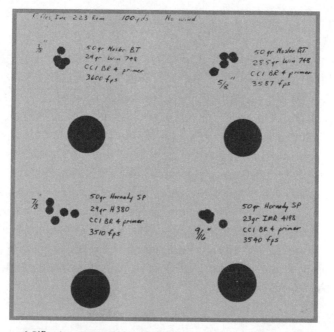

A Rifles, Inc. custom .223 produced these excellent groups from the bench at one hundred yards. Imagine what they'll do in the field. Rifles and ammo this accurate are real confidence builders.

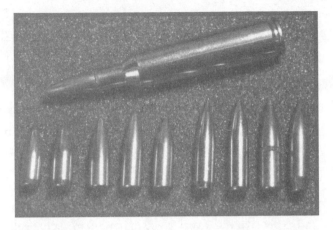

6mm Rem. cartridge and .243 bullets from 60-grain V-Max to 100-grain boat-tail spire points. Lighter bullets shoot flatter. Heavier ones drift less in wind.

Winchester, a necked-down version of the .308 Winchester. In the past two seasons I've gone 11 for 12 on coyotes out to 350 yards with a sweet little .243 Win. Kilimanjaro bolt-action that weighs just under six pounds, carries like a baton, and whips into action fast to catch coyotes running flat out. A rifle like this is perfect for hunting deer and coyotes simultaneously. It's a bit overpowered for fox and bobcat if you're hunting for fur. For maximum speed and flat trajectory, load it with any of the 55- to 70-grain plastic-tipped varmint bullets. For a higher B.C. and less wind drift, go with an 80- or even a 100-grain bullet. The Berger 115-grain Match VLD is rated .545 B.C., but you'll need a 1-7 twist barrel to stabilize it. Pelt damage can be significant, but you will reach out with this one.

6 mm Remington

Anything the .243 Winchester can do, the 6 mm Remington can do slightly better. It'll churn out about one hundred feet per second more speed with the same bullets. This cartridge was originally released as the .244 Remington in 1955, but rifles chambered for it wore barrels with a 1-12 rifling twist rate that wouldn't stabilize many long, 100-grain bullets. This cost it sales to the more versatile .243 Winchester with its 1-10 twist rifling. Remington changed the .244's twist rate, but not soon enough. Slumping sales inspired them to reintroduced the .244 in 1963 as the 6 mm with 1-9 twist barrels. Despite these efforts, the .243 Winchester remains the more popular. This classic example of bad public relations does not mean the 6 mm is faulty. It remains a superb cartridge for coyotes, though few rifles are chambered for it. I have a Rifles, Inc. custom 6 mm Rem with a 24-inch Shilen barrel on an M70 action mated to a fancy walnut stock carved by Show Me Gunstocks of Warsaw, Missouri. I had it built as the ultimate coyote rifle that could double for deer or antelope. It will drop nearly any 55-to

80-grain bullet inside an inch or less at one hundred yards, day after day. Unfortunately, I neglected to specify a 1-10 twist barrel, and its 1-12 twist tube spreads 100-grain bullets like a kid tossing gravel.

.240 Weatherby Magnum

This belted cartridge could represent the ultimate in long-range .243 medicine for coyotes. It will throw bullets three hundred feet per second faster than the 6 mm Rem and four hundred feet per second faster than the .243 Win. That can create a lot of hide damage at close range, but if you need to reach to two hundred yards and beyond with minimum drop, minimum wind drift and maximum impact, this is your baby. On the downside, loaded ammunition is hard to find and expensive, but if you reload, no problem. The Weatherby PredatorMaster is a superb, modern rifle chambered for this screamers, and in 2012 had a MSRP of just $599.

.243 Winchester Super Short Magnum

This cousin to the .223 WSSM is the same case necked up. And it suffers the same problems as its narrower kin, although the barrel burning issue is way overblown. This cartridge consumes no more powder than the standard .243 Win, but it can kick up about 100 feet per second more speed. There's no significant advantage of one over another, so stick with the older version unless you handload and can find a used WSSM dirt cheap. For long-range shooting, this one will reach out and touch.

.257 Roberts

Before the .243 cartridges came along in the 1950s, the Roberts was king of the medium-bore deer cartridges. Like the .243 Win, it is a mild shooter with more than enough oomph for coyotes. With a muzzle velocity of 3,100 feet per second, it'll throw an 85-grain bullet almost as flat at the .243 Win will sling a 75-grain pill. I see no reason to choose the Roberts over any of the .243 cartridges, but if you already have one, there's no need to replace it. By the way, the Roberts, like the 6 mm Rem, is based on the 7 mm Mauser case, while the .243 Win, .260 Rem, and 7 mm-08 Rem are all based on the .308 Winchester case. The WSSMs are made from the .300 WSM case, which was itself concocted from the fat .404 Jeffery, a British dangerous game round from long ago.

A version of the .257 Roberts popular with handloaders is the .257 Roberts Improved. This is the standard Roberts case with straightened side-walls and a 40-degree shoulder, which adds seven percent more powder capacity and 150 feet per second more velocity. Nice option. Have a gunsmith rechamber a .257 Roberts barrel to Improved. Fire-form factory loads to the new shape. Then handload. Or just buy a .25-06 Remington.

.25-06 Remington

I know western coyote hunters who consider this the quintessential long-range coyote getter. While it recoils more than any of the previously discussed cartridges, it's not violent enough to cause flinching in most shooters. More importantly, it'll push an 87-grain pill along at a brisk 3,550 feet per second, good enough for four hundred-yard performance if rifle and shooter are up to it. Better yet, this bullet will drift slightly less than a 75-grain .243 or any 55-grain .224 in a crosswind—about an inch or two less at three hundred yards. This isn't a huge difference, but worth considering when you need to make an extreme-range, head-on shot. For even less wind deflection, try 115- to 120-grain projectiles. They're deadly to at least five hundred yards.

.25 Winchester Super Short Magnum

This is a .25-06 Remington in a really short fat case, the same case as used in the other two WSSMs. And, like them, it is probably already obsolete. Of the three, this is the most efficient and reasonable, giving good performance all the way around. Handloaders can really make this sing, and a used rifle could be had cheap. Not a bad option for predators and most big game. And you'll have a conversation piece at every hunting camp.

.257 Weatherby Magnum

Ouch. This is the .25-06 on steroids. It'll add two hundred feet per second to most .25-06 velocities. It's certainly more horsepower than any coyote needs, but that means you can misjudge range badly and still make hits out to 350 yards or so with no holdover. Know your trajectory and this is your baby way beyond boy-howdy. With the right scope, knowledge and skill, you could use this one for seven hundred-yard work. As with all Weatherby cartridges, ammunition is expensive and not commonly stocked in many retail stores, but you can handload your way around both problems. In today's market, this is the ultimate long-range coyote getter, but hell on pelts. But if you need to hit a coyote at any distance under the worst conditions, this cartridge will do it. I'm an unabashed .257 Wby fan, but admit the round is better suited to big game than predators, especially if you call them close.

.260 Remington

This 6.5 mm version of the .308 Win cartridge offers slight wind-drift and drop advantages over the .243 caliber version of the same case, but not enough to get worked up about. Its real value is realized in deer and antelope hunting, when the extra energy in its 120- and 140-grain bullets serves a need. Again, if you own one, it'll work for coyotes, but if you're buying specifically for predators, the .260 Rem offers no advantages over the .243 Win.

6.5 Grendel, Creedmoor, Swede, et. al.

The 6.5 mm bullet size has never done well in the U.S. even though it's a popular military round in various countries and a major big game round in Europe. In recent years it's caught on because of its long, high B.C. bullets combined with relatively low recoil when used with reasonable doses of powder. Some 6.5s were designed for maximum target competition efficiency (the Creedmoor), some for superior functioning through the short actions of AR platform rifles (Grendel), and some are just plain good hunting rounds for nearly anything. The fastest is the old .264 Winchester Magnum followed by the 6.5 Remington Magnum and then the 6.5-284 Norma, perhaps my favorite. All make good coyote rounds, but none are what I'd consider pelt protectors—or even necessary. If you need a big game rifle to serve double duty on predators, the 6.5s will suffice. If you need to shoot past five hundred yards, one of these could work, too.

.270 Winchester

Like most of the mid-power deer cartridges, the .270 is a great long-range coyote killer, but too much for close-range fur harvesting. Sure, it'll shoot nearly as flat as a .22-250 and resist wind drift slightly better, but at a significant increase in recoil, noise, and expense. Use it if you want, but don't fool yourself that you're packing any great advantage. Compare the 130-grain .270 bullet against a 120-grain .25-06 bullet and a 100-grain 6 mm Remington projectile, and you'll see that there is virtually no difference in trajectory or wind drift, so why put up with the extra noise, recoil, and pelt damage? Lump this one in with the faster 6.5 mm above.

.280 Rem, .30-06, .300 Win Mag, et al.

Overkill. In my experience, all cartridges more powerful than a .25-06 Rem are excessive for harvesting predators smaller than black bears. You can march up the caliber/power scale as far as you want and justify each cartridge, but all provide more recoil, noise, and expense without offering any improvements over the smaller calibers except reduced wind drift with high B.C. bullets like the 150- to 175-grain .284s and 165- to 180-grain .308s driven at top velocities. This is a close thing, but if you shop carefully for the sleekest, pointiest projectiles in these larger calibers (how about a B.C. of .475 in the Nosler 165-grain Ballistic Tip .308 or the .515 B.C. of the .284 Scirocco 150-grain pill?) and drive them to top velocities with magnum cartridges, you can realize several inches less wind drift than even the efficient 100-grain .243 and 120-grain .257 bullets can deliver at three hundred yards. If you do most of your predator shooting at extreme range in wind, this advantage might justify use of a larger magnum caliber. Study trajectory and wind drift tables carefully before deciding. And get ready for some recoil.

The only other reasons I can justify employing the bigger calibers for predators are that 1) it's the only suitable rifle you own, 2) you prefer to use your big game rifle in order to become totally familiar and deadly with it, or 3) you simply enjoy shooting big guns and want to use them. These are all great reasons.

By the way, large calibers don't necessarily mean major pelt damage. A substantial controlled-expansion bullet like a Swift A-Frame, Trophy Bonded Bear Claw, Nosler Accubond, Barnes TTSX, Winchester XP3, and the like usually punch through a coyote with minimum expansion, leaving a reasonable exit hole that can be sewed shut rather easily. Such bullets are quite expensive, though.

.22 LR AMMO

Small differences in .22 LR bullets make surprisingly big differences in impact. Some of today's .22 ammo seems to hit harder than it should. One of the best is Winchester's Power Point with a 40-grain hollow point starting at 1,280 feet per second. The flat meplat and hollow nose seem to upset much more dramatically and kill much more quickly than did hollow points of the past.

CCI's Stinger load with 32-grain hollow point at 1,640 feet per second is a hot cartridge worth trying. The Velocitor HP from CCI also holds promise of something special. Its 40-grain, notched hollow point roars to life

.22 cartridge is ideal for fox and bobcat hunting.

at an impressive 1,435 feet per second, faster than any other 40-grain bullet on the market. Remington's Hyper Velocity Yellow Jacket (33-grain hollow point at 1,500 feet per second) is another good bet. Remember that all lighter bullets, even though they start their journeys two hundred to three hundred feet per second faster than high-velocity 40-grain bullets, lose speed and energy faster, so that at one hundred yards the "slower" slugs have the power and trajectory advantage. Reserve lightweight hyper-velocity bullets for shots under fifty yards.

Rifles–Actions, Sizes, and Styles

Saying that a .223 Remington is the best rifle for hunting predators is like saying an eight-cylinder car is the best for drag racing. We're confusing power plant with vehicle. The two have to be considered together for each style of hunting/shooting.

Break-Action Single Shots

I see no advantage for the predator hunter in a rifle that requires pushing a lever aside so that a breech can swing down to expose the chamber for loading. Reloading in this fashion is slow. It completely interrupts aiming, and the design contributes nothing to improving accuracy over any other common action. This is not to say break-actions are inaccurate. They can be tack-drivers, but there's a misconception that the action-style itself contributes to enhanced accuracy. Not true. Break-action single shots can be, and often are, extremely accurate. Still, there is no need to put up with such slow reloading to realize this degree of precision. However, those who enjoy the adrenaline rush and extra challenge of one-shot hunting don't give a tinker's damn about reloading speed. By exercising control and waiting for perfect shooting opportunities, a careful man or woman can take more predators with a single-shot than an excitable shooter might bag with an autoloader. Examples of currently produced center-fire break-actions include Thompson Center Contender

A combination gun like this Savage M24F in 12-gauge and .22 Hornet might be perfect in habitat where shots may be far or extremely close.

Falling block action rifles include Dakota Arms' Model 10 chambered for the .220 Swift.

and Encore, Blaser K 95, and H&R Single- Shot. Buy additional barrels and you can convert these into big game rifles.

Falling Block or Drop Block Single-Shots

Falling block and rolling block actions are easier to reload than break-actions because there is no need to hinge a heavy barrel away from the breech/buttstock. You thumb back the rolling block breech to open its chamber. A lever, usually under the trigger guard, cams down the falling block breech. Because butt, action, fore-end, and barrel all remain firmly connected, rolling and falling blocks are inherently more accurate than break-actions. Again, these actions offer no advantage over repeating actions, but many fine, accurate rifles are built around falling blocks. Examples include Ruger No. 1, Dakota Model 10, and Browning Model 1885. The rolling block, most famous as the Remington Model No. 1, is not strong enough to handle high intensity cartridges, so it isn't chambered for modern, high-velocity rounds.

Lever Actions

Despite its rapid firepower, this traditional "cowboy" action has never shined as a varmint rifle. A Winchester M94, with its tubular magazine, can hold seven .30-30 cartridges and ram each into battery with a quick flick of the wrist. Unfortunately, like all tubular-magazine rifles, the M94 and its functional cousins, the Marlin M336 and Mossberg 464, are restricted to ammunition loaded with ballistically inefficient, flat-nosed bullets. Sharp tips resting against the primers ahead of them in the magazine would act as firing pins during recoil, initiating an unappealing chain reaction. Hornady's "rubber" tipped Monoflex and FTX bullets get around that restriction, but aren't built for classic varmint calibers.

Traditional lever-action rifles like this Winchester M94 aren't usually as accurate as bolt-actions, but they recycle faster when a pack of coyotes rushes you in heavy cover.

An autoloading 12-gauge like this 3-inch Winchester Super X2 is big medicine for predators in thick cover.

On average, lever rifles have never been quite as accurate as bolt actions, nor have many been chambered for fast, efficient predator cartridges. Clip and rotary magazines, however, allowed Savage to chamber its vaunted M99 lever action for fairly fast, powerful rounds like the old .250-3000 Savage, parent cartridge for today's hot .22-250 Remington—but the M99 is no longer manufactured. Browning, however, makes an excellent, modern, clip magazine BLR that can be had in a pair of superb varmint chamberings—.22-250 Rem and .243 Win. Ruger builds its Model 96 lever in .22 Win Mag and .44 Rem Mag.

Autoloader Actions

How things have changed! A mere decade ago autoloading rifles were just beginning to catch fire among predator hunters; now they're truly hot. Gunmakers have worked on the military-style AR platforms until they shoot as accurately as the best custom bolt actions. With 10-, 20-, and 30-round clips available for the ARs, we're talking serious fire power. Whether anyone needs it remains moot because people simply like ARs. And when a pack of seven coyotes comes calling, a high-volume, autoloading firearm is the one to be holding. Everyone from Mossberg to Smith & Wesson builds ARs these days. You're restricted in calibers depending on basic rifle size. True AR-15s are designed with a magazine just long enough to fit the .223 Rem. In order to shoot a .243 Win, you need a longer action usually known as the AR-25. Remington calls theirs the R-25.

Another big advantage of AR platforms is their modularity. By changing uppers, stocks, fore-ends, etc. you change the look and performance. You can mount a .450 Bushmaster for hogs, a 6.8 SPC for deer, a .204 Ruger for foxes. Or convert your .243 Win to a .338 Federal. Lots of options.

If you prefer an auto in more traditional styling, Browning's BARs have been reported to shoot sub MOA. The Lightweight Stalker version is chambered in .243 Win. Ruger's Mini-14 in .223 Rem can be tuned for fairly good accuracy, much as its 10/22 rimfires have been. Remington's M750 Woodmaster centerfire remains popular with auto shooters and comes in .243 Winchester.

Pump Actions

Once popular across America, pump-action rifles have lost fans due in part to declining interest in pump shotguns. Learn to shuck one, and you can handle the other with aplomb. Many good pump shooters can cycle their actions faster than autoloaders can load. And both Remington's 7600 and Browning's BPR can be tuned to shoot remarkably tight groups. Alas, Browning discontinued its BPR in 2002 and Remington's 7600 is chambered only for .243 Win and larger cartridges.

Bolt Actions

Here's your winner—today's most widely used rifle action. The bolt is not the quickest to cycle, but it's quick enough. Its biggest selling points are strength, durability, dependability and potential accuracy. Because of its straight axis of bore bolt movement, stiff-action walls, one-piece stock, and relatively simple, easily tuned trigger, a bolt action can easily be fine-tuned to shoot miniscule groups, even as tiny as half an inch. Right out of the box, many factory bolts will shoot MOA. They can be had with fancy walnut, laminated wood, molded plastic, and handlaid fiberglass stocks in a variety of styles from heavy benchrest to ultralight sporting. And they're chambered for virtually every high-velocity center-fire cartridge manufactured today. If those don't suit you, a gunsmith can rechamber a barrel for almost any wildcat round. Bolt actions can be cleaned from the breech, too, reducing muzzle crown erosion and accuracy loss. Virtually every manufacturer builds a bolt action at a reasonable price, and used ones can be found everywhere.

Rifle Styles and Their Application to Predator Calling

Heavy Target/Varmint Rifles

Many predator hunters have been deluded into thinking they needed one of these wide-stocked, heavy, long-barreled target rifles for taking coyotes or foxes. Not true. The big guns will certainly work for open-country shooting, but they're poor choices in most calling situations. The idea behind the heavy varmint rifle is to maximize accuracy for long-range, high-volume, precision shooting at small targets. Users usually set such rifles atop portable benches, or at least bipods, and lie in wait for rodents to show themselves. The overall mass of the rigs stabilizes them against tremors. The long barrels maximize the velocity potential of most cartridges. The flat forends anchor well on sandbags. The sharp, palm-swell pistol grips stabilize the trigger finger for precise, consistent pull. Finally, the heavy barrels remain accurate for more consecutive shots than do thinner barrels.

In my experience, though, applications for predator shooting with these big tools are limited and could just as effectively be handled by more responsive, sporter-weight rifles. Whether calling, glassing, stalking, or still-hunting, you carry a predator rifle more than you fire it, and when you fire it you rarely burn more than four quick shots—usually only one if you're any good. Your targets are two to ten times larger than those antici-pated for varmint rifles, and they're usually a lot closer.

When I was in my heavy-rifle phase, I found myself sitting on a Kansas sage-brush knob with a thirteen-pound Savage Model 12 BVSS .22-250 resting beside me atop a B-Square bipod. It was topped with a 6-20X Simmons scope. The height of the sage precluded use of the prone-length bipod, but not the call around my part-ner's neck. He blew it while sitting a few yards behind me and watching the oppo-site side of the knoll. A coyote appeared far out in the river valley, bounding up, down, in, and around the sage. I picked it up in the scope, lost it, found it again, lost it again. Each time I tried to fix the prairie predator in the cross hairs, it bounded

This Browning A-Bolt with Pentax variable scope epitomizes the kind of reliable, accurate rifle today's predator hunters prefer.

closer, until it disappeared under the roll of the hill. When it reappeared, it was close enough to swat with a badminton racket. Alas, I had no racket and had to let my quarry dash past, whereupon it bumped into Tom, swapped ends and came streaking back. Now that it was spooked, I felt free to swing my battery into action, and when I did, said coyote nearly tripped over the 26-inch barrel before disappearing down-slope. I took advantage of this opportunity to twist the scope down to 6X and raise the rifle into a somewhat ready position pointed in the general area the coyote had crossed during its approach. They usually leave the way they come in, and this was no exception. Despite considerable wobbling, I managed to align the cross hairs, swing them forward, and roll the coyote. In retrospect, I can honestly report that my big rifle/scope was more hindrance than help.

However, there have been times when I've spotted a coyote at great distance, unaware it was under observation, and thus pausing regularly enough for me to set up the bipod, align the sights, and even power up the scope before putting a 55-grain spire-point precisely on its shoulder. Similarly, there have been times when a coyote responding to a call has inexplicably stopped at three hundred yards or more and sat down to watch, again giving me time to set up my long-range hardware and make the shot.

Nonetheless, such instances have not been common enough to convince me that this is the ideal calling rig. For that we need to consider the sporter-weight center-fire that follows.

Sporter-Weight Predator Rifles

This category describes a traditional medium-weight "deer rifle" chambered for predator cartridges. Such rifles weigh from six to eight pounds without scopes, seven to ten pounds with glass sights aboard and sling attached. Barrels are usually medium weight and twenty-two to twenty-four inches long, stocks are trim with semi-open pistol grips and hand-filling forends. Fitted with medium-size scopes in the 3-14X range, these all-around tools seem the ideal compromise for a variety of predator-hunting situations. When you're calling, they are light and compact enough to whip into action quickly, yet stable enough and long enough to put bullets on target out to four hundred yards if the accuracy is in them and their operator. When you're hiking, glassing, and stalking, they don't cut into your shoulder or unduly test your stamina. I find them easier to hold steady than a heavier rifle while I'm awaiting perfect alignment with a target. Their narrower, more rounded fore-ends snuggle into various shooting yokes and bipods better than fat, sharp-edged target stocks, too.

Short Lightweights

These rifles fill a rather narrow purpose—quick, close shooting, something one tries to avoid when predator hunting but often can't. In most cases a shotgun will serve better, but if you prefer a rifle—for whatever reason— and call or jump most of your predators in heavy cover where shots rarely stretch past one hundred yards, this could be your best bet. Autos, levers, pumps, and short, handy bolt-actions like Remington's Model Seven with eighteen and a half- to twenty-inch barrels fit this category. Close-cover rifles need to whip into action quickly and really throw lead. As ranges are short, high velocity isn't much of a concern. Think .22 Hornet; maybe even some of the pistol or old "cowboy" rounds like .44- 40. But standards like .223 Remington make these rifles more versatile. ARs can be effective in these "tight cover" situations, given their quick follow up shots.

Single-Shots, Muzzleloaders, Handguns, and Other Inefficiencies

Don't let the subtitle fool you. I enjoy single-shots and muzzleloaders and (when I have earplugs screwed in tight) handguns, but even their most ardent fans must admit they aren't ideal for most predator hunting. Anything they do, a bolt action or other repeater can do better. However, if one-shot rifles, revolvers, or hand cannons bring you pleasure and job satisfaction, they may be your ideal predator shooter. The name of this game is Fun, not High Score. Partner up with whatever firearm, bow, or spear turns your crank, and you'll get the most satisfaction out of your predator hunting. Truth be known, the vast majority of predator shooting opportunities involve one shot. You either make it or wish you had, because your game gets gone before you can say, "Where'd he go?"

Best All-Around Rifle/Cartridge for Predators

This is a tough one, but almost everyone asks it at one time or another, so here's my take on it. Remember my premise at the start of this chapter: There is no perfect predator rifle. But each of us can select what we think is ideal for our style of hunting.

Were I forced to choose but one rifle and cartridge for all my predator hunting, I'd settle (grudgingly) for a sporter-weight bolt action with a 22-inch barrel chambered for a .22-250 Remington. For long-range work, I'd load one of the plastic-tipped, 55-grain, high B.C. bullets. When doing a lot of calling and close shooting, I'd load down in velocity to reduce pelt damage and switch to a premium bullet like the Barnes X or Trophy Bonded Bear Claw if the plastic-tips proved too destructive. Readers should note that I do most of my predator hunting by calling or glassing and stalking in open country, where coyotes are the

Long barrels for open terrain and maximum velocity, short barrels for close cover and quick handling. From left: 26-, 24-, 22-, and 20-inch barrels.

most likely responders. If I hunted eastern woods, Texas brush, or Arizona desert scrub, I'd choose different tools— which, again, takes us back to the beginning of this chapter.

Bullets

Any old bullet will kill a predator. Some will do it more efficiently than others. If pelt collection is your primary goal, try super-frangible bullets at the highest allowed velocities. These usually punch a tiny entrance hole, then break into tiny fragments that kill quickly and don't exit. Because the jackets of these deadly pills are thin, some cannot be driven to maximum velocities. The limit is usually 3,400 feet per second or less. Check with bullet manufacturers for these restrictions.

Examples of bullets that usually break up and stay inside a coyote (your results may vary) include Berger Varmint in .17, .20, .22 and .24; Hornady SPSX (Super Explosive) in .22 and V-Max in .17, .20, .22, and .24; Hornady NTX (lead-free) in .20 and .22; Speer TNT and TNT Green in .20, .22 and .24; Barnes Varmint Grenade and Varminator in .20, .22, and .24; Sierra Blitz King and Blitz in .20, .22 and .24; Nosler Ballistic Tip Varmint in .20, .22 and .24; Nosler Ballistic Tip Lead-Free Varmint in .20, .22 and .24. Be forewarned: any of these fragile pills can do considerable pelt damage if they strike near the "edges" of game where there is insufficient muscle to absorb the bullet's energy. The explosive force then blows large holes in hides.

If you don't handload, study factory ammunition carefully to see which varmint bullets they carry. Winchester loads Nosler's Ballistic Tips, including the Lead-Free versions. Federal loads the Nosler Ballistic Tip Varmint and Speer TNT Green. Hornady loads its V-Max and NTX. Remington has the Accutip-V. Norma puts the Hornady V-Max aboard its .22 centerfire ammo. In Black Hills ammo look for V-Max and Varmint Grenade bullets. Any of this can change at a moment's notice, so stay abreast of developments. The current (2012) buzz surrounding lead in bullets may lead to more alternatives. Non-lead bullets are now available in .22 and .17 rimfire rounds, too. They pack plenty of punch at close range, but shed energy much sooner than do heavier, lead-core bullets.

A poor alternative to the high-speed, frangible bullet is the full metal jacket. The idea behind these nonmushrooming projectiles is to make two small holes, in and out, with no explosive damage. Full metal jackets will do this unless you strike major bone, fragments of which can tear hides. The downside to FMJs is minimal tissue damage leading to runaways. A neat .22 hole—even a .308 hole— through a tough coyote's lungs often does not stop it. Which leads to the third school of thought.

Big game bullets. More or less. The idea here is to use a heavy, rugged, expanding bullet that mushrooms to about twice its caliber but stays together to plow through the target animal. The expanded bullet transfers considerable energy to the critter's system, while its enlarged frontal area rips vital tissue. The exit wound, golfball to baseball size, aids in leaving a blood trail without creating too much pelt damage. Examples include most mid- to large-caliber "deer" bullets as well as all premium controlled-expansion big game bullets, including Barnes TTSX, Federal Trophy Bonded, Winchester Power Max Bonded and Power Core, Nosler Partition, Accutip and E-Tip, Hornady GMX and Interbond, Federal Trophy Copper, Remington and Copper Solid (which is really a hollowpoint,) Swift A-Frame and Scirocco and others.

Personally, I lean toward the super-explosive bullets. Over the years I've had excellent luck with Hornady's 55-grain SX in my .22-250. To get this performance I have to throttle back horsepower to 3,400 feet per second, negating much of the potential of this cartridge. Recently I've found that the 75-grain V-Max, fired at 3,450 feet per second from my Rifles, Inc. Custom M70 6 mm Rem, will remain in a coyote hit dead center. Winchester Silver Ballistic Tips fired from .25-06 Rem and .270 Win blow through and necessitate major tailoring after skinning. Nosler Ballistic Tips in .22-250 have given me mixed results depending on how close the critter was. Terminal velocity is the key to most bullet performance. You'll have to experiment with bullets and initial velocities to determine which system works for you and your style of hunting.

Scope Sights

Today's high-velocity, long-range rifles are only as good as the telescopic sights that aim them. Take away that bright, magnified target, and even the .220

A variable scope is versatile. Dial it down for close work, up for long-range sniping.

Swift becomes a 150-yard rifle. You can't hit what you can't see.

In my not-so-humble opinion, the ideal scope for a general-purpose, sporter-weight predator rifle is a 3-9X variable with 36 mm or 40 mm objective lens. Not too heavy and bulky, bright enough for dusk shooting, wide enough for tight-cover action, magnification enough for four hundred-yard sniping, if it comes to that. I've found that most of my shots come well inside three hundred yards.

Funny thing about scopes. Twenty years ago, the average hunter complained about too much magnification providing a sight picture that was "nothin' but hair in the scope"—usually said of a variable cranked up to 8X or so. That was gross exaggeration, of course. I used to shoot running jackrabbits with a 10X Weaver Target scope inside forty yards. The whole bunny fit inside. A sheep mount on my office wall just thirty feet away fits shoulder to shoulder inside my Swarovski Z5 set at 8X.

These days hunters can't get enough magnification. Deer hunters—even elk hunters—have begun clamping 6-20X telescopes onto their rifles. As if that weren't sufficient overkill, they get them with objective lenses the diameter of your average trash can. Who's carrying all that bulk? Glad it's not me.

Big objective lenses, the ones out front, do let in lots of light, just like a picture window does. But magnification reduces the light that gets through to your eye (through-put). Internal lenses also reduce light through-put. So don't assume that a huge objective scope alone is going to give you the most usable brightness. You've got to balance it with magnification. Basically, above 10X a 50 mm objective can add useful brightness. Below 10X, you rarely need it.

Listen, here's what you need to know about scopes. Fully multi-coated air-to-glass lens surfaces do more for brightness than do huge objective lenses. Uncoated glass reflects about 4 percent of the light that strikes it and another 4 percent as it leaves. You lose 8 percent of the light with just one lens. The bad news is that scopes usually have five to eight lenses. You could lose nearly 70 percent of the light! But, coating the glass with a single layer of anti-reflection materials (magnesium fluoride is a big one) cuts that loss in half. Additional coatings of similar natural elements can reduce light loss to less than a 0.5 percent per lens.

Cory Lundberg often calls with a rifle
and shotgun on the same stand,
grabbing the scattergun when his
customers come extra close in heavy
cover, using the rifle when they stop
outside of shotgun range.

This is the good news. You get the most light for your buck when you spend it on scopes that sport fully-multi-coated lenses, meaning every air-to-glass surface has multiple layers of anti-reflection coatings. And, unlike big objective glass, coatings don't add weight or bulk. Beware: If a scope is advertised as "fully-coated," it could have but a single-coating on all air-to-glass lens surfaces. And if advertised "coated," it might have just the external objective and eyepiece lenses coated with a single layer. These are cheap scopes that look bright in the store or in broad daylight, but offer dim views in low light. Huge objective lenses won't make up for uncoated lenses. Fortunately, you can buy fully multi-coated scopes for as little as $200.

Now, let's examine those big objective lenses more closely. The diameter of the objective lens in millimeters divided by its magnification determines the diameter of a scope's exit pupil, the little window that lets the light (image) out of the scope and into your eye. You can see this exit pupil as a circle of light in the eyepiece when you hold a scope at arm's length and aim it at a bright surface. The exit pupil corresponds to the size of the pupil in your eye. Thus, a 6X scope with 50 mm objective would provide an 8.3 mm exit pupil. Wonderful.

The catch here is that the human eye can only open about 7 mm and this shrinks as you get older. You can't shove an 8.3 mm beam of light through a 7 mm hole. The 1.3 mm excess merely bounces off your iris, wasted. And if you are fifty-five years old and your pupils only open to 5 mm, 3.3 mm of edge light is wasted. So this is good news. You don't need to waste money on a huge scope that provides a 10 mm exit pupil. However, if you do get an oversized exit pupil, you'll find it easier to gain a full sight picture without that annoying edge blackout. Your pupils can literally shift around inside that extra-wide exit pupil without hitting the edges. This is why it seems so much easier to use a scope at 4X than 18X. It's not just the wider field-of-view downrange. It's the extra wide tube of light you get to wander around in. There's the potential for parallax trouble with that, but it's small and can easily be prevented, as we'll discuss a few paragraphs further.

If you're doing the math, you'll understand why so many variable scopes do come with 50 mm or larger objective lenses. At 10X a 50 mm yields a 5 mm exit pupil, more than adequate for targeting most predators roughly 45 minutes after sunset. In fact, a 4mm exit pupil in a fully multi-coated scope is plenty bright in such low light, but if you crank that scope up to 15X, its exit window shrinks to 3.3 mm. With excellent, fully multi-coated lenses, this is still enough light for our work, but it's reaching the ragged edge. At 20X the exit pupil squeezes to a tiny 2.5 mm hole and the image begins looking pretty dim. You'll have trouble putting a reticle on target 30 minutes after sunset. At those times an illuminated reticle can really help. Most scope brands offer these. Get one if you shoot a lot at dusk and dawn and definitely if you ever plan to hunt at night.

In dim light, it isn't often you can see, let alone aim at a predator so far away that you need more than 10X power. Remember, you have to first find them, and that's usually done with naked eyes. I use a binocular to scan for distant coyotes after sunset, but even then the majority are discovered within three hundred yards. Most will approach much closer if you're calling, so 6X or even 4X will magnify them adequately. At those powers a 42 mm and 28 mm objective respectively will provide a 7 mm exit pupil. Plenty bright enough. But if you hope to pick coyotes off at three hundred yards plus at dusk using 10X to 20X power, a 50 mm or even 56 mm objective definitely increases brightness.

Now on to those fat, 30 mm scope tubes. No, they are not usably brighter than one-inch tubes. Main tube diameter does not affect usable brightness. Objective diameter and magnification do. Anti-reflection coatings do. Below about 5X a 30 mm tube can pass slightly more light than a comparable 1-inch tube, but at that magnification any scope with an objective lens larger than 35 mm will be providing an exit pupil larger than our eyes can handle anyway. Again, it's wasted light. Many 30 mm main tube scopes look brighter because they're made with all the best ingredients, and there's certainly nothing wrong with that. But you can buy high-quality 1-inch tubes just as good. And you can find cheap scopes with 30 mm main tubes that don't give you any optical advantage over 1-inch tubes.

Beyond checking the magnification, objective lens size, and coatings, it's difficult to judge a scope, because most of what you see is its cover. You don't know how good or bad the glass, tubes, materials, or construction are. Rest assured that if the scope is inexpensive, so are its parts and probably its workmanship. Expect distortion and flare when you look toward the setting sun. In fact, looking into the shadows toward the rising or setting sun is a good test of any scope. Compare several. The best provide a clear, sharp image without the orange haze or fog covering the scene. This veiling glare is caused by light bouncing from lens to lens. Anti-reflection coatings stop this.

When the sun is down, look into dark shadows for detail and contrast. Can you pick out a brown coyote against a wooded background? If you don't have a coyote handy for this testing, conscript a friend wearing a dull or camouflage coat, or just use a taxidermy mount. But look for detail and compare it from scope to scope.

Eye relief, the distance your eye rests behind the scope when you see a full picture without blackout, is important for quick sighting and providing a complete field of view. The distance from the eyepiece glass to your eye when you see a full picture without blackout is the instrument's eye relief. It should run about 3 inches to as much as 5 inches. The shorter the eye relief, the more likely you'll get whacked by the scope under recoil. The longer the eye relief the less field-of-view. Don't worry too much about that. Field-of-view—the area you can see down-range—is vastly overrated. You don't need to see an 8X magnified image of half the county surrounding your fox—just the fox.

In some scopes eye relief shrinks as you crank up magnification. An eye relief of 4 inches at 4X might shrink to 3 inches at 10X. My old buddy John Barsness, author of *Optics for the Hunter,* the best book on sporting optics ever written for the layman (like me), describes an easy way to check any scope for eye relief. Lay a ruler on a table, place the scope on top of it, shine a flashlight into its objective end, hold a sheet of white paper behind the eyepiece, and move said paper back and forth along the ruler until the circle of light projected onto it is sharp. Note the distance. That's the scope's eye relief.

Parallax is a major problem in some scopes. This is the apparent shifting of the target in relationship to the cross hairs as you move your head around behind the scope. If you don't place your head and eye in the exact same position each and every time you shoot with a scope that has parallax problems, your aim can be off by several inches at two hundred yards. Most big-game scopes are adjusted to be parallax-free at one hundred to one hundred fifty yards. This means they'll show some parallax at nearer distances, but not enough to matter (maybe an inch) because targets are closer and precise aiming is less important.

Parallax is defined as "the apparent shifting of the target in relationship to the crosshairs." You can see this shift (if it's there) when you move your eye off the center axis of the scope, i.e. left to right, up or down. The target will appear to move off the crosshair's center. Here's how to understand parallax: Think of a mechanical speedometer on an old car, the kind with a needle that moved over an arched dial of speed numbers pasted behind it. Because the needle didn't touch that dial, but hovered in front of it, the driver would see the needle over the

60-mph number, but the passenger on the right would see it over the 50-mph marker because of the space between the needle and numbered dial. Were you to paste the needle smack onto the dial, this parallax would disappear.

A similar thing happens in a scope if the crosshair (needle) hovers in front of the target (dial). Shift your eye slightly left or right of dead-center (the driver's position) and, like the passenger, you are seeing the needle over a different place. So your bullet won't land where you think it will.

Don't freak out over parallax. It's significant in target shooting, but rarely messes up hunting shots. To check a scope for excessive parallax, set your rifle on sandbags at the range, center the reticle on a one-inch bullseye one hundred yards away, and shift your head around while watching the crosshair. If it doesn't move around—or the bullseye doesn't seem to move around in relation to the crosshair—you have proper focus and no parallax. But even if you do see parallax, it won't be a problem if you position your head perfectly every time you shoot. If you're worried about this, send the scope in to have it refocused. They just turn the front lens in or out slightly like focusing a camera lens.

You can buy scopes with adjustable focus and tweak the parallax at any distance. This is most useful with magnifications above 10X. Adjustable objective lenses (the front of the barrel turns to focus) can mess up a scope's zero if they get bent or knocked slightly out of alignment. Side-focus knobs are more dependable, but also more expensive.

Other things to watch for when evaluating scopes are construction (a one-piece main tube/turret housing is more durable than joined pieces); waterproof/fogproof guarantee; type of reticle (thick, thin, dual, multiple, illuminated); ballistic turrets; turret accuracy. Power and diopter rings should turn smoothly but fairly stiffly so they hold position. Turret knobs should click smartly into position. Test turret adjustment accuracy by running "around the horn," as we used to say in baseball. After zeroing, click your scope down four inches (sixteen clicks on a quarter-click scope). Aim at the same spot as your first shot and fire again. Your bullet should hit four inches lower. Then click sixteen right. The next shot should land four inches to the right. Go up sixteen clicks to put the next shot four inches above the last one. Finally, click left sixteen times and you should park the last bullet beside your initial hole. Allow for natural dispersion according to how well your rifle groups.

Test a variable scope by shooting the same target at various power settings. If the scope isn't tracking accurately, bullets will land in different places at different power settings. Unfortunately, stores won't permit such testing before you buy a scope, but you should be able to return it under warranty.

High resolution and contrast provide a better image than does an extra five percent of light transmission. Whether a scope transmits ninety or ninety-five percent of the light that enters it isn't as important as cross hairs that go where you click them and stay there. Eye relief is more valuable than a wide field of view.

I'd rather spend $1,000 on binoculars and $200 on a scope than vice versa. And I'd rather spend $1,000 on a scope and $200 on a rifle than vice versa. Cheap rifles often shoot MOA, but not if the scope atop them isn't consistent. I've shot lots of game using cheap scopes, but the ranch dog that looked like a coyote through cheap binoculars remained a ranch dog. This doesn't mean that I recommend you buy the cheapest scope down at the local discount mart. Quality costs. But don't feel you must rob your kid's college fund to finance a jewel-encrusted European optical instrument, either.

Three main factors set the price of scopes: materials, engineering, and labor. The first two are largely fixed for all manufacturers, but labor is wildly variable. Thus, it is possible for a company to assemble top-quality scopes in third-world factories for less than they can in first-world countries with union labor. Some $300 Japanese scopes are every bit as good as some $500 U.S. scopes and some $800 European scopes. Well, close anyway. The best news is that quality keeps going up and prices, relatively, keep going down. You can get a remarkably good scope for under $400 these days.

So how do you know which to buy? Reputation is a good place to start. If you've heard nothing but good reports about Brand X and bad about Brand Y, take a hard look at Brand X. Be aware that many scope makers build scopes in two or three quality levels. Leupold, for instance, offers its top-line VX-6, VX-3, VX-2 and VX-I, among others. Bushnell runs from Elite down to Banner. Vortex and Nikon host many lines from bargain to top-notch. Pay attention to the differences in lines as much as brands. Swarovski sells two lines of 1-inch tube "American-style" scopes at roughly half the cost of its 30-mm-tube European scopes. Even Zeiss is now selling scopes for under $1,000.

I'd stick with the highest quality within each brand. The low-price line might feature uncoated lenses except for a single coating on the exterior of the eyepiece and objective lenses.

LONG RANGE SCOPE OPTIONS

Long-range shooting is all the rage, and coyotes are a perfect subject for it. You can often spot them on open range at vast distances. Memorizing your bullet's trajectory is essential. Then comes a precise distance measurement, handled easily by a laser range-finder, after which you must judge and compensate for wind. An anemometer (handheld wind meter) can help with that. Finally, you need a sighting system to compensate for bullet drop and drift. We cover good old MPBR in the ballistics section (Chapter 6). This is simple and effective to about three hundred yards. Beyond that it's best to use a ballistic reticle or ballistic turret.

A ballistic reticle simply holds several hash marks along the vertical cross wire. You zero the center one for anywhere from one hundred to two hundred fifty yards or so, then use lower marks to aim at farther distances. The trajectory of your bullet determines where it lands in relation to these marks. The first sub-reticle down might represent a three hundred-yard hit, the next line a three hundred seventy-five- or four hundred-yard hit, etc. It doesn't really matter as long as you memorize what distance each holding point represents. Some reticles have three or four lines, some have literally dozens, including ends or dot marks on both sides of the vertical line. These usually represent holding points to compensate for a 10-mph wind drift at those ranges.

The beauty of multiple reticles is speed. If you practice enough, you can put the correct reticle on target without taking your eye off the target. But if you don't practice, you may select the wrong aiming point and miss. Also, with most American-style scopes with reticles in the second focal plane (so they don't enlarge with magnification), all these aiming points work only at a specific power, usually the highest. First focal plane reticles negate this and are the most sensible way to use ballistic reticles.

Ballistic turrets are known as "dial and smile." You adjust the elevation dial to compensate for bullet drop. You can also turn the windage dial to compensate for wind deflection. An alternative to this is 10-mph wind marks on the horizontal wire. This keeps the view uncluttered and reduces confusion about which crosshair to use. There's only one! But you must take your eye off the target to focus on the turret in order to read the numbers (practice and you can count the clicks you hear or feel, too). Turret dialing can seem complicated at first, but once you print out a trajectory chart in clicks or MOAs, it becomes quite fast and easy. Custom turrets can be ordered with numbers corresponding to precise ranges for your load. Dial to #4 for four hundred yards, #6 for six hundred yards, etc. This system mandates a precise, repeatable scope you can depend on, and you must remember to dial back to zero after long shots. Also be careful that you don't bump the dial while carrying the rifle.

No system is perfect, but all offer wonderfully effective ways to aim precisely at distances that seemed impossible just ten years ago.

Shotguns

Much as I love the precision challenge of picking off coyotes at long range, I have to admit a scatter-gun is deadly at close quarters, especially when two or more critters charge a caller simultaneously. You don't know excitement until six coyotes accept your dinner invitation and vie to be first at the table. A fast-cycling scatter-gun proves useful at such moments. A handful of pellets that enter but don't exit are refreshingly easy on pelts, too, particularly when fox and bobcats are the prey. Finally, in much good predator habitat—eastern woods, Rocky Mountain forests, southwest brush and desert scrub—shooting ranges are often limited to fifty yards or less. The smart hunter chooses a shotgun at these times. But which gauge? I'd recommend the 3-inch 12-gauge for its range, versatility and ability to handle large pellets, and a 3½-inch 12-gauge if you can handle the recoil. A 10-gauge will put a few more shot in the air and gain perhaps five yards of additional range over the 12-gauge, but ammunition will cost considerably more, and so will the gun itself, if you can find one. There aren't a lot of 10-gauges on dealers' shelves compared to 12s, which can be had by the truckload in any action from bolt to autoloader.

What about the 31/2-inch 12-gauge? It's certainly an option, but I can't see any great advantage to it. With a long forcing cone and back-bored barrel, it performs on par with a 10-gauge. With the 31/2-inch, you're limited to pump and autoloader actions, too. Shells will cost more, and you'll pay a substantial price in recoil. Youch! Even a 31/2-inch autoloader puts a major punch on your cheek and shoulder, as I discovered during a 2002 late-winter hunt with Kevin Howard and Gary Roberson. Roberson manufactures Burnham Brothers predator calls and tests them extensively in his Texas brush-country neighborhood. We were calling where a wall of thorn scrub bumped abruptly against an open pasture. "If they come out of that brush, they'll be on us instantly and back just as fast," Gary said. "Better use this." He handed me his Winchester Super X2 and a handful of 31/2-inch Winchester Supreme Steel BBBs. I felt as if I were stuffing sticks of dynamite into that magazine.

Gary sat just inside a screen of brush bordering a runoff creek. I sat with my butt against a mesquite log to his right, and Kevin took a position watching the big field to his left. Gary was wailing his second solo with a mouth caller when I saw a coyote loping along the wall of brush, angling to get our wind. If he caught it, three jumps and a yip would carry him to safety. That's why I shot when he stopped at what I estimated to be fifty yards. I figured that big load of triple-Bs would roll him. Instead, it launched him as if it had gone off under his tail. Unfortunately, it also launched me backward over my tail. By the time I'd rolled back up

Popular shotguns include both the 372-inch and 3-inch 12 gauges, like the Beretta Xtrema (left) and the Beretta Urika (right).

to a sitting position, El Coyote was racing from left to right across my front at about twenty-five yards and directly away from his escape cover. If I didn't do something quickly, it would overrun Kevin and cause him all sorts of emotional trauma. So I swung the black barrel past the dog's nose, pushed the magic button, and again felt myself rolling over like a kid's punching clown. I bounced back up, but the coyote didn't. The shot had flipped him tail over ears, and he lay as still as grass, only the tips of his lustrous fur shifting lightly with the breeze.

Subsequent forensics research proved I was a poor judge of range—the first shot had been taken at seventy yards. But enough pellets had penetrated to disorient our quarry and compel him further into danger. The second shot had placed at least eighteen pellets into the body, not only killing the animal instantly, but, to my surprise, breaking both a front and back leg. I would not question the killing power of the 31/2-inch 12-gauge and steel BBB shot inside twenty-five yards, but I'd want heavier pellets for longer shots.

Despite the success of that enterprise, I stand by my choice of the 3-inch 12-gauge as more versatile, less expensive, more available, and more than adequate, especially when loaded with #4 lead buckshot. These pellets are .24 inch in diameter compared to .18-inch for BB shot. One in the boiler room is sufficient to terminate the orneriest coyote, and forty-one of them fit inside a 3-inch shell. These heavy pellets will retain more than ten footpounds of energy at fifty yards—enough to punch through that first layer of predatory fur and hide and disrupt the engine. The hitch with #4 buck is patterning. Some guns do a decent job of spreading those forty-one pellets evenly, but others clump them, leaving gaps through which a fleeing coyote can escape. For this reason, it's imperative that you pattern-test your prospective coyote scatter-gun on a few life-size paper coyote targets if possible. A rectangle of paper or cardboard nine inches square will suffice. This roughly represents the vital zone of a coyote's chest, as well as its backside going away.

If your gun doesn't handle #4 buck, try BBBs and BBs. Either is deadly, and if they hold an even, dense pattern to fifty or sixty yards, sign 'em up for duty. Certain guns may pattern #4 buck or BBBs well enough to stretch killing range to seventy yards, but this is pushing the envelope. Be aware that trying to stretch range with full and super-full chokes can be hazardous to your shotgun's well-being. The large pellets tend to bind and clump in the constriction—like two clowns getting stuck in a narrow doorway—raising pressure and bulging barrels. With modern shot cups and plastic buffering, tight choke is often superfluous. Start your tests with minimum choke and work your way up.

Inside forty yards, #2 shot will suffice for coyotes. You'll find #4s adequate for fox and bobcat inside forty yards. Go to #2s for longer shots.

If you're interested in speed, firepower, reliability, and minimum cost, shoot a pump. Remington, Winchester, Browning, Mossberg, Benelli, Beretta, Weatherby—they're all rugged and reliable. If you want to spend a bit more and enjoy slightly less felt recoil, choose an autoloader. Today's models are nearly as reliable and foolproof as pumps. Keep them reasonably clean, and they won't let you down. I've seen Remington, Browning, and Beretta autoloaders handle hundreds of rounds during high-volume dove shoots in Argentina. If they can tolerate that kind of abuse, they should stand up to a lifetime of predator hunting. Double barrels can suffice, but with only two quick shots, they may not provide the firepower you'll need.

GREAT SHOTSHELL LOADS

Shotshell load development progressed markedly in the last ten years as manufacturers searched for high performance, non-toxic substitutes for lead. Some new shells pattern better and hit harder than lead ever did. Winchester Xtended Range Hi-Density turkey, waterfowl, and coyote loads are a prime example. Because the pellets are 10 percent denser (heavier) than lead, they carry more energy farther downrange. State-of-the-art wads protect loads and work with modern choke tubes to throw tight patterns, which in turn extends effective range. Muzzle velocities of 1,250 feet per second also increase punch. Winchester's Supreme Double X Buckshot loads with copper-plated, plastic-buffered shot in #00 Buck is a deadly coyote load in two and three quarters-, three-, and -inch 12-gauge.

Remington is currently out of the tungsten shot market, but could join in again anytime. Keep your eyes open. Meanwhile, its Premier High Velocity Magnum Copper-Plated, buffered turkey loads in #4 and #5 shot for 3- and 3.5-inch 12-gauge should be deadly on fox, bobcat, and close coyotes. Try buffered Nitro Mag loads in #2 for extra range.

Federal stuffs its Heavyweight Coyote shells with BB pellets cradled in a FLITECONTROL wad for dense patterns and a hard punch far downrange. This is another heavier-than-lead pellet material for added punch and reach in a 3-inch 12-gauge. Muzzle velocity is rated a stiff 1,350 feet per second. Premium Vital-Shok Buckshot shells in 20-, 12-, and 10-gauge throw a variety of buckshot-sized, copper-plated lead pellets from 1,100 to 1,325 feet per second.

Kent Cartridge Tungsten-Matrix Waterfowl shells in 1-, 3-, and 5-shot should be deadly on called predators. They are available in all lengths for 20- and 12-gauge guns.

6

Basic Ballistics for Better Field Shooting

Simplified Explanations About Wind Drift and Sighting In

Few things are more frustrating than getting game within reasonable shooting distance and then missing. Most poor shooting is due to insufficient practice and buck fever. So put in lots of time at the range and in the fields. Eventually you'll calm down.

The other reasons you miss are gravity, drag, wind drift, and weird angles flummox most people. A basic understanding of ballistics will help you eliminate ninety-nine percent of these shooting mistakes.

The Answer is Blowing in the Wind

Wind blowing bullets off course is not a major concern when you're shooting at called predators. Even open-country coyotes will usually approach within two hundred yards or less before hanging up or circling downwind to catch the caller's scent. Most will get within one hundred yards, and at that range a 20-mph wind will push a relatively inefficient, 50-grain .224 bullet (launched at 3,000 feet per second) only three inches off point of aim. A 30-mph gale will move that same bullet 4.5 inches off course at one hundred yards, which is a problem when you're aiming at targets as small as the neck or brisket of a coyote facing you. This diffi-culty is self-correcting to a large degree because roaring winds encourage most predators and predator hunters to stay home. Even the loudest calls are muted,

Long, sleek bullets drift less in wind than do short, blunt bullets.

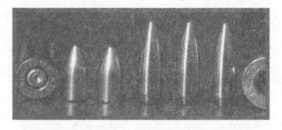

tattered, and generally ineffective. Last but not least, it's hard to aim a rifle accurately in buffeting gusts. However, it is possible to shelter behind haystacks, cutbanks, old barns, or walls of trees to gain a steady aim while your quarry stands far away, rocking in the wind, so it pays to know how fast-moving air affects your bullets once they've left the barrel.

The easiest way to minimize wind drift is to shoot to maximum velocity the longest, heaviest, smoothest, most sharply pointed bullet your rifle will handle. Such bullets have a high ballistic coefficient (B.C.), a numeric rating that quantifies a bullet's ability to slip through the air with the greatest of ease. Short, fat, blunt bullets (with low B.C. numbers, like .200) push or "buck" a lot of wind, which slows them down. The longer it takes for a bullet to reach its target (time of flight), the more time crosswinds have to push it off course. Long, skinny, sharp bullets (with high B.C. numbers, like .400) slice through the air and overcome much of its resistance, reaching targets before crosswinds have time to drift them far off course.

A high B.C. rating for most applicable predator bullets would be .260 in a 55-grain .224 caliber, .400 in a 100-grain .243, .460 in a .257, .480 in a .260 (6.55 mm), and .480 in a 150-grain .270. Even though lighter bullets in each of these calibers can be driven to higher initial velocities, the poorer ballistic efficiency of those lighter slugs will permit air resistance to slow them. Here are examples for low and slightly higher B.C. bullets fired from a .220 Swift in a twenty-mile-per-hour crosswind:

Bullet	Muzzle Velocity	Drift 100 yd	Drift 200 yd	Drift 300 yd	Drift 400 yd
50-grain Hollow Point					
B.C. .207	4,000 fps	2"	8.9"	21.3"	41"
60-grain Spitzer					
B.C. .266	3,800 fps	1.7"	7"	16.3"	30.7"

Many shooters think larger calibers with heavier bullets give vastly superior wind drift resistance, but the following examples should shed some light on that misconception. The crosswind in these examples is twenty miles per hour.

Bullet	Muzzle Velocity	Drift 100 yd	Drift 200 yd	Drift 300 yd	Drift 400 yd
75-grain .243 Spitzer					
B.C. .303	3,500 fps	1.6"	6.8"	16"	30"
87-grain .257 Spitzer					
B.C. .300	3,500 fps	1.7"	6.9"	16.3"	30.5"
200-grain .358 Round Nose					
B.C. .200	3,500 fps	2.6"	11.2"	27.3"	53.4"

As the 200-grain, round-nosed .358 bullet with the rather low B.C. of .200 shows, weight alone does *not* mean less wind deflection. Weight and form, or a bullet's shape, work together to create a high B.C., and that plus high velocity minimizes the nasty effects of wind. Time-of-flight, then, is *the* critical component in wind drift.

For a more complete understanding of what wind does to your slugs, test-fire them on windy days at big paper targets at long range. The holes in the paper will quickly teach you what happens. The faster the wind and the farther the target, the farther the bullet holes land from where you aim. Wind at your back or in your face doesn't nudge bullets off course at all, nor does it speed them up or slow them down enough to worry about. Wind blowing at a forty five-degree angle to the bullet's path shoves them less than the same wind at a ninety-degree angle.

Remember all this and apply it afield, and perhaps you'll have better luck than I've had.

Over the years, big winds have blasted my bullets so far off course that I've missed coyotes standing broadside. But I've also missed them by adjusting my aim to compensate for the wind. One

A sleek, high B.C. bullet like this .308, 180-grain Swift Scirocco is ideal for resisting wind drift, but expensive and larger than necessary for most predators.

raging January afternoon in South Dakota, I shot at a coyote 250 yards away, and missed. So I held a foot into the wind and fired again. The coyote looked around in confusion. I held another foot into the wind and shot again. This time the coyote simply shook its head and slunk away.

That episode inspired me to read and study wind drift tables in the backs of reloading manuals. While I couldn't keep extensive charts in my head for varying wind angles and speeds, I'd figured that a six-inch hold into a twenty- to thirty-mph gust would compensate adequately for most situations out to 250 yards or so. Using that assumption, I aimed my .22-250 Ruger an inch or two off a Kansas coyote facing me from about two hundred yards in a powerful left-to-right blast of wind. Imagine my dismay when the bullet kicked up dust exactly where I'd aimed.

Compensating for wind drift is anything but a science. There are too many variables, such as inconsistency in wind speed, slight to major changes in wind direction, mistakes in guessing velocity and angle, and probably even the height of last week's solar flares. The only modus operandi I've used with any success is partly described above: I use the highest B.C. bullet I can and drive it to top speed. Then I try to get my quarry as close as possible before shooting. And I always hold on hair for the first shot. Well, almost always. When conditions are extreme and the range is long, I'll still try that six-inch hold into the wind. And sometimes it even works.

WIND EXPERIMENTS

Some simple experiments will help you comprehend B.C. and wind drift. Coast down a hill while sitting upright on a bicycle. Feel the wind (air resistance) against your chest. Now make the same run bent double. You feel less resistance, don't you? That's because you improved your B.C. Now you know why bike racers wear those silly nylon tights and pointy helmets.

Wind drift (more accurately "deflection") is a bit more difficult to understand. Common sense suggests a heavy object would be hard for wind to blow off course, but that's false reasoning. The wind is not like a man trying to push a cinder block across a driveway. It's more like a river carrying twigs and logs in its current – light or heavy, they'll both go with the flow equally. Here's an experiment that demonstrates wind drift:

Cut two 6" lengths of 2x4 lumber and carry them to the edge of a moving stream. Lay one broadside to the current, the other beside it lengthwise to the current. Push both across the current. Obviously the piece pushed "nose first" is going to reach the opposite bank sooner with minimum drift downstream because its leading edge is pushing less water out of its way. The wood pushed "broadside first" is going to meet a lot of water resistance, slow quickly and remain in the current for a long time, drifting far downstream.

Similarly, the sooner any bullet reaches its target (gets out of the river), the less it will be carried off course. But that isn't everything. There is also the changing angle of departure that plays a big role. When the wind nudges a bullet slightly left or right, it sets it on a new direction of travel. It gives the bullet another vector or direction of motion. This means the farther downrange your bullet flies, the farther it moves off your point of aim. And if the wind blows consistently the entire time, the angle of departure continues to widen. All of this can be calculated *if* you know the precise direction and speed of the wind. Ballistic calculators for cell phones are effective for doing the math and wind gauges (anemometers) can measure wind speed, but nothing guarantees consistency. By the time you check your charts and gauges, the wind speed could shift 10 degrees or decline 10 mph, which is why judging wind is considered as much art as science. The more you practice, the better you get. And practicing on coyote-sized steel plates or paper targets is the best way to practice.

Know the Angles

Angled shooting has its ups and downs. Sorting them out could increase your effectiveness. A lot of shooters get confused by this. Do you aim low when shooting uphill and aim high when shooting down, or vice versa?

Actually, bullets strike higher than normal when fired uphill *and* downhill. Really. But in the hunting fields you rarely have to worry about this unless you're aiming more than 30 degrees from level and at a target more than 200 yards away. The good news is that this rarely occurs when predator hunting. The better news is you can largely overcome it by using a high B.C. bullet at maximum velocity.

To avoid confusion and overcompensation, my rule is to aim on the lower edge of a target but *not off the hair* if the predator is at an extremely steep angle above or below me *and* more than 200 yards away. If I miss, I'll aim under the target on subsequent shots. But listen: angles of 30 degrees or more are extremely rare, even in the mountains. You can buy software apps for your phone to measure angle or a dial unit that clamps to your scope. Or just use a protractor and a small weight on a string. Aim the straight edge of the protractor downhill and not where the string hangs. Pretty simple. Most shooters learn to judge angle in the field just by holding their arm out at a 45-degree angle and comparing that to the line of the slope. Works well enough for nearly all field shooting out to 400 yards

Now, if you want to know *why* projectiles strike higher than normal when shooting uphill and downhill, keep reading.

When shooting up or down, the pull of gravity only matters over the horizontal distance, not the vertical. Thus, if a coyote is 350 yards away at a 60-degree angle uphill, only half that distance will be horizontal, so your bullet would drop as if it were only traveling 175 yards. In reality gravity *is* pulling that bullet down over the entire 350 yards—just as much as it would be if fired perfectly horizontally—but the angle of this pull in relation to line-of-sight, as opposed to axis-of-bore, accounts for the difference in impact.

So here's more detail: when launched horizontally to the earth's surface, a bullet is pulled at a right-angle from its axis-of-bore or line-of-departure, i.e. straight down toward the center of the Earth, if you will. Gravity's pull (32 feet per second each second) against this line-of-departure is maximized at this right angle. A bullet launched straight up or down, i.e. on the same line as gravity's pull, is pulled exactly as much as one sent horizontally, but since this pull is directly in line with the original flight path there is no drop AWAY from the axis-of-bore. The bullet going up is slowed slightly. The bullet going straight down is accelerated slightly. With this vertical flight path in mind, it's easy to visualize what happens when the axis-of-bore is angled slightly away from vertical. Gravity begins to pull the bullet away from its axis-of-bore, changing its line-of-flight and its relation to line-of-sight. The greater the angle, the greater the effect until the 90 degree, or right angle, is reached. Thus, bullet drop below line-of-sight is maximized when shooting horizontally and minimized when shooting vertically, so when you shoot up or down, your bullets strike higher than normal in relation to point of aim.

The Perfect Sight-In Distance

If you understand nothing else about ballistic performance, understand maximum point-blank range (MPBR) and sight in your rifle to take advantage of it, because this will do more to increase

Any rifle/ammo combination that groups this tightly is more than adequate for predators at all ranges.

your hits than super scopes, laser range finders, computer printouts, and voodoo dolls.

In practical terms, MPBR refers to the total distance over which your bullet will strike your target if you aim for the center of its vital zone. MPBR can vary from two hundred yards to nearly three hundred yards with most popular predator bullets, velocities, and targets. You do not need to hold over, under, or guess the range. Just aim for the center of the vital zone and shoot. Here's how it works:

Every bullet fired from every rifle begins to drop the instant it leaves the muzzle. It does not rise above the line of bore, but it does slice through the line of sight, because we angle our barrels at a slight upward angle compared to line of sight. We do this for the same reason we throw a baseball upward—it goes farther. Of course we don't want to throw a bullet so far above our line of sight that it strikes a foot high at one hundred yards. The idea is to sight it just high enough so it never rises above the vital zone of our anticipated target (like a coyote's chest).

For this reason, it makes sense to sight a high-velocity rifle to strike higher than point of aim at one hundred yards. Sight a 50-grain Nosler Spitzer fired from a .223 Rem at 3,300 feet per second one inch high at one hundred yards, and it will "top out," (reach its maximum ordinate—peak distance above line of sight) at 1.07 inches at 114 yards. At three hundred yards it will fall 8.5 inches below point of aim. Increase the one hundred-yard hit to two inches high and maximum ordinate will be 2.35 inches at 140 yards and the drop at three hundred yards will be just 5.4 inches. Are you beginning to see the potential here?

If you aim for the vertical center of a coyote's chest and your bullet strikes two inches higher, you're still going to kill it. The vital heart/lung/spine area on a coyote is around eight inches in diameter. So why not sight your rifle for a maximum ordinate of 2.5 inches and aim for the center of the chest? That will stretch considerably the distance before the bullet falls more than 2.5 inches below point of aim, which is also still in the vitals. This distance is your MPBR.

A 2.5-inch maximum ordinate sighting fits a five-inch target zone. You could accept a six-inch target zone for coyote shooting and extend your maximum ordinate to three inches. This would increase your MPBR, but would also leave little room for sighting error. Jiggle or pull your shot slightly, and you'd probably shoot over your subject.

A graphic way of thinking about MPBR is to imagine shooting down the center of a pipe the diameter of your vital zone target. Adjust your sights so your slugs just miss glancing off the top of the pipe. When they graze the bottom, you've reached your MPBR.

Here are some examples of MPBRs for a five-inch target zone taken from the Sierra Rifle Reloading Manual, 50th Anniversary Edition:

- .22 Hornet, 45-grain Spitzer, 2,600 fps, MPBR is 215 yards, set zero at 185 yards.
- .223 Rem, 50-grain Blitz, 3,300 fps, MPBR is 275 yards, set zero at 235 yards.
- .22-250 Rem, 55-grain Sierra Spitzer Boat Tail, 3,700 fps, MPBR is 310 yards, set zero at 265 yards.
- .243 Win, 85-grain Hollow Point Boat Tail, 3,300 fps, MPBR is 285 yards, set zero at 245 yards.
- .25-06 Rem., 100-grain Spitzer, 3,300 fps, MPBR is 295 yards, set zero at 250 yards.

Computer ballistic programs like RCBS.LOAD also calculate MPBR. If you don't have access to such resources, a bit of target shooting will show you your MPBR. Start by sighting to hit 2.5 inches high at 150 yards. That's roughly the maximum ordinate for most high-intensity cartridges like the .223 Rem. Then test-fire at twenty-five-yard increments from one hundred yards out to three hundred and record your results. You may need to adjust your scope setting slightly up or down to prevent shooting higher than 2.5 inches at any range. If you are hunting fox, you might want a maximum ordi-nate of only two inches.

Once you've set up your outfit for MPBR, practice holding on the center of a life-size fox or coyote target and shooting at a variety of distances to

There are software programs that compute trajectory, winddrift, and more.

train yourself to resist holding over targets. Repeated hits will build confidence.

7

We All Need a Little Support

Supply Packs and Rifle Supports

Asmall backpack can simplify your predator hunts by organizing your supplies and keeping them handy. A pack also makes a good rifle rest to steady your shooting. A large enough pack can serve as a solid backrest to make your wait more tolerable and improve your aim by reducing muscle tremors.

Before buying your predator pack, consider what you'll haul in it. I guarantee it'll be more than a spare call and a sandwich. If you hike a lot, you'll end up wanting to stuff your coat or insulated bibs inside when the day warms. You might wish to keep a rain suit for emergencies. Spare gloves and an extra stocking cap are good ideas. Then there are binoculars, camera, film, extra ammunition, snacks, spare calls, maybe an electronic caller and battery, flashlight, scent bombs, decoys, skinning knife, and a few plastic garbage bags in which to isolate fresh pelts. A full-size backpack (about 5,000 cubic inches internal space) will provide more than enough room with space left over. Day packs usually measure under 3,000 cubic inches in volume. An internal frame model will be most comfortable, bending and flexing with you as you cross fences, sit, crawl, and so on. An external frame won't bend much and make you feel clumsy, but the hard frame can double as an elevated shooting support adequate for sitting and kneeling positions. Small frameless packs are usually only high enough for prone shooting support.

Most of us can get by with a small daypack if it has external straps, buckles, etc. on which to tie a spare coat or a bag of pelts. Those items take up the most space. Whatever size pack you get, I recommend that it have several zippered pockets in which to organize gear. You won't want a camera clanking around with a dirty knife and flashlight. Nor will you want to dig to the bottom of a single-compartment pack to fish for a flashlight in the dark. Look for no-rattle zippers. They use a nylon string-loop pull instead of noisy metal tabs. The smaller the zipper teeth, the quieter they'll close. Packs and pack manufacturers come and go so often that it hardly pays to mention brands and models. Every hunter has his or her own ideas about the ideal pack. Here are some things I like: External, Velcro-closed knife and flashlight pockets. I like at least one zippered pocket on each side of the pack and one or two on the face, plus the main compartment. I don't recommend open pockets of any kind, or those closed by an elastic band. Gear inevitably falls out of these, while rain, snow, and debris fall in—rarely a fair or welcome trade. Drawstring closure pockets are quiet and can suffice if you remember to cinch them tight. I like these for water bottles, as they confine leaks outside the pack. Padded shoulder straps and belts shouldn't be necessary unless you plan to hike for miles with a lot of fresh hides aboard. When I carry 20 pounds or more I like a padded waist belt both for transferring weight to my hips instead of neck and shoulders and to stabilize a pack laterally. If you've ever tried running with a pack aboard, you'll know what I mean.

A few innovative packs include foldout chairs or seats that use the main pack as a back rest. These are wonderful for keeping your butt out of mud and snow while steadying your shots. Some have rifle holders incorporated into the straps and belt for handsfree carry as you hike. Most pack builders make hunter packs, most from camouflage fleece, micro-fleece or saddle cloth. A few feature Scent-Lok liners, too, and that can help as long as you remember to wash the external surfaces from time to time. Experiment with your pack to discover different positions in which it can help support you while you shoot. Lying prone over them is obvious, but the back rest trick helps, too.

A backpack that holds essential supplies makes a day of predator hunting easier. You should be set to travel miles and handle any situation.

A Vested Interest

An alternative to a pack is a well-designed vest with enough pockets to organize your gear. A large game bag pouch in back will serve to haul a jacket. I don't recommend vests for prone shooting, but they're fine for sitting and kneeling unless you overload the upper pockets. Today's turkey vests, with their padded seat flaps, large game bags, and multiple pockets, are ideal. Fishing vests are generally too confining and their pockets too small. Safari vests with multiple pockets can also work. Their green or tan colors blend pretty well with most predator-calling environments. Don't get the oiled (waxed) cotton versions, which carry a strong odor.

Support Your Right to Keep and Aim Arms

Unless you're in this game strictly to hone your field-shooting skills, consider including some kind of rifle support in your kit. With it you'll hit more of what you shoot at. Don't depend on the old fence post, tree limb, or dirt bank rest. All have a nasty habit of disappearing when you need them most. In a lot of prime coyote and fox country, anything taller and more substantial than a clump of grass is rare.

The easiest support to carry—you never forget or lose it—is your own body. Properly applied, your butt, belly, insteps, legs, and arms can be positioned to settle a rifle amazingly well. Shooting manuals traditionally describe four major field-shooting positions which increase in stability in this order—standing, kneeling, sitting, and prone. Contrary to popular opinion, I find sitting to be more effective than prone for the vast majority of predator calling. Prone may reduce wind buffeting and your own body tremors maximally, but it will reduce your shooting flexibility even more, and unpredictable predators demand flexibility. To quickly understand this, lie prone on your living room floor with an unloaded rifle. Now pretend a coyote is approaching not directly toward your muzzle, but ninety degrees to your left. Can you get

A turkey vest is a good carryall and seat.

While prone shooting is stable, it limits your shooting flexibility when predators come in from any other angle than head-on.

your sights on him? How about ninety degrees right? Behind you? What if he comes over a hill? Can you effectively aim six feet up the wall? See, that's the problem with prone. It's like shooting in a straightjacket. Add interference from grass and brush (there is a lot of this outdoors these days), and prone becomes untenable.

Contrast that with a solid sitting position. Knees bent, legs tipped slightly to each side, elbows inside your knees—not right on top of them. Notice how your rifle wants to line up at an angle slightly away from the direction you're facing—about thirty degrees to the left for a right-handed shooter. Now pretend that a coyote's approaching over your left shoulder. See how easily you can twist to align your sights? You'll have to give up your knee support, but if your quarry's close, you shouldn't need it. You can't twist nearly as far to the right, but a lot farther than you could if you were prone. Notice also how smoothly you can swing at the waist to follow running game through a wide arc. Sweet, isn't it? But that's not the end of sitting's benefits. If you detect predators while they're still hundreds of yards away, you'll have time to spin on your butt and realign. Push off with your feet and you won't even have to take your hands off the rifle. I've spun 180 degrees numerous times without unduly spooking approaching coyotes, even those

within one hundred yards in the open. Some callers actually sit on those rotating ice-fishing bucket lids, but they're a bit squirrelly for my tastes—liable to shift when I'm putting the final squeeze on the trigger.

The sitting position can be stabilized additionally by pushing your back against a trunk, post, cutbank, backpack, or even a few stalks of stiff vegetation. Add a hiking staff or cross-sticks

A solid sitting position allows greater flexibility to adjust your shooting position.

under the forend stock, and you're practically a living benchrest. My absolute favorite location for sitting is inside a shallow, V-shaped cutbank facing the opening of the V. This enables me to rest my elbows on the ground, my back against the apex, even my legs against the walls. Steady as a rock cemented to a mountain.

A neat option for additional sitting stability on flat, open ground is the backpack seat already mentioned or a stadium cushion/seat with the adjustable nylon side straps. You can find insulated camping pads that include straps and snaps that convert the pad into a legless backrest chair. Therm-A-Rest markets a conversion kit that turns their sleeping pads into a similar back support. A bonus with these seats is that they keep your butt off the wet ground. In lieu of any accessory backrest, you can always sit back-to-back with your partner. Just arrange some kind of nudge or verbal signal to indicate you're ready to shoot so your living back-support can freeze into position.

Lastly, a loop of rope or nylon strap around your back and legs will stop leg quivers. As your legs fall to either side, they tighten the loop and stop muscle fatigue. It's a simple system that weighs next to nothing and is easy to get on and off.

What about kneeling or standing to shoot? Don't forget them, but avoid them if possible. Neither position is particularly stable for accurate shooting, and both make you more obvious to approaching game. Where cover is too high to shoot over while sitting, however, you may be forced to stand. Try to lean against brush, trees or posts—anything to add support, break your outline, and help you stand still. Most situations that force standing or kneeling are suitable for shotgunning, and that reduces your need for maximum accuracy. The ability to shift positions and swing quickly in heavy cover is more valuable than pinpoint accuracy.

Mechanical Shooting Supports

Muscles are convenient, but metals are permanent. If you want to support your rifle's forend without inducing muscle fatigue and the shakes, stick a post under it. Bipods that attach to a rifle's fore-end sling stud are as sturdy, steady, and reliable as they are popular. Most feature telescoping legs that adjust, within a narrow range, for precise shooting levels. To switch from prone to sitting to standing, you usually need to attach specific bipods designed for each use. The prone models are the most stable, but, again, they suffer from limited range of motion and limited application in grass or brush. Sitting-length bipods are more versatile, in my experience. Standing models? I'd rather use a walking stick, which doesn't unbalance a rifle.

Poor balance is one of my complaints against stock-mounted bipods. Even if the legs fold out of the way, their weight near the end of a stock ruins a rifle's feel and makes it more difficult to shoot without first extending the legs. I also don't like the limitations a bipod puts on shooting angles. Remember our little experiment with prone shooting? Shooting off an attached bipod is similarly constraining, if not worse. Just last week I was trying to do some varmint shooting with a gun mounted bipod. At the prone setting, the legs were so high I had to lift my right elbow off the ground to align the sights. But when I sat and

Jointed shooting sticks set up instantly and adjust quickly for a variety of shooting heights and angles. And there's no bulky weight hanging from the stock.

extended the legs, they were too short. I was forced to scrunch my back and shoulders and lean my head sideways to get the cross hairs on a target. A bit of rise or fall to the ground made things even worse. Many long-range coyote and fox shooters love attached bipods. More power to 'em.

I prefer simple shooting sticks carried on a belt sheath or even in the hands. Shock-corded aluminum poles (like arrows) joined near their tips by a flexible rubber block weigh about six ounces and carry easily and deploy quickly. Spread to varying degrees, they are instantly and infinitely adjustable from prone to thirty-four inches, tall enough for kneeling shots. I can whip mine into position so fast that I use them while still-hunting or jump-shooting deer. My hunting partner Tom Berger simply wraps a length of bicycle inner tube around a couple of laths or dowels to build his shooting sticks. Simple, inexpensive, and effective. I'll admit stock-mounted bipods provide slightly steadier holds, but not enough to matter at hunting ranges and certainly insufficient to offset the speed and versatility of cross-sticks. It takes a bit of practice to use cross-sticks to their full potential, but once you become proficient, you'll swear by them.

Monopods don't offer as much horizontal stability as cross-sticks, but are even more versatile. Get one head-high, and it'll serve for all shooting positions and double as a walking stick, handy in broken, steep country. I've never liked the side-to-side sway inherent in monopods and rarely used them until last year, when I took one on a mountain goat hunt. It surprised me. I found it quite useful for remaining erect on mountainsides, pole-vaulting over streams, steadying my

AR-15-style automatic rifles are becoming a go-to favorite for many coyote callers who like the fast, extra rounds when more than one coyote approaches at once--or when they screw up a shot and need backups. After the author miffed an easy shot, he and Rob Lancellotti took full advantage of the R15's firepower to finally lay this coyote to rest.

binoculars while glassing, and steadying my rifle. Experiment with a monopod, and you'll discover little tricks for increasing its stability. For instance, shove its point in the ground and lean its side against a boulder or limb for two-point stability. Push it against the inside or outside of your legs while sitting to steady them. Lean it backward or forward to adjust your vertical angle. Rest it at a severe angle from atop your head or shoulder and down to your boot instep and press your rifle against it. A simple stick can make a major contribution to marksmanship.

Heavier, more complicated but infinitely steadier than a monopod, is a tripod. These three-legged devils are the ultimate in field stability. With one and a good backrest I can sit and shoot accurately to 450 yards—or at least I have, several times. For speed, tape two legs together; this converts the tripod into a bipod. Extend the legs, tape all three together with Velcro and use as a hiking staff. Most tripods will adjust from sitting to standing lengths, a few from prone to kneeling lengths. Leg locks come in clamp or twist styles. Both work.

Slings

Everyone seems to carry their rifles on slings these days, but almost no one steadies a rifle with a sling anymore. The military sling was designed so a right-handed shooter's left arm would be slipped through two straps that then tightened around his biceps. Properly adjusted for length, the strap pulled tightly between upper arm and rifle forend, reducing shake. Two-pronged hooks fit into a series of double holes along the length of the strap so it could be adjusted to a variety of arm lengths. You'll spend a little trial-and-error time setting up such a sling, but once you've found the ideal length, you're set forever. Works great sitting or standing. Military straps were one and one-half-inches wide, but a one-inch wide Whelen version is sufficient for hunting.

If you don't want to improve your shooting with a military sling, at least don't handicap yourself with one of those overweight cobra-style carry straps. These are popular way out of proportion to their usefulness, which is primarily to make money for the seller. I know, I know, that wide strap is supposed to make your rifle easier to carry by distributing its weight over a larger surface, but do you honestly think a simple one-inch-wide nylon strap is going to permanently maim your shoulder if you sling an eight-pound rifle off it for a walk of a few hundred yards from your truck? Try a versatile Quick-Adjust sling and see if you don't find it more useful and less interfering than those heavy cobras. If you do use a heavy sling, remove it before calling so it doesn't get in the way. If its pendulum swaying doesn't throw your shot off, it may alert your incoming predator.

Little things like slings and shooting sticks might not seem significant compared to rifles and scopes, but they can make a big difference in your ability to hit distant targets. Personally, I'd rather have a rifle that groups 1 1/2-inches at a hundred yards plus a shooting support than a MOA rifle that I had to shoot freehand. Field accuracy is more a product of your ability than your rifle's.

Rifle slings can be used to help steady your shot while sitting or standing.

8

Hear No Evil, See No Evil, Smell No Evil

How to Become the Invisible Hunter

When reduced to its lowest common denominator, predator hunting is quite simple. Don't let your quarry hear, see or smell you, and you can walk right up and grab it. None of us is about to become the invisible (or should we say undetectable?) man or woman, but with today's quiet fabrics, camouflage patterns, and scent-absorbing clothing, we can come close.

Hush Hush, Sweet Caller

Keeping quiet is relatively easy when predator calling. Just sit still. Even when you raise your gun to shoot, you rarely make enough noise to spook a predator responding to the dinner bell. They're expecting a wounded animal—and probably the predator that caught it—so a bit of rustling will usually either stop them or inspire them to run in faster; it rarely frightens them. One cloudy November afternoon, I was sitting back-to-back with my old calling partner, Tom Berger, south of Dodge City. We'd been pulling in coyotes like crappies all morning and getting pretty lackadaisical about it. For this setup, we hiked from the truck a few hundred yards over a low ridge and sat bold as you please on a grassy slope overlooking a woolly maze of draws. "You cover the north, I'll watch behind us just in case," I told Tom. That was akin to giving him the shot, because the wind was out of the north and we'd just come from the south. Anything approaching from that direction would see the truck or smell us and spook.

Tom was just into his second series when the coyote with the lowest IQ in Kansas loped over the ridge. Each time Tom let loose a cry, that dog kicked himself into a higher gear. "Stop!" I stage-whispered, half at the coyote, half at Tom. Apparently neither heard me, 'cause Tom kept blowing, and El Coyote shifted into overdrive. "Stop!" I tried again, louder. Same response from both Tom and the coyote. This forced me to raise my rifle in self-defense. My attacker saw this, mistook me for an oversized jackrabbit, and put the pedal to the metal. Tom felt me move, pulled the caller from his lips in time to hear my third and final "Stop!" and nearly jumped out of his coveralls when I fired at what had become a blur of pink tongue and gleaming teeth. The coyote collapsed in mid-lunge and collided, quivering, against the toe of my boot.

Despite noisy success stories such as this, most hunters like to remain quiet on stand. The whisper of brushed cotton, wool, fleece, or micro-fleece clothing helps. I find these soft materials useful when I'm listening for approaching game in tight cover. The rasp of hard nylon on a collar or sleeve obscures a lot of natural sounds like creeping cat paws—not that you can hear a cat until it steps on your ears, but fox and coyotes thump the ground pretty loudly. I once sat against a wall of tall Indian grass at the base of a healing cutbank overlooking a gamey-looking valley. I'd seen a big bobcat in the area the evening before, but couldn't get a shot at it. I was prepared to sit and call for an hour in an attempt to get it to show, but never got that far. After my third series, I heard grass rustling over my left shoulder. Fearing I was about to feel claws on my neck, I slowly turned, leading with the rifle's muzzle, prepared to use it as a bayonet. There stood a coyote, towering over me, with its head cocked like a puppy listening to a squeak-toy. I shot it from about ten feet.

If quiet garments are useful to callers, they're essential to stalkers. Why go scraping and slapping through sagebrush or greenbriars when a soft fleece pant will enable you to ghost along as quietly as a kitten? To my aging ears, no fabric is quieter than long fleece, but few fabrics grab as much debris, either. The micro-fleeces aren't as messy, but they aren't nearly as quiet. Wool ranks right with long fleece as a bur magnet, but is quieter. Brushed cotton—think flannel shirts here, not blue jeans—rates an A for keeping a secret; a B or C for picking up hitchhikers. Cotton's dark side is moisture retention. Sit on wet grass with cotton pants and you'll feel it the rest of the day. Save cotton for desert climates or warm weather.

A quiet-fabric coverall makes a versatile all-season garment. Alone, it's adequate for warm weather. Pull it over pants, bibs, or coats as temperatures demand. No need to buy several outfits for the same purpose. And you can store the thing in an airtight plastic bag or box in your rig, where it can remain bur-laden but free of unnatural odors, hunt after hunt. Get one with lots of pockets so you have easy access to calls, gloves, spare ammunition, etc.

Oh, Say, Can You See?

Unlike children, predator callers are meant to be heard and not seen. Fortunately, disappearing is almost as easy as remaining quiet. Again, callers sit still, and that alone is enough to fool most predators. Unlike humans, furbearers do not have good color vision or the ability to decipher motionless, abstract shapes. If we see just the leg, tail, or ear of a fox in cover, we can rather quickly surmise the rest of the

Fleece camo is soft, quiet and warm, but debris and snow stick to it like stink on a skunk. Fortunately, it doesn't absorb water and dries quickly.

shape and conclude that a fox is there. Old Reynard cannot return the favor. This is why we can shift position, raise a gun, reposition our glasses, and still have time to shoot at the puzzled red fox standing thirty yards away. Predators approach a call expecting to see a struggling bunny anyway, so a bit of motion is natural. What seems unnatural is that a sharp-eyed, wary predator can't differentiate between a crippled hare and a two hundred-pound hominid.

I've given up being surprised when a four-legged critter practically trips across my extended legs. Deer, elk, boar, coyote. Doesn't matter. So long as I remain still and at least partially concealed, they miss the big picture. And it doesn't matter what colors I'm wearing. Numerous times while big game hunting I've seen or heard coyotes, called to them, and watched as they approached as close as fifty yards—even though I was dressed like a neon pumpkin in blaze orange vest and cap. Duh!

According to research, mammalian predators aren't completely color blind, but virtually every wavelength on the red end of the spectrum appears yellow to them. An October cottonwood leaf—yellow. Blood—yellow. Red Corvette—yellow. Blaze orange hunter—yellow. Hey, a lot of grass and brush I hide in during predator

Burnham Brothers electronic caller (in camouflage bag on ground beneath left bobcat) included all the sounds necessary for this mixed bag of coyotes and bobcats taken with a Kimber 84M in .204 Ruger and a Browning BLR in .22-250 Rem.

A gray fox is not big, but it inspires a big jolt of adrenaline when it charges a call. The Savage Mark II-LV .22 Long Rifle was perfect for this little dog at close range.

A half hour after the author left his hunting partner, Marty Malin, the big Texan spotted this mountain lion chasing some wild sheep. He called, the cat came more than three hundred yards, and one shot from a Model 70 in .270 Winchester Short Magnum with 140-grain Fail Safe bullet ended the show.

The author admires a pair of eastern coyotes dropped within yards of one another. The dogs approached together and when the first one fell, the second stood staring. Gunshots do not necessarily frighten predators.

A coyote catches one of its most common and dependable meals-meadow vole. Soft, high-pitched squeaks mimic these animals and lure coyotes, foxes, and bobcats that are close enough to hear them.

Hitting predators at long range isn't easy, so assume a solid field position that gets you above grass and brush. This hunter's kneeling position is not quite as steady as sitting, but adequate. He'd be better off with that heavy sling wrapped once around his arm to stop its swaying.

Predators provided sanctuary in man-made structures and kept fat and sassy on a variety of man-supplied foods place unnaturally high mortality losses on songbirds and game birds like this pheasant. Trimming predator numbers can be an important tool in reaching a more natural predator/prey balance.

Ranchers and farmers often welcome predator hunters who alleviate stock losses. These folks are a wealth of information on predator densities. Ask and ye shall discover.

A wolf in the calf pasture isn't common, but this Montana marauder illustrates why ranchers often welcome predator hunters.

Finally! Tom Berger celebrates the taking of an Oklahoma coyote after a long day of calling, proving again that persistence counts.

Midwest foxes hunt wide-open cornfields long after the stalks have been cut. Lay prone in appropriate camo and you can call them close right from the middle of the field.

Camouflage isn't essential, but it helps. Brad Deffenbaugh blends nicely into these snowy eastern hardwoods, and he'll have a steady log to shoot over should the anticipated gray fox arrive.

Kevin Howard thinks a bobcat is the perfect end to a long day of predator calling.

Superb camouflage and a handheld speaker for directing digital prey sounds enable this hunter to work with a shotgun in fairly brushy habitat where predators can approach closely.

seasons is—yellow. But a lot more of it, in all seasons, is brown, gray, and green—just like most camouflage patterns on today's market.

A shortage of cone cells (the cells that detect color) in the retina gets the blame for abbreviated color perception in predators. Humans have a lot of them. Most mammals, however, have an abundance of rod cells, which enhance low-light vision. Thus, they get to hunt at night while we huddle by the fire.

This being the case, why bother with camouflage? The obvious answer is why not? It can't hurt, and it might help. In fact, it does. The closer a critter gets to abstract shapes, the better he begins to see and/or decipher them. Some hunters state smugly that any varmint close enough to make them out is close enough to be shot, har har, so why bother with camo? I say, "Better safe than sorry."

There's another good reason to go camo. Birds. Crows, ravens, magpies, bluejays, and similar predatory birds often outrace furry carnivores to the sounds of an anguished varmint. And these birds see color better than we do. If they recognize us for the dangerous bushwhackers we are, they spook,

Ground blinds offer additional cover to hide movement. However, they can be cumbersome to carry from one set up to another throughout the day.

perhaps even alarming approaching wild cats and dogs in the process. But if they don't recognize us, they often hang around, flying, diving, and calling excitedly to add realism to our setups. This is why I advocate (but don't always practice, more's the pity) complete camouflage, especially gloves and face mask. The three parts of a caller's body most likely to move during a calling sequence are face, right hand, and left hand. If they are white and shiny, you might as well be waving semaphores.

What about eyes? Should they be camouflaged? Do prey animals "feel the eyes of the hunter upon them?" Or is that just an old wives' tale? I've seen no research on the subject one way or the other, but I've stared at lots of game up close and personal, sometimes for nearly an hour without it spooking them. Birds—particularly crows—do often spook when I turn a big telephoto lens on them—even "tame" ones in city parks. But I've never witnessed mammals do this, not even whitetails during hunting season. I have, however, seen them react to a human's flickering eyes at close range. That makes sense. A dark pupil outlined in white and dancing side to side should draw attention. But how do you hide eyeballs without obscuring vision? Camouflage contact lenses? I don't think so. You could confine them behind dark glasses, even a thin veil, but I don't recommend it. It's too easy to miss a shot while trying to aim through any sort of sheer cover. No, when it comes to hiding eyeballs I subscribe to the philosophy, "If they're close enough to see the whites of my eyes, they're close enough to shoot." Har har.

What about blinds as an alternative to camouflage clothing? Honestly, I don't see the need. It's a lot easier wearing your cover than carrying it. Considering how often one moves from setup to setup, dragging a blind around could get old in a hurry. I have seen some simple rolls of tattered camouflage fabric attached to slim fiberglass rods that are convenient. You unroll the material, poke the sticks into the ground around you, and sit behind the resultant low camo screen. The visual block allows you to shift about and twiddle your toes if you want, but again, you can do most of this in blaze orange pants without ruining your chances. A blind might be useful when calling bobcats, though. Although cats are notorious for walking up to callers who are practically dancing the jitterbug, they're equally notorious for sneaking in unseen, sitting for long periods, and watching carefully. I suspect that many more slink away unseen than prance in like idiots.

If finances demand that you choose between an elaborate camouflage outfit or blind and a higher-quality binocular or scope, spend your money on the optics, and call in any old clothing that'll keep you warm. Camo is nice, but it isn't essential.

You Little Stinker

Keeping quiet and remaining unseen are child's play compared to remaining scentless. Bobcats and lions will often ignore man-stink, but one whiff of it turns every wild canine and bruin inside out in its rush to get away.

The best defense against your quarry's olfactory powers is the wind. So long as it blows away from approaching predators, you're as safe as if locked in a plastic bag. But wind, sad to say, is fickle. Here today, gone tomorrow. Out of the west one minute, out of the east the next. Years ago I sat on a call site and, as an experiment, ignited one of those sawdust sticks that have been soaked in deer urine and gland scents. The smoke began drifting slowly south on the barest whiff of a zephyr. But it hadn't oozed more than thirty yards before it turned on itself and came back. When it was about ten yards north of its smoldering source, it suddenly turned east and snaked directly toward me. This variable drifting continued until the punk had nearly burned itself out.

With winds like that, who needs enemies? Even with steady breezes, predators often circle to intercept the scent trail of what they assume will be a dead or dying rabbit. Red fox usually do this, and shy coyotes often do, sometimes beginning as far as 250 yards out. On the wide-open plains, a hunter with a flat-shooting center-fire can usually handle this; just bark to stop your quarry, aim, and fire. But in short-range situations, where responding predators may approach within fifty yards unseen, your personal perfume will ruin many of your chances.

One of my old tricks for outguessing shifting breezes is to carry several plastic pill bottles filled with cotton soaked in some sort of animal scent. Fox or deer urine, gland scents, even skunk scent, though that's a bit riskier than required. A freshly killed rabbit or squirrel or chunk of any old meat can work. Anything natural and aromatic that will quickly catch a critter's nose should suffice. Before calling, I toss these scent bombs out at four points of the compass in hopes that anything responding to my audio entreaties will hit the outrider scent trail before cutting mine, regardless of which way the wind is drifting at the moment. As they probably say at Microsoft, it ain't a bad system. Other hunters use just one scent bottle and set it by their side. Less trouble than dispensing and retrieving four bottles and, they claim, just as effective.

Personally, I doubt any cover scent can fool a wild dog's nose. If they can hire dogs to detect drugs inside locked containers surrounded by onions, I don't think a wolf or coyote would have trouble smelling me through a haze of skunk perfume. But it could confuse them just long enough. And if they intercept the scent bomb before hitting my scent line . . . Success.

Another tactic for eluding olfactory detection is to tightly manage personal body odor. This can be a major pain in the bath. First you have to shower with some sort of scent-free deer hunter's soap, then dry with towels washed in scent-free deer hunter's detergent, then rub scent-free deer hunter's antiperspirant under your arms and over your feet and maybe in a few other places I won't mention. Then you don underwear and clothes washed in scent-free soap and eat a scent-free breakfast. Do not go within a half-mile of frying bacon. You put on your special driving coveralls washed in you-know-what soap and drive to your call site, where you take

Scent-free soap eliminates perfume laundry odors and human stink from your clothes.

from your trunk or truck bed a scent-free plastic bag or cooler in which you've stored your special hunting clothes washed in scent-free soap. Remove your car coverall and house clothes. (Hope it's not snowing.) Put on your hunting clothes. Remove your special knee-length rubber boots from their scent-free plastic bag, but don't put them on. First sprinkle scent-adsorbing crystals in them. Then pull them on. Spray them liberally with deer hunter's scent-eliminating spray. Give your hat a good douse while you're at it. Hit the rifle a blast or two as well. Okay, now go have fun, but don't walk fast enough to work up a sweat or you'll contaminate the whole outfit.

If all this seems a bit extreme to you, sign here _____ to join my "Some Folks Take This Way Too Seriously" club. If it doesn't seem extreme, I've got a few bottles of scent-free soap you might want to buy.

Look, controlling scent is well and good, but consider what you're up against. Bird dogs have been known to stop and point a quail while carrying a dead quail in their mouths. Bears are known to detect human scent from a mile away. Deer can smell an acorn under two inches of autumn oak leaves. I'm sure keeping clothing as clean and scent-free as possible will help, but it's asking a bit much to expect to make yourself nose-proof to a fox or coyote. The very attempt, as outlined above, could become so onerous that you might eventually prefer going to the mall. So take the easy way out. Get a scent-blocking suit. If you still believe those things work.

Scent locking, blocking, adsorbing, and absorbing clothing has been huge in the deer hunting market for about fifteen years, but recently someone sued a manufacturer for false advertising, proving in court that the suits did not block, adsorb, or cover 100 percent of odor as reportedly advertised. The manufacturer was forced to change his advertising claims, but he's still manufacturing. Now he promises reduction in human odor, not complete elimination.

So now what? Do we abandon all these no-scent clothes? I'm just lazy and old-fashioned enough to trust my success to playing the wind, but common sense also tells me that any scent-reduction is better than none. While dressed in "scent-proof" garments, I have had coyotes catch a slight whiff of me without running off. It was as if they'd smelled such things before, but since it was so faint they perhaps assumed the danger had moved on. Their hesitation gave me time to aim and score. Reason enough to wear the stuff? Only you can decide that for yourself.

The various brands of scent-reduction clothing use various methods for achieving their objectives. Some put carbon or charcoal in the fibers of the cloth. These are supposed to work like a giant industrial filter to suck up and hold scent molecules within thousands of miniscule cavities. Once the cavities are stuffed, you can supposedly drive the stink out by heating the garment in a drier. Critics claim that for this to work you would need to raise the temperature so high the item would burst into flame. Others claim regular drier temperatures for two hours or more does the trick. Caveat emptor. Do your research.

Another way to minimize odors is to prevent them in the first place. This is the "bathe often" and antimicrobial method. Manufacturers treat fabrics with antimicrobial "stuff" that prevents bacteria from growing. The bacteria are what stink. Essentially they're "passing gas" as they digest sweat and skin cells from your body. Silver—the metal that dimes used to be made of—is a natural antimicrobial, which is why royalty dined with silverware. Manufacturers sometimes add silver fibers to their clothing to control odors, but given the rising value of silver, we're not seeing much of this anymore. I doubt that many could afford even a sock that contained enough silver to make a difference anyway. Whether or not the antibacterial treatments work any better than the carbon remains to be determined. Some hunters say, "No way." Some say, "Any little bit helps." I say, "Do whatever you think helps." The one thing about scent control I do know is this: keep yourself downwind from your prey and you will remain undetected.

I know some hunters who brazenly call downwind and claim they have great success. Most of them sit above the areas into which they are calling and try to shoot while their customers are still 200 yards away or more, but some report coyotes running right to them inside 50 yards without catching a whiff of bad odors. That's encouraging news, because completely eliminating human odor removes a major barrier to predator calling success.

You might never become completely invisible to critters, but with careful selection of quiet, camouflaged, scent-free clothing plus thorough bathing, careful choice of your stand location and minimal movement on it, you might pass undetected while your quarry approaches quite close. Or at least close enough.

9

Haven't I Seen You Somewhere Before?

The Hottest Decoys for Fooling the Wariest Predators

At first blush, the idea of decoying a predator seems quite novel and clever, but it's not. Humans have been decoying animals for centuries. You've probably heard about the Native American reed duck decoy found in a Southwest cave. Crow hunters figured out the use of a stuffed great horned owl decades back. Even dress-shop managers are smart enough to place mannequins in store windows. It just took us awhile to apply this knowledge to predators.

Adding a visual lure to the auditory appeal of prey-in-distress calls fleshes out the ruse. I first heard about predator decoying in the late 1970s, when a few South Dakotans reported coyotes charging spreads of Judas Canada geese and carrying the plastic fakes off by their necks. In retrospect, that seemed inevitable, what with all the wild flocks feeding in new irrigated cornfields near the river hills. Local coyotes quickly learned to charge feeding flocks and pick off any cripples. Still, hunters watching from pit blinds were surprised when the wild dogs ran brazenly through open fields where hunters fired 12-gauge shotguns almost daily.

I remember thinking "What would they do if they saw a moving cottontail near the sounds of a predator call?" The idea was intoxicating. Hang a cottontail skin on a short stick, push this into the ground forty or fifty yards from your hiding place, run a string to it, and simply pull to attract an approaching coyote's attention. If the wind were blowing, you wouldn't even need the string. The movement would both reassure a hesitant predator and distract it while you moved

Bobcats and coyotes respond to ordinary turkey calls and decoys in places where these big birds are abundant.

into position to shoot. Combine such a visual aid with a scent lure and you had the whole show. How much more convincing could you get?

Turns out, quite a bit. I've subsequently heard of callers who take children's stuffed toy bunnies afield. They work just as well as the real thing. A few have been snatched and spirited off when shooters missed or their guns failed to fire. One fellow used a stuffed toy dog instead of bunny to decoy coyotes. He figured correctly that coyotes would believe the little dog was competition for the "rabbit" they'd heard screaming. Or maybe just a bonus meal. "Super-size that, please."

Once turkey decoys came into common use, coyotes attacked them, too. One spring, Mark Kayser and I hunted Merriam's gobblers on a Montana sheep ranch. The owner, Randy, showed us a narrow range of forested hills in which the birds roamed. Several coyotes used the same cloistered hills and canyons as a fortress from which they'd sweep down at night to devour lambs. "Shoot every blamed coyote you see," Randy instructed us. "Don't let one go by because you're afraid you'll spook a turkey. I ever find out you did that, I won't let you come back." He was serious. With that bit of information, you can pretty much guess what happened the next morning. After a protracted conversation with a gang of jakes, I finally talked them over for a look at two decoys standing twenty-five yards in front of us. The jakes liked what they saw and were whispering sweet nothings to the stuffy hens, adding authenticity to our ruse. We could hear a mature tom gobbling just down the valley, coming closer to see what all the fuss was about. "Get ready," I whispered. "He could pop over that little ridge any second."

"Coyotes," Mark replied. "A pair." A flicker of pale gray caught my eye. Sure enough, out in the bordering grassland, two coyotes were running right toward us. The fastest popped over the rise where we'd anticipated a red head only seconds before. A surprised jake burped a half-choked warning and flew straight up into the sheltering arms of a Ponderosa pine. Three of his buddies followed suit. The little glade was alive with the sounds of "put"-ing. Mr. Coyote, seeing his breakfast options dwindle, switched his attention to the decoys. Mark waited as long as he could for the second coyote to appear, but it must have gotten sidetracked. "A coyote in the hand is worth two in the bush," he said when the smoke cleared.

Next morning, on a similar setup a quarter-mile away, my hen calls brought the surviving mate on the run, and Mark grassed her as she raced toward the decoys. The rancher very nearly gave us the deed to his property. "You boys come back anytime. Anytime."

Plastic geese, plush bunnies, and foam turkeys all suggest that predator decoying possibilities are wide. Replicate any natural scenario, and you should be able to fool a predator. Decoy makers seem to agree because they make just about every decoy you can imagine from three-dimensional deer foam and plastic deer to nondescript rags and synthetic tails on stakes that quiver, shimmy, shake, and dance. Obviously one would use different species to match local conditions, adding the appropriate sounds. A lower-pitched jackrabbit/fawn bawl should work better with a fawn decoy than a turkey decoy. But it wouldn't surprise me if the opposite would work just as well. The more I hunt and watch predators, the more I think any sound and nearly any decoy in any combination can and will attract them. But I still recommend doing this the "right" way. Rabbit sounds with rabbit decoy, deer sounds with deer, etc.

Black bears are one of the major predators of elk fawns in parts of the Rocky Mountain West each spring. An elk decoy and some low-pitched bawling ought to work there. I've called black bears in spring with regular rabbit squealers, but I make them sound more like bear cubs in distress. Brings both protective sows and hungry boars. Bruins are so near-sighted, however, that I'm not sure how important a decoy would be. Can't hurt to try.

But what about the decoys that look like rags? Motion. That's all. They're just something designed to move and attract the attention of an incoming predator. This means it isn't as likely to notice you. It can also encourage a reluctant critter to charge right in. However, (I hate to ruin your enthusiasm) this doesn't always happen. For whatever reason, hungry cats and coyotes will as often ignore a decoy as charge it. Why? Who knows. But don't assume that the sight of a decoy, moving or standing, automatically means

A fawn decoy combined with fawn distress cries is the perfect ruse in deer-rich eastern woodlands.

fur on the stretcher. You still need to remain quiet, relatively motionless, down-wind of your quarry, and ready to shoot at your best opportunity. No decoy will compensate for mistakes in other critical parts of your presentation.

You don't have to buy a decoy. Make your own. If you live in forested country, tie a squirrel tail to a low branch, manipulate it with a string, and blow one of those whistles that mimics a frightened young squirrel. Get an old car antennae, the springy style, and rig a stuffed bunny or a few feathers atop it. Poke one end into the ground and yank the top with a string when you want your customers to see it. One creative decoy ruse I like involves mounting a crow decoy or two on a post near your calling site as a confidence decoy. Call-wary or otherwise shy foxes and coyotes apparently see the familiar black form and assume the coast is clear. Out west a black-and-white magpie might be more appropriate. And guess what? A few companies sell those. Or at least they used to.

There are also moving wing decoys. Flap, flap, flap. I think MoJo started these. I've seen one shaped and painted like a pileated woodpecker. Should work well in the woods and equally well atop a cornfield fence post. I doubt any fox or coyote knows the difference between a pileated woodpecker and a titillated tit-mouse. Those nylon bird windsocks goose hunters use can be added for a little attention-getting action on breezy days. Another idea is to set up a crow/great horned owl decoy spread and blow crow-in-distress calls instead of rabbit screams. A dying crow call carries well. Given the constant bickering between crows and owls, wild dogs and cats must be familiar with the potential for dead bodies. Shucks, my brother once saw a host of frantic crows peck a horned owl right out of the sky, and he doesn't spend nearly as much time outdoors as your average red fox. I played around with this setup in North Dakota one winter without any luck, but traditional rabbit calls weren't working that day, either. We ended up making thirteen sets before finally calling in one coyote. I'm eager to stage the crow/owl production again this fall, but probably won't for the usual reason: traditional calling usually works well enough. Seriously. A standard calling session brings most critters close enough to be taken with a typical center-fire predator rifle without all the fuss of scents, decoys, and elaborate ruses. Now, in some parts of the country where predators are particularly shy or cautious, decoys and scent attractants could spell the difference between success and failure, so don't discount them out of hand. Predator hunting is a competitive business these days. The team with the most options often scores the most. It never hurts to improvise; try something new or go the extra mile.

A perfect example of this is to mix crow decoys and calls with traditional rabbit screams. It seems a natural. A hawk or fox catches a rabbit, it screams, a crow responds and starts calling to summon his buddies. All of this piques the interest of furry ears within hearing, and you're in business. The more natural the sounds, the better. More than once we've set up for coyotes, played a bunch of coyote howls, and brought in a bobcat.

A creative old-timer I once hunted with had come up with a simple, easy, novel motion decoy. He put a visual lure—I think it was a stuffed toy bunny—on a stick and shoved this into his boot laces. When he wanted to catch a client's eye, he just wiggled his foot. I've seen other hunters twirl a feather or bit of fur in their fingers. Some simply wave a gloved hand slowly. I've tossed a glove through the air to convince a reluctant bobcat to come closer. Obviously, you want to be well camouflaged before trying this. The downside to wiggling decoys on your person is drawing direct attention to yourself. A remote decoy distracts your quarry, increasing your chances for shifting into position for an easy shot.

Competition Decoys

A relatively new idea is the predator itself as decoy—instead of the prey. A fake coyote standing on the lonesome prairie is bound to excite a real coyote that sees it in his territory. Let the fighting begin! This tactic risks spooking shy pups, but generally they aren't so gutless that they'll run the other way. They might hang up at two hundred yards or approach more cautiously, but their attention will be riveted on the Judas coyote, not you. And their confidence will be high, too. If another coyote is hanging out, what could be wrong? This attitude should help you line up some easy shots.

Mating season in late winter is when a coyote or fox decoy really shines. Mated pairs will want to drive it out of town. Unpaired singles will perhaps want to speed date it. Either way you win. Some of these decoys even wear three-dimensional fur tails that blow in the wind, but if they don't, you can add one of your own.

Mixing coyote howls with full-body coyote decoys can really work wonders. It's a one-two punch that brings dominant, territorial dogs charging. We've had them practically run us over. I don't know of any fox sounds that work this well, but foxes do bark and yap. I'll bet if you could find those calls on a digital caller they'd give you an extra advantage. Ditto for bobcat in heat calls. I haven't seen a bobcat decoy yet, but I'll bet one is either on the market or about to be.

Wolves should be another perfect candidate for a fake of its own species. These powerful wild canines are infamous for attacking and ripping apart not only other wolves, but dogs, coyotes, and foxes. No canine defiles the sacred territory of a wolf pack without being challenged. Again, I haven't seen any full-sized wolf decoys, but I don't doubt a coyote decoy would suffice. Combine it with a howl and you should bring any wolf pack within hearing on the run.

Doggone Good Idea

A unique variation of decoying involves live dogs trained to sit or play near a caller. Coyotes see the dog and focus attention upon it, giving the shooter plenty of time to do his job.

I accidentally discovered the usefulness of an attractor dog years ago when I turned my English setter loose in hopes that she could sniff out a wounded coyote I couldn't find. As she bounded through the grass, she attracted another coyote. I first saw this animal as a flash of tan above the grass about one hundred yards away. I focused on the area and soon saw its head pop up, study the leaping setter, then drop back into the grass only to reappear twenty yards closer seconds later. Old Jesse, her plumed tail flagging, thought she was hunting birds and never did see her wild cousin, but when it popped up for the third time, I leveled the cross hairs and made a lucky head-shot at about sixty yards. Proof that curiosity killed more than the cat.

Larry Symes, an equine dentist from Oklahoma, partners with an Airedale that doubles as a coyote retriever. Usually the dog just sits at Larry's side, ready to run down or sniff out any wounded coyotes, but fairly often it moves at just the right time to draw the coyote's attention. Larry is then pretty much free to shift into position for his shot.

Training a dog to sit near you or parade out front may not be necessary. Some hunters simply stake the family mutt to a short lead in front of their calling spot, whistling to it when necessary to get it to jump, whine, or wriggle. To encourage walking back and forth, stake a ground cable between two anchors and attach a short, sliding lead from the cable to the dog's collar. Rover is then free to romp between the stakes. You might need to place a shooter at each end of the line, just beyond Rover's reach, and call him back and forth. If you do any work with a tied-out dog, it's best to carry a shotgun. Reports have it that some dominant, territorial coyotes will flat-out charge a small dog and attack it. Be prepared to intercept.

Don't expect a charging coyote to stop short of your dog and offer an easy shot. And don't tell your kids you're using Fluffy as a living decoy.

Larry Symes uses his dog as coyote bait and retriever.

While we're discussing decoy dogs, I might as well put in a word for tracking dogs. Careful, selective shooting should result in instant kills of most predators, but now and then all of us end up with a "dead" critter that isn't lying where it should be. It may have run off, temporarily stunned, or it may have crawled a considerable distance before succumbing to its wounds. Finding it can be a real chore, especially in thick brush or grass. A dog with a nose for trouble can really help. You don't need a full-blooded hound or a fierce fighter. Any mutt willing to pick up a scent trail and follow it will suffice—even Fluffy. You might want to keep it on a leash to prevent tooth-and-claw ambush. You can train nearly any dog to follow a scent trail by laying one down with a freshly killed coyote or fox, guiding the dog along the trail, and rewarding it with effusive praise and a tasty treat when it discovers the body at the end of the line. Let this scent-hound of yours ride along in a kennel box during your hunts, and when you need its services, there it is.

The possibilities for decoying are limited only by your imagination. Think creatively, and use your ideas to attract predatory attention and/or divert it from yourself. Your success should improve markedly.

PREDATOR DECOY MANUFACTURERS

Predator decoys have flourished like fungus in the past ten years with manufacturers popping up thither and yon. Most can be found on the Internet where they maintain websites with the latest products and prices. Just type the name in the search engine, or do a general search for Predator Hunting Decoys. Some companies listed here may be out of business before this book gets printed. Some new ones might pop up. I found the following companies listed as manufacturers of predator hunting decoys:

Cass Creek www.casscreek.com
Expedite Edge www.edgebyexpedite.com
Flambeau www.flambeau.com
Foxpro www.gofoxpro.com
MoJo www.mojooutdoors.com
Montana www.montanadecoy.com
Phantom Decoys www.phantomcalls.com
Primos https://shop.primos.com/c-93-decoys.aspx
Western Rivers www.western-rivers-sales.com

10

Where, Oh, Where Can My Little Dog Be?

Scouting for Your Subjects and a Place to Hunt

Finding a good place to hunt predators can be as easy as walking into the woods or fields, calling, and seeing what answers. But that might not be the most efficient use of your hunting time. To maximize encounters of the furry kind, it pays to hunt densely populated habitat, and you find that by scouting.

Visual Sign

You can pretty much bet there's a bobcat in the area when you see one. You probably didn't need to buy this book to figure that out, did you? Unfortunately, most predators are shy about showing themselves, so you have to walk the grounds looking for visual clues like tracks and droppings. Tracks in snow are the easiest to find. They show up best when low sun casts shadows in them. You can see trails from hundreds of yards away in fresh snow at sunrise. If roads cross your scouting area, drive them slowly,

A well appointed 4-wheel drive truck in good working order with plenty of tools in back is a perfect horse for getting in and out of remote predator habit. Glassing gives hunters a quick overview of the landscape to reveal suitable calling sites.

watching the shoulders or ditches for prints. I once spotted the spoor of a wolf crossing a highway in Alberta. With my binoculars, I was able to trace it more than a mile as it climbed a snow-covered mountain and disappeared over the top. Each paw print was the size of my palm.

These days wolf tracks decorate nearly every trail and road in Idaho, but that doesn't mean there's a wolf behind every bush. The big dogs often range over dozens of miles a night and could be much too far to hear your calls the next morning. But tracks do reveal their territories and travel routes, so pay attention.

An old fox hunter's trick is to drive country roads at dawn after a fresh snowfall until you see a fox track. Then drive the nearest roads that encircle the area into which the track headed. If no tracks come out, Bingo. You know where the fox is. Go get it. Seriously— good trackers do this, using snowshoes or skis if necessary.

Coyotes like to leave calling cards on roads and trails. Watch for them.

Of course, instead of tracking, you can try calling. Either way, you'll hunt cautiously and with confidence, knowing your quarry is near. The same thing can be done with coyotes, wolves, bobcats, and even cougars.

Without snow, you'll have to make a closer study of dusty road shoulders, cow trails, cultivated field edges and muddy shores. If you have the gumption, you can build "track traps" by baiting a chunk of freshly swept, dusty soil. Just place in the center of the dusty area a powerful animal gland scent, a chunk of redolent meat, or a visual lure such as a feather blowing on the end of a pole. Check each morning for fresh tracks, and you'll have some idea of what's in the area.

Droppings are another handy clue. Bears and coyotes love to make deposits along trails and roads. Cats will use loose road soil for covering their toilets, too, so cruise slowly with your eyes peeled. In South Dakota, we used to find fall fox-hunting grounds by watching for dens in early summer, then hunting within a mile of them in fall. Road kills are good indicators of predator numbers, especially in summer, when pups are beginning to move about. If you're seeing good numbers of fox and coyote flattened on the highway, there should be survivors in the area. Remember where you see hit-and-run victims.

Another good sign for locating wolves are urine posts. All dogs squirt on isolated posts, tree stumps, boulders, or other obvious objects in their territories, but wolves travel in such numbers that they sometimes leave visible urine marks, especially in snow. I once found a moose antler lying on the tundra, its basin damp with redolent wolf urine. One February in Jackson Hole, I spotted yellow pee on a steep bank of snow pushed off the gravel road. Close examination revealed wolf tracks all around it. I followed them for less than a mile before spotting seven wolves trotting across Antelope Flats in the distance. Alas, the season was closed.

Audio Sign

Coyotes and wolves, bless 'em, are a bunch of loudmouths. They make scouting easy. Cruise roads and trails in potential coyote habitat at dusk and dawn, stopping every mile or so to either howl or crank up a police siren. Then listen for replies and take notes. Mark a map, perhaps with a small red check for each wolf or coyote heard. Put the mark close to where you think the animal was. Sometimes they sound much closer than they are, but you should be able to guess within a mile, and that's close enough. Coyotes sound like sopranos. Wolves sound like baritones bemoaning a death in the family—long, low, drawn out howls that might send shivers up your spine. Two or three coyotes can sound like a small army yipping and yowling.

Don't assume that one audio scouting trip will cover you for a season. Coyotes often move suddenly—and a significant distance—in response to fires, crop harvest, logging, deep snow, and livestock movements. I've often noticed that pastures with cattle hold more coyotes than pastures without cattle. The same goes for wild ungulates. Coyotes will hang around wintering herds of antelope, deer, and elk. When the elk leave, the coyotes leave. Wolves will frighten elk right out of the country. Deep snow will drive coyotes from high country or broad expanses of short grass into lower-elevation brushy cover, where they can hide and find prey. Obviously, no predator is going to hang out where all his meals are buried and frozen.

Livestock feedlots can be a coyote magnet in winter. The little song dogs aren't much of a threat to mature cattle, but they sometimes eat undigested grain

Coyotes will stay near wintering herds of deer, elk, and antelope.

from cow pies and molasses cakes from feed bunks. They also find pigeons and starlings in the area, and perhaps cottontails attracted to the cattle feed. Winter pastures in which cattle are being fed are similarly attractive. When a rancher rolls out a big, round bale for the cattle, coyotes will hunt for mice where the old bale sat and see if any birds or rabbits are drawn to the hay scraps. The entire area is a center of activity and can't help but attract opportunistic predators. Once cows start calving, coyotes are right there to eat afterbirth, stillborn calves, and now and then a live calf if they can get it away from mamma.

The most dependable audio scouting is done immediately before hunting. Cruise your hunting grounds about an hour before dawn and howl. Then go back and call where you got responses. Some hunters like to howl immediately before calling any area. If they don't get a response, they move on. I wouldn't trust this. Often coyotes don't howl back, especially at midday. Then again, howling coyotes don't always respond to calls. A buddy and I set up across a wooded creek from what sounded like at least four, possibly six howling and yapping coyotes last December. They couldn't have been more than 600 yards away, yet none loped in. And we played them durned near every call on our digital player. There are no guarantees in predator calling.

Audio scouting rarely works for other species, but at odd times while camping, fishing, or hunting other species, you may hear fox bark or cats yowl. Don't waste the opportunity. Hunt such areas as soon as possible.

Rumors

When it comes to game scouting, the postman doesn't ring just twice. Day after day, week after week, year after year, he or she travels the same route, seeing not just mailboxes, but red foxes and coyotes and bobcats and bears, oh my. The same can be said for the UPS driver, school bus driver, and the guy checking gas wells in the area. If you want to know what they know, get friendly. Talk wildlife. Tell about the turkey you saw cross the road; the cougar your neighbor claims to have heard scream in the night. Prime the pump and see what comes up. You may soon discover a cornucopia of critters in your backyard.

You can pull similar intelligence reports from farmers down at the local cafe, feed store, or livestock sales barn. Hang out wherever country folk gather, and join the gossip. Spread some of your own if necessary to bring the conversation around to wildlife sightings. Once it's known you hunt livestock killers, you're likely to get a steady stream of reports.

Some fish and game department biologists and conservation officers may be able to refer you to landowners who've been having predator depredation problems. Your deer-, rabbit-, and bird-hunting buddies can also keep you informed as to when and where they've seen predators. Bowhunters in particular see and hear a lot during their long waits in trees. Don't be afraid to ask.

The speed and ease of digital communication via laptops, tablets, and smart-phones these days make it possible to set up a "party line" of informants. Arrange for farmers and landowners along your hunting/calling routes to text or instant message you whenever they hear or see predators. Then get out as soon as you can. Keep records to discover patterns. You may figure out a bobcat or mountain lion crosses a certain road on a certain day every week. The more intelligence you have, the better.

Natural History and Habitat

If you know the natural history of your subjects, you can do a pretty good job of finding them just by looking for their habitat. Experienced bobcat hunters know better than to waste their time in a bald prairie or heavily farmed land-scape, but coyote hunters might see potential in the prairie and fox hunters in the farmland. Think food and shelter for each species and you're halfway there.

Captain May I

Tougher than finding game to hunt is finding land to hunt. North America, sadly, is rapidly becoming Western Europe—overpopulated and overdeveloped. Some days it seems that new houses are sprouting like dandelions on every hill and valley. Most new rural residents erect No Hunting signs faster than their new roofs. Farms and ranches that aren't sold as hobby farms are increasingly leased for exclusive hunting rights. You may be able to gain access to some of these by offering to alleviate predator overpopulations. Pilgrims who lose Muffin and Boots to coyotes and a sweet corn patch to raccoons soon modify their anti-hunting positions.

Determining who owns what property can be difficult. Ease your pain by going to the

Big predators live in big country, but if you scout and research before going out, you should have something to shout about at the end of the hunt.

local courthouse and buying a plat map. These maps show property ownership and boundaries.

Whenever requesting hunting permission, call first, explain that you want to remove a few excess predators to ease pressure on local songbirds, and so on and request a face-to-face visit. Show up neat and clean and get to know your potential host. Offer to patrol the property for poachers and perhaps help repair a gate or fence. If you have children, bring them along. Show that you're a responsible family man or woman, not some wild-eyed redneck.

Because private land access is shrinking, everyone is turning to public lands. Who can blame them? These lands are your lands, these lands are my lands. And they still provide some excellent predator hunting. Just expect more competition than existed twenty years ago. Public land varies from vast spreads of federal forests and grasslands in the West to small state hunting tracts in the Midwest and East. The western Forest Service and Bureau of Land Management properties offer virtually unlimited hunting for coyotes, mountain lions, wolves, bears, bobcats, raccoons, and red fox, but it's big country far from where most of us live, and huge chunks of it are relatively barren. You've got to do your homework and put in your time, but you can enjoy productive hunting if you do.

Closer to home, however, you can play it smart to maximize the potential of even small public hunting areas. For instance, the Dakotas are dotted with Waterfowl Production Areas leased to the U.S. Fish and Wildlife Service and opened to public hunting. Some WPAs are less than three hundred acres and are mostly water, but a fox hunter can sit on a fringe of upland, call a fox off private land, and legally take it when it crosses the fence. This opens hundreds of thousands of acres to the creative hunter. Most states have similar public hunting areas. Explore them for predator potential. Most are used intensively by bowhunters, waterfowlers and upland hunters, but once those seasons close, they get pretty empty. Local predators might be chased out onto bordering private lands, but they are accustomed to scouring the public areas after hours for crippled game. Get the picture?

To find public hunting lands, contact your state fish and game agency and request maps or brochures listing them. The DeLorme Mapping Company (www.delorme.com; 1-800-561-5105) sells excellent state atlases and gazetteers that show public lands, roads, trails, hunting lands, and natural features and include addresses for public land management agencies you can contact for site-specific maps. Many book stores and sporting goods stores sell these maps. Most good hunting stores and hiking/canoeing shops sell local public land maps, too. DeLorme also lets you download USGS top maps and DigitalGlobe Satellite Imagery high resolution maps.

One of the most exciting mapping systems I've discovered is Hunting GPS Maps (www.huntinggpsmaps.com). These are statewide digital maps on a microchip you load into a Garmin handheld GPS unit. While you are in the field, you punch up a variety of overlays that show topography, land features, and, best of all, land ownership. The unit will clearly show you if you are on Forest Service land, BLM land, state school lands, timber company lands, or private land. In most states and counties it will even list landowner names so you can find the folks to request hunting permission. These maps are wonderful for exploring new areas. As you drive and assess new habitat, you can simultaneously determine who owns what. It's refreshing to check your Hunting GPS Map and see that the coyote you just saw cross the road has gone onto BLM land open to hunting.

You can find traditional paper maps for virtually any United States national forest by going to the Web site www.fs.fed.us. Maps for Bureau of Land Management lands must be ordered from individual state offices. For a directory of addresses, phone numbers, and state Web site addresses, go to www.blm.gov.

Paper or downloadable digital topographical maps can be purchased from www.store.usgs.gov; or:

USGS Information Services
Box 25286
Denver, CO
80225
Phone: 1-888-ASK-USGS or 303-202-4700
Web site: ask.usgs.gov

Other sources for a variety of maps include: www.maptech.com; www.digital-topo-maps.com; www.mytopo.com.

Finally, download Google Earth on your computer and zoom in for a satellite image of virtually any plot of ground. Vegetative cover may have changed due to fires, construction, or farming, but you should get a good feel for the lay of the land.

11

Making the Call

If You Blow It, They Will Come

Once you've collected your calls, assembled your kit, tuned your firearm, scouted a game-rich area, and donned your cute little camo outfit, you're ready for your big debut. It's opening night off Broadway. Let the hunt begin!

Like a Thief in the Night

One of the biggest mistakes many callers make is approaching a calling site like a bull in a china shop. Predators are alert and sensitive to strange stimuli in their territories. Unless you're out to drive them away, try a little tenderness. Standard operating procedure starts by driving or hiking as quietly as possible into the wind and behind cover. On the Plains, this usually means staying behind hills and ridges. In the East and Midwest it can mean approaching calling sites from behind woodlots, shelterbelts, old farmsteads, even rows of big hay bales. Most of this is common sense and you'll quickly figure it out as you gain experience. If you can see a lot of open fields, valleys, pastures, and meadows, assume any predator in them can see you. Often they can't because they're busy nosing around behind vegetation or in a low spot, but always assume they can. Since you've already exposed yourself, continue driving and return to call the area later. An hour's wait should be plenty, sometimes just a half-hour will suf-

A silent approach resulted in a coyote-bobcat double.

fice. Just don't hike out and call while the memory of your intrusion is still fresh in the minds of your quarry. That will only teach them a dangerous relationship between humans and distressed critter cries. Ideally, whenever you call you want to terminate every predator that hears you. Otherwise, you're just making it harder to call them the next time. Don't worry. You aren't going to get them all.

If you're cruising along a normal traffic flow, such as a public road or frequently driven ranch trail, predators may accept you as harmless so long as you don't stop. Drive until out of sight of the call area and even beyond hearing before stopping as quietly as possible. If the wind is right, you might be able to slip back for a successful setup. Obviously you don't open the doors with music blasting or partners talking. And don't slam the doors when you leave. You're in stealth mode here.

You can slip into position right away, but they say dogs have about a ten-minute "memory" for current events, so waiting ten minutes before setting up and calling might improve your odds of success. They should have forgotten all about your vehicle by then. While driving public roads, I've often seen a coyote in the distance, driven out of sight, sneaked back, and called it right in, but only when it wasn't alarmed by my passing. Critters that flee as you drive by are not likely to come galloping back to the area just because they hear a possible luncheon entree.

Experienced callers learn the lay of their hunting grounds and the best ways to move through them depending on wind direction. Ideally they map out loop tours with standard parking places and calling sites sprinkled along the way. Not all sites will be viable under all wind conditions or approachable from all directions. It is best to simply skip them rather than risk educating area predators with a sloppy approach. Those that see you move into position and then hear you squallerin' like a stuck pig aren't likely to rush to that call or any others for quite some time.

If you call a lot of terrain in different areas, you should maintain a map of your best calling sites. You could use a topographical map or create your own basic outline map showing critical trails, landmarks, parking spots, and calling sites, marking each of these in a different color corresponding to wind direction. Yellow stands for west winds, red for south, etc. Pencil in useful information such as "sit against dead pine," or "sun in eyes before 10 AM." Place a green tally mark by each stand when you call something there, red when you shoot something, blue when you miss. Over time you'll discover your most productive stands.

When approaching stands, consider how sound as well as sight and smell might expose you. On windy days you can stop a vehicle closer to a calling site than on calm days. When atmospheric conditions transmit sound well, stop farther away than usual. Don't let laziness mess up your chances. Do what you can to silence your vehicle, too. Stick on a quiet muffler. Fix squeaky brakes. Turn off the radio. Pad or remove rattling tailgates, doors, jacks, and shovels in the bed, etc. Think submariner and rig for silent running.

When you park, open and close doors softly. Most modern cars and trucks are so well built you can push doors fully closed with a "click." Hold the latch in and you might even avoid that. No need to slam. If you're in an area where no one is likely to rob you blind, leave doors open and avoid any chance of noise. Just be certain an errant gust won't slam them later.

With a ridge between you and your call site plus a good breeze laying down cover noise, you may be able to drive within fifty yards of it, but it's safer to stop several hundred yards away and walk in. Hide your rig in a low spot, clump of trees, etc. Stand beside it and look all around. Any high, open ground you can see represents areas from which approaching cats and dogs will spot your shiny vehicle. Sometimes they won't care, but most times they'll chuckle at your stupidity and walk away. Why give them the option? If you must leave a vehicle exposed, leave it visible on your downwind side.

Most callers drive their routes to maximize efficiency. You'll call more places per day when you travel thirty miles per hour than three. Some terrain, however, can't be accessed effectively by truck. This can make it quite productive because fewer hunters will disturb it. I'll happily hike a mile or two to reach otherwise inaccessible terrain. It's almost like hunting virgin ground. Tom Berger and I hunt a wide, long, flat Kansas pasture surrounded on two sides by a high plateau cracked and broken with a series of deep, woody draws. Almost no one calls it because the only wheeled access is across the open flat. We hunt it by walking the base of the sloping plateau wall, calling up each major draw. The deep, twisting canyons seem to contain our cries and limit interest from coyotes and bobcats in neighboring draws, but some days we'll suck 'em out and over the tops, so we set up to watch all possible approaches. Because those canyon slopes also muffle our shots, we regularly suck animals from adjoining canyons during back-to-back calling sessions only a few hundred yards apart. The circuit is about a four-mile hike, but well worth the time.

A critical time during your approach to a calling stand is when you are exposed to the target landscape. This usually happens when you cross the horizon or line of brush that hid

Sit in front of brush, to break up your silhouette, and make sure you have a good field of view and clear shooting lane.

your initial approach. Every big game hunter knows that standing on a horizon against a bright sky is tantamount to wearing a bikini to church. You tend to stand out. Avoid horizons when possible, minimize them when impossible. Try to cross in a saddle, beside a tree, shrub, amid boulders, or even tall grass. Use anything to break your outline. Crawl like a snake if nothing else. And cross quickly. Don't stand there looking about like a tourist on the lip of the Grand Canyon. Slink down the slope and sit in front of a shrub, boulder, cutbank—anything to break your outline and provide back support. Make sure you have a good field of view and clear shooting lane. Don't sit behind large obstructions. Sure, they'll hide you, but they'll also hide your customers and block your shots. Sitting still with something at your back will camouflage you adequately. Whatever you do, don't waltz atop a hill, sit on it like a zit on the prom queen's nose, and start blasting on your call. Any locals that missed your dramatic entrance or didn't spook from your too-loud calling will see you perched up there like Sir Edmund Hillary on Everest.

Over Easy

There's an alternate school of thought on crossing ridges. Instead of hurrying over to get out of sight quickly, you cross one step at a time, thoroughly glassing all new terrain that has opened to view. Then you take another step up and repeat. This virtually eliminates spooking critters that are close enough to spot you as you cross. While this takes time, it pays handsome dividends.

A few years ago I was crossing an isolated ridge in order to call a copse of trees in a creek bottom surrounded by a huge, hilly pasture. The quiet wood was a popular bedding location for deer and coyotes. The grassy ridge bordering the bottom offered a commanding view, but was impossible to cross without sky-lining yourself. In previous attempts I'd hurried across, low and quick, only to glimpse coyotes or deer sneaking out the far side. Even if the coyotes didn't see me, deer often would, and the effect was the same. So, this day I edged over cautiously, glassing the narrow strip of new ground that opened with every step. And that's how I happened to spot two reddish ears in the grass. A coyote. I inched higher, saw the back of its head about eighty yards away. The wind was in my face and loud enough to cover the rustling of a 179-pound body sliding over dry grass, so I crawled until I had a clear, prone sight picture. There lay my dog, napping. It stayed in dreamland forever.

Most hunters are surprised at how often they spot unalerted coyotes, fox, and even bobcat just over a hill. I often catch them within one hundred yards, sometimes within bow range. You can shoot these without calling and without messing

If you hear coyotes howling, take advantage of the opportunity. Set up and call immediately.

up the site. A single gunshot rarely ruins an area for calling. It might alert game within hearing, but, unless they've been shot at and missed a few times, they calm down and return to business within five or ten minutes. If you spot and shoot something, sit down and wait for ten minutes, then sneak to a good calling position nearby and go to work.

If you hear coyotes howling nearby, set up for them, even if it means altering your stand site drastically. Get the wind in your favor with as long a view as you can find and toot your horn. I was once preparing to call down a Montana mountainside—in fact I may have sucked in a big breath for the first blow—when I heard a howl at my back, close enough to shiver my timbers. There was no breeze, so I spun on my bun, hit a quavering high C twice, and spit out the call just in time to plaster a prairie wolf at twenty paces.

A Higher Calling

When looking for a call site, I'm like an old bighorn ram—I want elevation, even if it's just a few feet. Every inch aids in seeing over cover and lifting your scent over incoming noses. If there are bulging hills to either side, I try to slip to the point of one in order to prevent a sneak attack. All of this will make sense to you when you start calling. The more ground you can see, the better. When you sit down, study the lay of the land. Are there many blind spots? Could a wary cat sneak close, unseen? Could a fox dive behind a small rise and run out of range without exposing itself for a shot? Which patch of ground provides the best command of the landscape without overly exposing you? A single bush or boulder should be enough to break your outline. Again, do not skyline yourself. You don't have to be on the crest of a ridge or top of a hill to do this. Even halfway down a hillside you might appear skylined to an animal looking up from the bottom.

The Performance

Once you've settled in, donned your gloves and facemask, set up your shooting sticks, and chambered a round, look around again. Note any anomalies that look like game so your heart doesn't miss a beat each time you pick them out during the calling. Some callers like to scan carefully with a binocular just in case there's a distant subject watching. If they spot one looking back, they don't call

Shooting sticks are a must in open country.

until it moves off or resumes normal activity. Otherwise it won't come in but might learn a thing or two about humans and rabbit cries. Coyotes will bark warnings that alert all other coyotes within hearing, screwing up a lot of country.

If the coast is clear, start by playing or blowing a soft, short series, perhaps only ten seconds. This should entice, rather than scare the hell out of, any nearby critters. Red fox are particularly sensitive to excessive volume. You might start them with a mouse squeaker. Wait a minute or two for anything to show, then blow at slightly higher volume for fifteen to twenty seconds and wait another five to ten minutes. You may add volume and several more series at your discretion. Give cats thirty minutes to an hour. Most coyotes appear within the first three series. In heavily called areas, they might not show for twenty or thirty minutes. Usually the later the season, the slower the response. You have to decide whether waiting or hurrying to your next site is the best use of time. Some folks like to cover as much ground as possible and appeal to the "hot" critters. Others prefer to entice the shy ones out of hiding. I gotta tell you, though, spotting your quarry slinking away after you stand to leave is a major bummer. So look carefully all about before departing. Then move away as unobtrusively as possible. This last bit of advice is significant. Dance away singing or talking and you could educate a client that you hadn't seen hiding in a distant thicket, perhaps a late arrival just popping into view. The fewer chances a predator has to associate distress cries with humans, the more chances you'll have to call it in someday.

Time is of the Essence

High wildlife activity periods, usually early and late in the day, are the best times to call, but that doesn't mean midday calling is a waste of time. Even sleeping bobcats may perk up and slink in to investigate an easy meal, especially if it's only a short distance away. Many, many times

A red fox circling at a distance. He'll try to get downwind of you before coming any closer.

my calling partners and I have awakened the "free lunch" impulse in drowsy predators. One excessively warm December day at high noon, in what appeared to be the worst conditions for a successful calling session, Doug and I sat beside a small cedar in a pasture near the mouth of two brushy draws. We had planned to eat lunch, but the sight of a coyote trotting along the rim of one of the draws inspired us to try one more call.

"Close as he is, he should come running," Doug said. I agreed. So once the dog had trotted out of sight, we scrambled to that cedar and let 'er rip.

"You watch that other draw in case something comes out of there," Doug said.

"No problem. But you be ready because that coyote is going to come screaming out of your draw. Sit quiet after you shoot. Maybe we'll get a double."

Well, it appeared the late hour and heat were working against us because I was deep into my fourth series of calls and our "sure thing" coyote hadn't appeared. Doug gave me the "give it up" nudge, so I cast one last glance around and spotted a bright, white object atop the ridge of the "other draw."

"Don't move," I whispered. "I've got one way over here to the right."

I had to turn more than 90 degrees to set up for the shot, and when I got the Swarovski on target, it resolved into a bobcat. A bobcat! At high noon and at 70 degrees up in the grass instead of down in the brush? Oh, yeah. Never look a gift cat in the mouth. I concentrated extra hard on the trigger and squeezed off a perfect shot from the .260 Remington, taking the prime cat center brisket as it faced us.

The coyote never did appear, but we left that site more than amply rewarded for delaying our lunch.

The point, then, is to call all day. The more open and remote your calling country, the better chance it'll produce. Where human traffic is intense, predators may rarely, if ever, come out to play before dusk and after dawn. But in vast, western landscapes, or even eastern woodlands and meadows that rarely see human activity, cats and dogs may readily leap from their beds to check out what sounds like an easy meal.

Efficiency Experts

Hunting is supposed to be fun, so set your own pace. But if you want to maximize your chances for success, don't dawdle. Work quickly and efficiently. Keep your gear in tune and in the same place where you can quickly grab it and hustle to your calling location. Charge caller batteries each night before a hunt and carry spares. Replenish your ammo each night before a trip. Carry at least

one spare box in your truck. Keep spare mouth calls in your pack, as well as on a lanyard around your neck. You'll feel pretty stupid when, sixty miles from home, you discover your batteries are dead and the reed from your one mouth call has fallen out. You have a lot of time and money invested in your hunts. It would be a shame to be shut out by something as basic as a broken call. Ditto for a malfunctioning truck. Keep it in good repair and haul a few basic tools and spares. In some locations two spare tires are a good idea. Sometimes it's a spare battery or at least jumper cables. And always have at least one stout shovel and a winch or come-along. You're going hunting for the day, not shopping. Even if you can get AAA to respond, do you really want to sit and wait for that? Prepare to dig out, jump start, and make your own basic repairs.

After you reach a calling site, set yourself quickly and efficiently for a steady shot from the most likely direction. Check your scope so it's set on a low power for close work. You can always zoom higher for distant game, which is less likely than close subjects to see your motion. Set up your shooting sticks and back support. Chamber a round. (Make it a habit to always carry your gun with an empty chamber, loading only after seated and ready to call. Before you get up to leave, unload the chamber. I've yet to see a predator that was so fast I didn't have time to bolt in a round before shooting. Loading from magazine to chamber takes but a split second. But I have seen guns "accidentally discharge" as hunters got in and out of vehicles. It's just not worth it. Carry guns with empty chambers.)

When finished calling a site, don't stand around talking about what did or did not happen. Hustle quietly to the truck, drive away, and then talk. Drive quickly to your next calling site and repeat. Do this and you should squeeze in as many as 15 calling sessions per twelve-hour day. (This means you drive to your first setup in the dark and finish your last call just as the last shooting light dims.)

A Moving Experience

During the average predator hunt you call, retreat to your vehicle, drive at least a quarter mile, and set up to call a fresh area. Sometimes you drive several miles before reaching a suitable site. But sometimes you're better off walking through the area you just called to reach another that's inaccessible by wheels, particularly when calling bobcats and fox which don't usually travel as far as do coyotes to reach a call. Only experience and common sense will inform you when walking becomes more productive than driving. Last year, Gordy Krahn and I called a small, isolated butte on the Wyoming plains two consecutive days. It curved in a long, gentle C and couldn't have been more than a mile long, end to end. It stretched three hundred yards to no more than six hundred yards across its top. Both sides plunged quickly to wide, shortgrass plains and sagebrush creek valleys.

We slipped along the west base of this ridge in the morning shadows and set up in a small erosion cut. Gordy called progressively louder and on his third series a white form appeared far out in the valley. "One coming from way out there," I said. It was a pretty approach, the sun shining on the pale fur as the old dog trotted in, dodging sage clumps like water sliding around boulders. He veered south to catch our wind, but the breeze was angling it steeply uphill and he was both too confident and lazy to climb for it. With the sun in his eyes he never saw us until Gordy barked. The old bunny eater raised his hackles and glared. Gordy shot. The dog churned gravel and ran. I shot. He kept running. I swept the crosshair through him and kept swinging on my second shot, pushing the 130-grain Winchester Silver Ballistic Tip through his chest.

"What happened?" I asked, a bit surprised that Gordy had missed, even though he was handicapped with a Cabela's replica .45-70 Sharps buffalo rifle with open sights. "He couldn't have been more than 20 yards away."

"I forgot I left the peep set up for long-range shooting from yesterday. I tried to site down the barrel. Didn't work too well." The dog was deep-chested, its canines worn to rounded pegs. We'd fooled a veteran.

"Let's go over top and try the other side." Here we sat in the sun on a naked slope, but we each hugged a sage partway down the ridge and promised not to move. We were about to give up when two candidates appeared at the base of the far end of the ridge. "They must be more than a mile away, but they're coming," I said. "Keep calling." Gordy blew and those dogs raced in, a double in the making. But one held up at least four hundred yards out, progressing in fits and stops while the more aggressive one just bee-lined for Gordy. I picked it up in the scope and waited for as long as I could stand it, finally shooting when it appeared ready to cut our scent. It's partner was still far enough out to make good its escape.

A successful end to a day afield.

That high ridge made it possible for us to make two calls such a short distance apart, even though we had shot three times at the first location. The sound waves, both call and shots, must have bounced off the slope and away, barely registering on the opposite side. Such audio separation isn't mandatory for close call setups to work. Some days you can call in and shoot three coyotes from the same site, one after another in a matter of fifteen minutes. I guess this is nature's way of making up for those days when you can't call a politician to a fundraising dinner.

Tom Berger and I nearly killed three-for-three at the junction of a winter wheat field, milo stubble field, and big pasture. Our first customer came hopping the stubble rows, our second glided quickly over the wheat, but a long way out. I shot the milo hopper and Tom laid into an emotional series of puppy yipes and cries. These stopped the wheat field coyote in midflight. "He's turning. Keep working him," I whispered. The dog was nervous, sitting and watching for long moments, but slowly working closer in fits and stops. While watching, I caught movement in my peripheral vision and turned to spy our third client angling in from the pasture. It closed to within three hundred yards, so I slowly turned and put it in the crosshairs. "How's yours doing?" I asked.

"Still hung up. About four hundred."

"Mine's angling to catch our wind at about three hundred. If he stops I might take him." He did. I did. Then I spun around and joined Tom in saluting the third and most cautious coyote as it laid a dust trail toward the horizon.

"Probably won't call that one again anytime soon," Tom noted.

12

Time and Weather Wait for No Man

The Best Conditions and Times for Calling

Whether or not you call in predators depends on weather. Call during a downpour all you want, but you're unlikely to entice any visitors. Blizzards, extreme heat, and big winds will also ruin your chances. Ah, but light breezes, fog, low pressure, high pressure, and something as simple as cloud cover can make or break your day.

Foggy Philosophy

My favorite calling weather is calm fog. I don't know what it is—the increased sense of security perhaps—that fires up predators on quiet, foggy days, but fire up they do, charging the call with enthusiasm. My favorite foggy-morning call-down happened late one November when my partner Tom and I awoke in our pickup camper on the broken grasslands of western Kansas. While Tom heated water for breakfast, I stepped out to water the landscape, whereupon I discovered two things: thick fog and the frantic cries of a cottontail bidding farewell to this cruel world. I was supposed to go deer hunting, but changed my mind. "Let's call the Hell Zone pasture," I suggested. This was a huge flat on which we regularly saw coyotes hunting but couldn't call because there was no place to hide the truck or sneak within range. In the gray soup, we simply drove to the fence, walked out a few hundred yards, and plunked our buns in grass no taller than our left big toes.

"Good a place as any?"

Calling in fog-even ice fog-can be pure magic. You can sit in big, open fields and pastures impossible to approach on clear days. They'll never suspect you out there.

"Yeah." We sat side by side. I covered the southwest, Tom the southeast. We ignored the north, because that's where the truck was. That's also where the first coyote came from—a huge, dark dog that announced its arrival with heavy footfalls drumming the prairie. When they sounded as if they were about to run up my back, I spun on my butt. El Coyote's eyes just about popped past his nose. Rather than waste time turning around, he kicked in the afterburner and veered right, leaning like Lance Armstrong on a hard corner in the Tour de France. I swung through the air, slapped the trigger, and won the yellow jersey in that little race. As I came out of recoil, I caught sight of a pale-colored bitch turning back into the wall of fog. She disappeared before I could get the cross hairs on her. Both coyotes had come from the direction of the truck. I love fog.

Tom quickly cranked out a series of yipes and wounded coyote cries, waited a few minutes, and started up another wounded-rabbit series. This was too much for a little bitch that must have been dying of curiosity. She came sneaking up a fence line from the south, pausing and peering until Tom got a clear sight picture and dropped her at thirty yards. I stepped fifteen paces to the old dog I'd laid out with a neck shot. It weighed thirty-five pounds, the heaviest coyote I'd ever taken.

Before the fog lifted at mid-morning, we had three more coyotes to skin. Have I mentioned I love calling in fog?

If you find yourself in atmospheric soup, use the opportunity to call sites you can't normally approach without being seen. You may be pleasantly surprised. Even coyotes and fox that are slightly call-wary may fall for a distress cry if it comes from an area in which they've never been spooked before. Follow weather reports so you can plan where to hunt if fog seems likely.

Cloudy Outcomes

I have no firm statistics, but personal recollection tells me that cloudy days have produced more coyotes than clear days. A North Dakota Game and Fish Department survey of some three thousand predator callers confirms my suspicions. Respondents claimed they tolled in more coyotes in cloudy weather than bright. Red fox didn't seem to care a whit whether clouds or sunshine ruled the day. They responded equally. No information was available on bobcat response.

What should you do with this information? I wouldn't let either blue or gray skies keep me home, but given the option, I might head for coyote country on gray days, fox habitat on clear days.

Clouds blanketed Kansas on the most productive coyote hunt of my life. Again, I was out with my good buddy Tom Berger, and we could do no wrong. Sit, call, shoot. Sit, call, shoot. We brought in thirteen animals and killed seven. We'd have tallied more, but my rifle was shooting high and I whistled 55-grain slugs over four coyotes. I clipped a big puff of hair off the last one, and that's when I recognized my problem.

I suppose coyotes feel a bit more secure in the dim light that filters through clouds. It's almost as if the entire day is an extended dawn and protracted dusk. Certainly they are harder to see then, blending into grass and brush. They shine like beacons when struck by morning and evening sun.

When backlit, they stand out as nearly black semi-silhouettes. Perhaps hunters are merely seeing more coyotes on clear days and the actual response rate is no different. Either way, cloudy or clear, I'm going hunting.

Don't Be a Blowhard

Wind is the mother of all weather curses. The roar of moving air mutes your calls, disguises their direction, and prevents you from hearing howls or approaching feet. Buffeting gusts ruin your aim, blow bullets off course and discourage predators from even getting up. Wind snaps and rattles clothing and gives you away. When the wind blows over fifteen miles per hour, I often stay home or switch to duck hunting. Sometimes, however, you're committed to a hunt, wind or no wind. Your best option then is to search for quiet habitats such as canyons and forested valleys. In flat country, try working the lee sides of long, wide shelterbelts or at least rolling country. I once called half a day in a big wind without ringing up any customers. Then I drove to some sand hills. With all those dips and holes and hollows, I figured the hills might hide a coyote that could hear me. At my first setup, a coyote popped out of a plum thicket less than one hundred yards downwind. I don't think I'd blown more than two notes before it appeared. It must have been lying just to the side of my scent trail.

Sometimes wind in one place means calm in another. I awoke in Dodge City one November to feel the house shaking. Went out anyway. Sixty miles south the wind was sliding along at an unbelievable ten miles per hour. Practically dead calm for Kansas. I brought in five dogs that day.

Let it Snow, Let it Snow

Conventional wisdom holds that one of the most productive calling times is the day after a blizzard. Makes sense. Having been confined for a day or two, predators are hungry and

A good dump of snow buries prey and makes predators hungry and eager to answer your dinner bell.

itching to travel. The only problem with that theory is that it's never worked for me. My least productive days have been those following snowstorms.

Well, guess what? That North Dakota survey mentioned above revealed that coyote responses rated lower in deep snow, so maybe I'm not imagining things. Interestingly, fox responses were higher with deep snow, but you couldn't prove that by my experiences.

A few years ago I walked a South Dakota shelterbelt bordering a natural wetland and jumped a fox. This pleased me, because I hadn't seen a fox in that locale in years. During the 1970s, it had been crawling with the little red devils. Then coyotes moved in. Well, after seeing that fox run off (and missing it with the .22 rimfire I was carrying for potting cottontails), I had to check its trail. I discovered that it had been curled up behind a little nest of cattails out of the north wind. Doubly encouraging was a second fresh fox trail that had run out of my view along the line of trees. It was late December, so they were probably paired. For the next three mornings I sneaked within two hundred yards of that shelterbelt and called. Nothing. But always fresh tracks in the area. The third morning, after my calling again failed, I quietly walked toward the trees. It was my last day to hunt the area, so spooking my clients wouldn't matter. And spook them I did. Or at least one. The snowy expanse was empty one second, illuminated by a fiery, furry

comet the next. Fortunately, that comet made the mistake of interrupting its out-
going trajectory for a quick look back. A 52-grain satellite from my .22-250 made
sure it would never make that mistake again.

I suspect that one of the reasons I haven't called many predators in snow is that
their ranks have been thinned and the survivors educated by the time snow falls.
Early fall critters are much more gullible than late-season veterans. One of these
years I'm going to have to skip deer, duck, and bird hunting in order to take advantage of an early snowstorm. First snow of the year—now that should be good!

Under Pressure

If a falling barometer can shut down the bass bite, why not the predator bite?
Well, it just might. That North Dakota survey revealed that red fox respond to
calling better during a rising or falling barometer than a steady one. Coyotes,
however, liked what they heard better during a steady barometer. This is precious
little evidence on which to base a hunt, but while you're out giving it the old
Yankee try, why not keep track of atmospheric pressure? In time you might discover some firm correlations that can guide you on future hunts. If you're limited
to a few hunts per season and can choose which day to take them, choosing a
good barometer day would be wise. On the other hand, if you're limited to hunting
specific days of the week, to heck with pressure, cloud cover, and all the rest. A
bad day in the outdoors is better than a good day cleaning the garage.

Time Is on Your Side

I don't need surveys and studies to figure this one out. The best time to call is
dawn to mid-morning. The second best is dusk. This correlates with high activity
times for all predators and minimal activity times for air. Usually. Once the sun
rises and begins heating the
ground, wind kicks up. Near
sunset, it'll often settle down
again. So get your licks in early.
The only better time would be at
night, but that entails either a full
moon and snow or spotlights.
Where legal, spotlight predator

**Head for sheltering woods when wind rages
and snow blows. Predators, which lay up in
the calmer cover, might hear your calls and
investigate.**

145

hunting can be quite productive, but it's never been my thing. Watching those dogs and cats come in is more than half the fun for me.

To maximize your effectiveness during prime calling hours, depart early enough to be on site for your first call when it's light enough to see critters approaching. Go to your most productive areas and hit them fast and hard. Try to plan a route that will take you to a series of calling spots that are close together. The more places you call, the more coyotes you'll toll. If you're working bobcats or red fox, you'll have to stay longer on each site,

Dawn and dusk are prime calling time.

so pick your best. Gray fox usually respond as quickly as coyotes but don't come as far. It's possible to call cover pockets a few hundred yards apart and get responses in each. Gray fox tend to be fairly concentrated in good habitat, so it should be possible to work several setups within a mile or two.

As your morning progresses, be alert for changing winds. A north zephyr at dawn can switch to a south breeze after sunrise. Choose your stands accordingly.

Midday is traditionally siesta time for predators, but even the sleepiest can be talked into a lunch break. The trick is to get close enough. Lazy critters appreciate a free meal, but walking half a mile to claim it means it's not so free anymore. My buddies and I have enjoyed amazing action at all times of day. A few times we've even gotten more responses at midday than in the early morning. You just can't predict what your quarry is going to do from day to day. The best approach is to keep trying. At the least, you'll learn something.

Cold, especially following a heat spell, can make predators active all day. As mentioned above, so can clouds and a changing barometer. Don't forget midday calling simply because you think it won't work. If you feel like hunting, hunt. If you feel like napping, nap. Over time you'll establish a hunting style that works for you.

Season's Greetings

Early fall is consistently the most productive calling season. Following annual brood rearing, populations are at their peak, and young animals are inexperienced and gullible. Once deer and bird hunters begin combing the fields, disturbed predators become more wary. Their routines are interrupted, their refuges invaded, and their senses alerted by shouts, whistles, odors, and shots. More than a few get shot at and killed, too. As fall moves toward winter, other callers go afield, educating the carnivores they don't shoot. By December, most predators are veterans.

Hunting early in the season seems the most logical, but it has a flip side: Pelts aren't prime. Why pick green tomatoes? Why serve a wine before its time? If fur prices are in the cellar, or you're taking predators to alleviate a depredation problem, prime pelts mean little. But when coyote hides fetch fifteen dollars and up, it seems stupid to waste them. Four or five coyotes a day will cover most of your expenses. How many skiers or golfers get that kind of deal?

I personally begin predator hunting in early October in the high Rockies, late October on the northern Plains, and mid-November at the latitude of central Kansas. I don't hit south Texas until late winter. On large private ranches where I know hunting pressure is carefully limited, I'll wait until pelts are fully prime before beginning to hunt. Let me tell you, seeing full-grown, fully-furred coyotes and bobcats racing to your calls in December is the ultimate predator-hunting thrill. Admiring their pelts stretched and dried and ready for the market is pure satisfaction.

Once pair bonding and mating begin, particularly among coyotes, calling can again get hot, but you have to speak their language. Barks, howls, and meows are the magic words. You want a dog to think you're making off with his vixen—or at least invading his territory. Bobcats and lions will respond to caterwauling. If you've ever heard a couple of male house cats engaged in a shouting match over a sweet young thing, you'll know what to say in the bobcat thickets. Yowser bowser—do they make a racket— long, drawn out yeows and rayows and similar angry and anguished permutations of meow. I'll confess I've never employed these to fool a bobcat in the wild, but I tried them on someone's pet free-roaming bobcat once and he bounced right over with hair standing. And

Sagebrush provides a backrest as well as visual cover as Eddie Stevenson watches a big sagebrush flat for approaching coyotes. He defends his turf with an AR-15 platform rifle in .223 Rem, one of the most popular predator rounds going. A Trijicon scope with lighted reticle handles the sighting chores and Predator Snipe Stix bipod steadies the whole rig.

when I was a kid on the farm, I regularly called curious tom and female barn cats by imitating their calls.

Here Kitty Kitty Lion

I sincerely believe these calls can work on lions, too, based on a Mexican adventure I had two years ago. I was hunting Coues whitetails in Sonora as a guest of Leica Optics and Rifles, Inc. Outfitter Rick Martin of Jemez, New Mexico, sent us into rugged, isolated, oak/grass/brush mountains with experienced local guides who spoke of cougars in abundance.

They weren't kidding. We found tracks regularly, and our third afternoon, while walking a ridge above a deep, wide mountain basin, we heard what sounded like an overgrown house cat pulling whiskers out of its face. My guide and I immediately began looking for the source of the new calls, knowing that it was a cougar. My instinct was to imitate the calls, but when I indicated this by pointing to the predator call around my neck (I spoke Spanish as well as my guide spoke English), my guide shook his head "no" emphatically. Yet neither of us could see the cat, despite its continuing calls. Again I pointed to my call. No. We glassed. Finally, my guide pointed excitedly. "Coogar! Coogar!"

"Where?" There followed a Keystone Cops pantomime of pointing and leaning and drawing word pictures until I remembered agua (water), meaning a stock pond in the valley below. Agua. I pointed left of the pond. No, senor. Right of agua. No. Downstream from agua. Si. Si. Si. I scoured the oak-studded valley bottom with my binoculars and still failed to see the cat. Then my brain kicked in, and I handed my sharp-eyed guide the Leica spotting scope on its tripod. Get the cat in the scope. He quickly did that, I peeked, saw a lion that was way, way farther down the valley than I'd been looking, and again pointed to my call. "I want to call the cat, imitate its calls. Meow. Meow."

"No no no. Tiro. Tiro!" Shoot, shoot. So, reluctantly and regretfully, I put the cross hairs a foot or two over the lion's head—it was walking left to right at some ridiculous distance—and fired. My custom Rifles, Inc., bolt action, chambered for .257 Weatherby, consistently spit three 100-grain Spire Point Weatherby factory loads inside a half-inch at one hundred yards, and that accuracy seemed to carry. I came out of recoil and got the lion back in the scope just in time to see it dart forward as a white rock the size of a softball rolled off the hill and nearly bounced onto its rump. Although there was no sign of a hit, we hiked down just to be sure. The distance was in the vicinity of seven hundred yards. Hindsight is 20/20, but man, I wish I'd defied my guide and called to that mountain lion. The manner in which he (it was a huge, red, pumpkin-headed male) was singing the blues convinced me he was trolling for a hot date.

Romantic Rendezvous—or Turf War?

Coyotes, because they are so vocal, are the easiest predators to talk-in during late winter mating rites. Find the territory of a mated pair, slip in undetected, and blow a dominant male howl or two. This is the classic howl, fairly low in pitch and drawn out for as many as ten seconds with a smooth slide down the scale near the end. No preliminary barks or yipes are necessary. Just that commanding howl. Then sit and watch. In fall, this call will frighten more coyotes than it attracts. None of the teenagers on the block want to mess with a big dog. But by January and February, every surviving male thinks he's a big dog and should respond with bravado, running in stiff-legged, with hair erect, maybe even growling and barking. This is no polite social visit, but a mission to run you out of town. Be prepared to defend yourself. You can usually stop hard-charging coyotes with a loud bark, but sometimes this only encourages them.

If you're doing control work for a rancher in summer, puppy yipes and family greeting calls work well. Adults are quite protective of their young in this season, so if they hear what they think is a pup in trouble, they'll charge right in. A coyote pup in trouble sounds just like domestic puppy with its foot caught in a fence. You can mimic it with an open reed rabbit call or diaphragm elk or turkey call. Electronic callers play elaborate recordings of pups in distress.

Storms, winds, phases of the moon. A confusing variety of conditions over which we have no control clearly impact calling success. Some we can work around, some we can work to our advantage, but some we just have to tolerate.

13

I Did It My Way

Alternative Tactics

There's more than one way to skin a cat, fox, or coyote. Calling may be the most popular tactic, but glassing, stalking, still-hunting, and stand-hunting also work. Plenty of hunters shot their first predators from tree stands during deer season. That's when most still-hunters bagged theirs, too. But these tactics can and sometimes should be employed specifically for predators, depending on location, habitat, and calling pressure.

Glass And Stalk

Coyotes

The wild, wild West is the classic locale for successfully spotting coyotes at long range and stalking in for a shot. You don't read about this much in the popular press, but it happens regularly in mountain foothills and on rolling plains where terrain is broken, ground cover short, and distances long. Hunters sit on knobs or high ridges, carefully searching with 8X to 10X binoculars or even 15X to 40X spotting scopes. At dawn they expect to find coyotes hunting mice in grassy swales or trotting from bottomlands and river valleys toward bordering

Glassing reveals a surprising number of coyotes and red fox.

hills and broken terrain to bed. From mid-morning on, they peruse grassy ridges and hillsides for sleeping dogs. Most incautious hunters—the ones who've never glassed terrain carefully before exposing themselves to it—would be surprised at how often a cautious hunter can spot sleeping coyotes.

Like many western hunters, I discovered coyote spotting while deer hunting. Virtually every day while looking for mule deer or whitetails, I'd pick out a coyote or two. Usually I wouldn't interrupt my deer hunt to pursue them, but sometimes they proved irresistible, as on one November day in central South Dakota near Badlands National Park. The clay soil hills bordering the White River here are cut into severe gullies, canyons, and spires with nearly perpendicular sides. In many places the upper edge of this rugged valley is a virtually perpendicular wall towering above a maze of broken hills, ridges, and alleys directly below. The top of this wall is flat and covered with just enough buffalo grass to hide an anorexic rattler, but that matters little, because coyotes at the bottom of the wall rarely look up. To hunt this terrain, I would ease to the edge and glass carefully below. If I didn't spot anything, I'd pull back from the edge and hike to my next viewing stand. On just my second lookout of the day, I spied a coyote trotting across a flat. He was too far away to shoot, and the badland's wall was too steep to negotiate, so I pulled out my call and sent him a dinner invitation. His head snapped up at the first wail, and he came running at the second, angling for what proved to be a gully he could climb to access the rim where I greeted him for the first and last time. He was a big, deep-chested male in prime condition. I skinned him on the spot and continued along the rim.

Roughly an hour later, I bellied to the edge and saw my second coyote of the day curled atop a narrow ridge of badlands clay. He was only 150 yards away, but half that distance was straight down, so I held the cross hairs low on his chest and anchored him permanently in dreamland.

My third and final dog of the day must have been getting an early start on rabbit hunting. He was trotting amid a series of gullies near the base of the wall, investigating clumps of sage and yucca. I readied the rifle, blew the call once to stop him, and punched his ticket.

Natural terrain advantages like the badlands' wall are not common, even in the West, but more typical landscapes can provide equally good glass-and-stalk hunting. Across much of the High Plains, upland flats bordered by gullies and draws are planted to alfalfa, wheat, or milo. Coyotes shelter in the broken ground, then hunt the fields for mice, rabbits, and birds. I like to slip up to these fields, glass them, drop back into the gullies, and sneak into position for the shot. In the foothills of many Rocky Mountain states, creeks run off the slopes in a series of more-or-less parallel draws divided by grassy ridges. By sitting high and glassing these drainages, you can spot coyotes hunting their way up them at sunrise. Using the ridge for cover, it's easy to sneak within range for a shot. Be sure to "lead" your subject so you don't pop over the ridge where it was rather than where it will be by the time you get there. Crawl into position carefully and be patient. If your subject isn't putting in an appearance, blow a low-volume call or squeaker to entice it into view.

Glass to study stalking routes before sneaking in for a shot.

In the Midwest and East, you sometimes find coyotes hunting grassy bottom-land fields surrounded by timbered hills, usually at dawn and dusk. These are most often isolated fields with limited hunter access. Coyotes aren't likely to hunt frequently-disturbed fields when the lights are on. The best method for hunting such fields yourself is to take a stand with a commanding view before first light or an hour before sunset. Use edge cover and terrain to stalk subjects too far away for a shot or try squeaking them in.

Red Fox

In much of the upper Midwest and northern Plains, glassing and stalking red fox is more popular and productive than calling them. The little dogs are nervous and cautious, usually circling far downwind before coming to a call. What with all the coyotes swarming the countryside—plus roaming farm dogs and even feisty bobcats—a ten-pound fox has to be careful. Whatever has caught that screaming rabbit is probably bigger than it is. Thirty years ago this wasn't the case. At least not in eastern South Dakota where coyotes were rare, bobcats were unheard of, and red fox were at the top of the food chain. As scapegoat for the pheasant decline, reds were bountied, harried, trapped, and poisoned, and still they thrived. If you blew a high-pitched cottontail call in the sixties, Old Reynard would often come charging. Not anymore.

By the seventies, fence-line-to-fence-line agriculture was wiping out South Dakota's pheasants, and coyotes were wiping out her red fox. Or at least helping. The sudden shortage of poultry dinners probably had a lot to do with it. At any rate, by 1973 it seemed that a coyote loped in every time I sat down to call a red fox. But once it snowed, the surviving fox glowed like ornaments on Christmas trees. It's their nature to bed right on the snow, usually in the lee of a brush pile, fence line, weed patch, or snowdrift. Here they can smell, see, and hear trouble coming in plenty of time to run away. Finding these bedded fox involves covering ground—the more the better— and this generally requires an internal combustion engine. I've never been a fan of road hunting, preferring instead

Red fox tolerate vehicle traffic on frequently traveled roads. Glass from them to minimize disturbance.

the intimate connection with nature that walking provides, but I'll admit that cruising is the most efficient way to locate red fox. You drive country roads slowly, watching distant landscapes for spots of rusty red. Roads are so common and close together in most of the Midwest that walking or even snowmobiling are mostly superfluous, but if you identify an area isolated enough that it can't be scouted from a road, by all means hike or ski into it. If you snowmobile, use a quiet machine, and stay as far back from likely bedding sites as possible.

Road traffic, being a natural part of the landscape, rarely alerts fox. They're used to the background hum of tires and engines. And, since farmers and postal carriers frequently stop along rural roads, fox tolerate motionless vehicles, too. Just don't be slamming doors and playing loud music. As a young man, I took most of my red fox by trapping. Pelts were bringing $35 back then, and I couldn't afford bullet holes. But occasionally an elusive fox would avoid my traps. One such animal lived on the edge of town, leaving plenty of tracks and droppings to entice me but refusing to take any interest in my scents and sets. One snowy morning, I drove out to run my line and thought I finally had him. From the road, I could see a red fur ball curled up in the lee of the ridge. Fox routinely went to sleep with traps around their toes, but this one didn't look quite right. Sure enough, through the binocular I could see the trap set, undisturbed, several yards from the snoozing animal. Thumbing its nose at me. The distance was just under three hundred yards. I leveled the 6 mm Remington and finally collected my elusive prize. And yes, I sewed late into the evening.

A good binocular isn't essential while scouting foxes, but it sure saves time and energy. One day in January, my heart kicked into overdrive when I passed a large shelterbelt and caught a flash of rust along its snowy eastern edge. I pulled my truck out of sight and was preparing to start my stalk when I decided to study the situation at 7X. That's when my fox resolved into a ringnecked rooster soaking up the morning sun, his bronzed breast aflame.

Corn-stubble fields aren't as common today as in my youth, but where they occur together with red fox, check them carefully. Reds love to lie against a stubble row just under the wind, with enough cover around to add a sense of security without hampering a running escape. You can peer down each row or get high and overlook the entire field. Some fox pelts are pale enough to color-coordinate closely with yellow cornstalks, but most show up as darker spots—usually rusty red, sometimes almost black.

If you identify a tangled section of land largely hidden from roads, still-hunt it into the wind, moving from high point to high point to glass. Expect fox to be bedded with their backs against cover and to the wind. When you spot a fox, plot a route to bring you within shooting range, using terrain, vegetation, and wind to cover your approach. Remember that ninety percent of a fox is support media for its ears. Crunchy snow, snapping twigs, and rustling leaves will give you away from farther than you'd ever guess. Be cautious. Settle for a long shot instead of trying to push your luck over noisy ground.

When you've crept as close as you dare and still don't have a good shot, consider adding calling to your offense. One of four things will commonly happen. The little vixen will ignore it, sit up and look toward you, come to the call, or run away. The last is unlikely unless you blast too loudly. Start by preparing your rifle to fire just in case you have to take a quick poke. Then, with a bulb or lip squeaker, send just a few notes over the airwaves. On a calm day, these will pull a bold fox from one thousand yards. Next, max out the volume of your squeaker. If you get no response, try a high-pitched cottontail squeal at low volume. If your opponent shows no indication of hearing it, increase the volume. If you see indications that the fox has heard but ignored you, it's probably not coming to the call. Crawl closer, or take the shot when it looks good.

Frank Heidelbauer, an innovative and incurable hunter, once spotted a fox mousing along an Iowa fence line. At the time, Frank was gainfully employed by the Iowa Conservation Commission. Atypically, he was without a rifle or shotgun, but he had his .38 service revolver and figured nothing ventured, nothing gained. The breeze was right, so he sneaked along the fence, lay prone just under a rise, and squeaked against the back of his hand. Within seconds, the fox popped over the horizon no more than twenty feet away. At that range, even a handgun was sufficient.

HUNTING BINOCULARS

You can't shoot 'em if you can't see 'em. Spending $2,000 on a custom rifle and $50 on a binocular is putting the cart before the horse. But what is a good binocular, and what will it cost? Like a good scope, a good binocular will have fully multi-coated lenses to ensure maximum light transmission. Eye relief will not be as long as on a scope because you needn't worry about binoculars recoiling against your brow, but you don't want eye relief so short that your lashes are beating against the eyepiece glass. If you wear glasses, eye relief must be long enough to provide a full view—no blackout around the edges—with the rubber eyepiece rim pressed against your eyeglass lenses.

Exit pupil in binoculars is the same as in a scope and plays the same role. You want an exit pupil that matches your maximum pupil dilation, roughly 7 mm in folks under forty years of age, perhaps 6 mm or even 5 mm for those over fifty. You can calculate exit-pupil size by dividing the objective lens's diameter by its magnification—thus 8x40 binoculars have a 5 mm exit pupil. That's adequate for all but the last fifteen minutes of light at dusk, especially in a high-quality optic with full multi-coating. You can get a 7 mm exit pupil in 7x50 binoculars, but they will be bulkier and heavier than 8x40. If you'll do most of your glassing near the truck, the big glass might be best. If you plan to carry them far, you'll want smaller objectives.What about mini-binoculars? The best can project a pretty sharp image, but because the objective lenses are so small—often only 20 mm— the exit pupil is tiny. They're good for daylight viewing, but not dusk.

All else being equal, a lower power glass will show a clearer image than a slightly higher power. In other words, a 10x40 won't resolve as much detail as an 8x40, but a 10x50 would. In my experience, the critical factor in binoculars is whether or not you actually carry them. The finest, brightest, clearest binocular in the world does you no good if you leave it in the truck because it's too bulky and heavy to carry afield. I find 8x42s a good balance between size and performance. Mid-priced 8x40s, fully multi-coated, are so close to the optical quality of most expensive 8x40s that you probably won't notice the difference. The more expensive ones might be built more ruggedly. In mini-binoculars, however, you'd better be prepared to pay top dollar to get useable quality.

Ergonomics plays an important role. Before buying any glass, test all the controls. Do they feel natural in your hands, easy to access? I don't recommend models with individual eyepiece focus. A single wheel moving both eyepieces is much, much faster. Beware diopter adjustment wheels located near focus wheels.

Diopter controls (for matching the focuses of the eyepieces before general focusing) should be on the eyepiece. If the diopter controls are on or near the focus controls, they should be lockable.

Convenience features like rubber coatings, waterproof housings, and Bushnell's Rain-Guard antifogging glass can add a lot of value.

Here's the big secret in value pricing of binoculars: You can buy Porro prism binoculars that are as good as roof prism binoculars for a lot less money. Porro prisms are the binoculars with the dogleg barrels; roof prisms have the straight barrels. The difference is due to the glass prisms inside the barrels and how they bend light. It costs more to build roof prisms right. The upshot is that you can buy a top-of-the-line Porro prism glass for $200 to $300, and it will project as sharp and bright an image as an $800 roof prism. Rules about exit pupils, multi-coating, etc. still apply. Porro prisms are not quite as rugged and durable as roof prisms, however.

Still-Hunting

Coyotes

I'll confess up front. I've shot quite a few coyotes while still-hunting, but not still-hunting specifically for coyotes. Most of the time I was hunting deer or moving between calling sites. Merely by staying alert and moving slowly, especially while crossing ridges, I've spotted coyotes before they spotted me. Just last winter, I hiked along the Snake River breaks in Idaho. My objective was to find long, weedy draws and call down them, but while I was slipping into the third one of the morning, I glimpsed a pair of sharp-tipped ears ghosting along just under the roll of hill before me. The wind was in my favor, so I dropped to my butt, raised my rifle, and waited. Within thirty seconds, a coyote emerged from a steep canyon, picking his way up the far slope. At forty yards it was a chip shot for the 6 mm Remington.

Some of my most productive still-hunts have been in mixed prairie, crop, and brushland in Kansas, where I do a lot of deer hunting. By moving into the wind across a series of ridges and draws, I surprise a lot of game that doesn't see me coming. The only trick is to constantly scan new ground as it opens, step by step. If you walk several yards without stopping to examine the new ground opened to view, you risk being spotted. A single step can make or break a hunt. The temptation in big, open country like this is to hike fast for fear you're missing something.

That usually leads to glimpses of coyotes streaking through the grass and over the horizon, tails streaming. Unless you're a superb running game shot, slow and steady wins this race.

Windy days prove best for still-hunting, because the rush of air masks your footfalls in leaves and dry grass. It also proscribes an obvious wind-in-your-face direction. If you can get the low sun at your back, you have every possible advantage. I've had sun-blinded coyotes miss seeing me

Keep the wind in your face and ease over ridges when still-hunting coyotes in open country.

as I stood against the sunset, caught in mid-stride. For all they reacted, I could have been invisible. I thought they should at least have heard my jaw drop, but they just continued trotting toward me, looking side to side, poking their noses into likely mouse homes. I assumed a shooting position when their vision was momentarily blocked. A few times I've hiked over rises to find myself trailing a coyote as it putters along, rump to me, oblivious. Paying attention pays dividends.

Obviously, the first and last hours of each day are best for still-hunting, because this is when coyotes are on the move. From mid-morning through late afternoon they're usually asleep, and if you see them at all, they're running because you surprised them. Oddly enough, I've gotten within shotgun range of sleeping coyotes quite often, even while bird hunting relatively flat grassland with dogs. The Brittanies and setters either go on point or slink back with an odd look on their faces. I don't know whether those coyotes were so dead to the world they didn't hear or smell us coming or they thought they could lie low and escape detection. Most did escape because— as I learned decades ago—6-shot applied to the rump of a coyote doesn't stop it. Broadside inside thirty yards it will, but few flushed coyotes offer such targets.

Fox

Fox are difficult, but not impossible, to still-hunt, mostly because they are small and usually live in tight cover. Despite their bright color, they're hard to see without a snowy background. Exceptions are the high Plains and Alaskan tundra. There reds stand out like nuns in a casino and can be spotted readily. What with

157

coyotes ruling the West, you wouldn't anticipate finding many fox in a place like southeast Montana, but a concentration of sheep ranchers there benefits the smaller canine. Because coyotes have a soft spot (their bellies) for lamb, sheepmen wage constant war against them. A pair of feisty coyotes can litter a field with dead and crippled lambs in a single night. Persistent coyote culling eventually opens these sheep ranges to red fox, which are free to go about their mousing without having to look over their shoulders for territorial gangs of prairie wolves. In Alaska, the Northern Rockies, and Great Lakes states, real wolves keep the coyotes in check, again leaving fox relatively free to run their rodent control businesses. In wide-open habitats, fox can be still-hunted in combination with glassing and calling. Just slip along carefully, trying to see before being seen.

In farm country, still-hunting is best combined with glassing and calling. If you've identified a fox's territory and know it intimately, you might be able to catch it as it forages in a meadow at dawn or trots along a field or woodlot edge on its way to bed. Years ago, I knew that a red fox was living and hunting on a half-section of my uncle's farm through which a creek traced a narrow line of grass, brush, and weeds. Fresh fox tracks laced in and out of this cover every time I checked it, so one Saturday I borrowed Duane Schragg's 5 mm Remington Rimfire Magnum rifle (yes, there was such a cartridge) and set out to shoot that fox. My plan was to still-hunt along the creek, glassing it carefully and perhaps trying a call or two. I hadn't gone three hundred yards into the wind with the sun off my right shoulder when I heard several crows calling excitedly. They were harassing something, and I could see them diving and rising behind a low hill. This was the kind of behavior I'd seen before when crows were teasing a fox, and I crept up to a fence at the top of the knoll just in time to see the rusty-red subject of their harassment trot from the creek-side grass. I estimated him at 150 yards away. He was so busy feigning disinterest in the crows that he never saw me raise the little rifle and level the cross hairs over his back. At the crack of the

Try to spot fox and sneak close before calling.

When following tracks in a fresh snow, anticipate where your quarry might go and scan ahead to see it before it sees you.

escaping powder gases, he leaped and ran, and I cursed myself for missing. But then he spun in a circle and fell over, deader than even the crows might have wished. The bullet had taken him through both lungs.

With snow cover, you can track fox. This is the most productive and challenging still-hunting variation. It demands caution, stealth, woodsmanship, persistence, and intimate knowledge of fox behavior. Don't get so enamored of the spoor that you forget to watch ahead. Scanning the distance for any glimpse of your quarry should be job one. Glance at the trail from time to time. Follow it with your eyes as far as possible. Then try to anticipate where it's leading and where in that landscape a fox might hunt (if it's early morning) or bed (if it's midday.) If Sir Fox sees you before you see him, you'll have a long hike before dark. Two or three hunters can improve odds for taking a tracked fox. While one follows the trail, the others post themselves along anticipated escape routes, i.e., farm trails along a brush line, saddles in ridges, or ribbons of riparian brush through open fields.

Stand-Hunting and Pushing

All Species

Waiting to ambush predators may be the least popular way to hunt them, but sometimes it's the only way that works. Eastern hardwood forests after leaf fall are usually so noisy you couldn't sneak up on a graveyard. Western conifer forests are often so dense that calls won't carry far through them. Sometimes your only option is to climb a tree and wait. Archery deer hunters know how effective this can be. They regularly see coyotes, bobcats, red fox, gray fox, raccoons—even black bears and cougars—strolling by. But they cling to the promise of whitetails in order to remain on stand day after day. Can a predator hunter keep the faith that long?

I can't. Not that long, anyway. But that doesn't mean you can't. Some folks are just cut out for waiting. If you're one of them, a tree stand or cliff roost might be your ticket to a few pelts. Obviously, any stand will be more productive if taken in heavily used habitat. This means you scout first, wait later. Look for natural runways, travel routes, trails, and droppings. Try to identify junctions where two trails cross. Saddles in ridges are usually productive. So are the low ends of two wooded ridges separated by a thin band of low ground, perhaps a crop field or stream. In farmland any self-protective predator is going to avoid the open ground and travel along linear cover such as narrow tree strips, weedy fence lines, and wooded stream courses. In the mountains, they'll follow ridge crests, game trails, and old roadbeds through dense timber and cross from basin to basin in low spots or saddles to avoid the long climb over flanking peaks. Four-legged hunters are as lazy as we are, so study terrain for the obvious, easy travel routes. These are the places where you want to take a comfortable seat, preferably above the action so you can see better and your scent will rise above all creatures great and small.

Last year I dedicated the first two hours of a morning to sitting on a ridge overlooking a wooded stream bottom which was always full of coyote tracks. The riparian brush provided a cloistered travel route from surrounding, barren pastures toward a dense, isolated thicket on the backside of the property far from any roads. At one sharp loop in the stream, an old sandbar created a large opening that was an irresistible shortcut. Critters could follow the stream for one hundred yards or cut across thirty yards of open ground. I'd been sitting about forty-five minutes when a flicker of white at the brushy edge of the sand flat caught my eye. My 8X binocular revealed one coyote scanning the opening and a second waiting in the shadows behind her. I rested my Rifles, Inc. .257 Weatherby Magnum in my cross-sticks, my elbows inside my knees, held the cross hairs on the nearest coyote's chest, and fired when she walked into the clearing. The second dog jumped out of the thicket and stood staring at his fallen partner, then joined her in permanent repose.

Moving targets are the norm when stand-hunting, because animals are traveling to and from bedding areas, but this doesn't mean you have to shoot moving game. You can stop fox and coyotes with a short bark or even a "Hey!" If you fear spooking them, try a squeaker or even a short toot on a distress call. Have your gun level and ready, and as soon as your sights are aligned, shoot. Some predators will stand for a long time, others only pause a second or two. If they look as if they are about to move off, squeak your lips. That'll usually hold them a few more seconds or entice them closer. Use your call to bring in game passing out of range or through heavy cover, too.

Don't be afraid to add attractions such as scent lures and decoys to your stand. A dead cow, horse, or deer gut pile should lure every coyote for miles. Set up nearby. Tom Berger and I were heading out to call a Kansas ranch one Saturday when the foreman intercepted us and suggested we check a dead cow behind the feedlot. We didn't want to interrupt our calling with a wild goose chase, but figured in the name of PR we'd better. "Right over that rise," the foreman said as he pointed from his tractor. "Must have been seven on it last night." Well, you know how some people exaggerate? This guy didn't. There were seven coyotes at that carcass, napkins around their necks, knives and forks in their paws. And when the smoke cleared we'd managed to kill only two.

A big carcass will lure coyotes at any time, day or night. We rechecked that cow at midday and found two more diners. Another year we found a coyote with his head inside a dead cow at noon. I'm telling you, if there's a large carcass in your neighborhood, watch it.

Wolves are arguably our wariest predators. Because they roam in packs, several are educated for every one fooled. You might call a pack once, but probably not twice. For this reason many wolf hunters try baiting, especially if wolves kill a steer or horse and are spooked off before eating it. Success here hinges on hiding effectively within rifle range, yet downwind. Staking the carcass in a wide-open field or frozen lake, a long rifle shot from a good hiding place, is important. Shooting may have to be done by moonlight. Take every precaution, sit absolutely still, and have your rifle resting on sticks. This might be one of the few situations in which I'd consider using a blind for predator hunting. Leave a carcass unguarded overnight and it could be cleaned up by morning.

If you see the potential in waylaying predators from stands but aren't crazy about the wait, combine stands with drives. If you know likely escape routes, place shooters along them and send drivers through cover to move predators out. This works well in Dakota shelterbelts and narrow river bottoms. In the mountains, saddles and side draws at the ends of big canyons are natural funnels. When I was a teen, my hunting buddies and I bowhunted deer in a two-mile stretch of wooded creek bottom cutting through a high ridge bordered by flat, upland cornfields and pastures. This cover was a natural bedding area and travel funnel. When we got impatient waiting on stand, we'd stage a drive. Two or three fellows would still-hunt up the wooded bottom, pushing deer, fox squirrels, cottontails, great horned owls, and sometimes coyotes ahead of them. We soon discovered which cow paths and side draws were favored escape routes and set up along them. "Let's shoot a coyote," I suggested one Saturday afternoon during a frustrating, fruitless pheasant hunt. "How we gonna do that?" Mike asked.

"Drive Ash Hollow. Two of us sit in our deer stands, one hunts up the creek."

"Can't do any worse than we are with these pheasants," Don said.

"What pheasants?" I asked.

"That's my point," Don said.

An hour later, Mike and I were sitting on opposite sides of the creek, halfway up the flanking hills along proven escape trails. Mike had drawn the longest straw and picked the west side. I settled with my back against an oak along a side draw that intersected a cow trail. An owl glided by first, indicating that Don was on the move. I heard footsteps in the timber below, then something running up the west side toward Mike. He didn't fire. Must have been a deer. Then, silently, a gray form trotted out of the timber and down my cow trail. Coyote! Calm and cool as a farm dog heading to the barn. I sat hyperventilating as calmly as possible. Mr. Coyote stopped, glanced right and left. Stared west toward Mike's position. Dropped his head and bounded into the draw. I lifted my 12-gauge and pointed it where the trail emerged from the draw, praying that the coyote wouldn't stay in the bottom and follow it down into the woods. My rare patience was rewarded. Up popped ears, head, shoulders, chest. Oblivious. Thirty yards away. Twenty-five yards. I fired an anemic 11/4-ounce of 6-shot and the coyote collapsed. At twenty-five yards, even a pheasant load will suffice.

I doubt that anyone knows what percentage of predators shot each year are taken via stalking, still-hunting, and stand-hunting. Perhaps ten percent, maybe twenty percent? It doesn't matter, really. For those of us who do it, the satisfaction is one hundred percent.

STALKING RIFLE AND RANGE FINDER

A benchrest-accurate rifle, ballistic turret, or ballistic reticle scope, a thorough understanding of how to use them, and a laser range finder will increase a stalking hunter's shooting success. Sleeping fox and coyotes are small targets and are often three hundred or more yards away. The latest laser range finders aren't much larger than a mini-binocular and weigh less than thirteen ounces. The cheapest models are effective to five hundred yards, the best to 1,600 yards. I recommend at least an eight hundred-yard model because non-reflective subjects reduce effectiveness by as much as 50 percent.

New laser rangefinding binoculars from Bushnell, Zeiss, Swarovski, and Leica combine fine optical quality with excellent rangefinding in single units that are fast, simple, and delightful to use. No more fumbling for the binoculars, range finder, and rifle. Just glass, find, range, grab the rifle, and shoot. Range finders are as valuable for telling when you need to stalk closer as for how high to aim. Remember that variable breezes and steep shooting angles compromise accuracy at extreme range. Wind can easily deflect bullets farther than the length of a coyote. Angles of 45 degrees or more uphill or down at targets more than two hundred yards away will park bullets higher than normal. Even a simple aiming error of an inch at one hundred yards can become four inches at four hundred yards. To minimize confusion in the heat of the moment, keep a trajectory table for your ammunition taped to your stock. It's easier to remember if your bullet drops eight inches or twelve inches at four hundred yards when you have the numbers right in front of you. If you use a ballistic turret or reticle, study how it works and practice with it until using it is second nature. Skilled long-range shooters can hit as well at five hundred and six hundred yards as some casual shooters can at one hundred yards.

Since a successful stalker has plenty of time to choose a clear shooting lane and set up for a prone shot, he can take advantage of a sturdy bipod, high magnification scope, and super-accurate rifle. One of the heavy-barreled, heavy-stocked varmint rifles might be perfect, but a sporter-weight that shoots like a house afire can be equally effective. Any rifle that consistently shoots ½-inch or better groups at one hundred yards is a candidate. I have a few of those that weigh less than eight pounds and are a treat to carry. If necessary, have a gunsmith hone and lighten the trigger. Test a variety of factory ammunition and handloads to find the ultimate accuracy. Then attach one of the prone-length bipods from Harris, B-Square, Versa-Pod, or Caldwell. Models with tilt and swivel mounts are best for leveling a rifle on uneven ground. Finally, practice shooting at three hundred to five hundred yards. Then be honest with yourself and limit your shots within the range you can honestly hit every time. A calm, experienced shooter with an accurate rifle and range finder should be effective to four-hundred-fifty yards.

14

Working On Your Night Moves

In the Heat of the Night

Vampires and rock stars aren't the only creatures that play at night. Most fur-bearing carnivores do the bulk of their hunting after dark. Perhaps we should, too.

Historically humans have clustered round fires to stay out of predatory clutches from dusk to dawn. These days, firearms and electric lights enable us to turn the tables and hunt the hunted in the gloom of night when they are most bold and most active.

"That's one. Off to the east," Mike Kibble whispered. The spooky cry we'd heard was answered by another far to the north. "Two of them. Maybe we'll get a bidding war started."

I leaned over the Land Cruiser's rail and clutched Mike's Anschutz .22 Hornet. Mike had control of the spotlight, ready to light up the night when he judged a predator was near. As ringleader on this midnight adventure in the desert of Namibia, my PH was attempting to prove up on his boast—that he could bring Africa's coyote-like jackals within easy shooting range of an open-bed truck parked smack in the middle of nowhere.

"Make the cries shorter," he'd instructed early in our kudu hunt when I'd demonstrated how we Americans blow cottontail distress calls. "The pitch is about right, but a duiker caught in a fence makes short cries, more like whaa whaa than whaaaaaaaaaa." I shortened my cadence. "Good. Now pause a bit more between each one. That's it! That sounds just like one." Duikers are small African antelope that weigh about thirty-five pounds after a full meal, just right for an aggressive, twenty-five-pound black-backed jackal to tackle—especially when

Even in low light, the highly reflective tapetum layer on the retina of cats and other nocturnal predators can kick back enough light to show as "headlight eyes."

already crippled or caught in a fence, a predicament Mike had seen more than once during his adventures afield.

"Blow some more," he said as we shuddered in the back of his safari truck. I did, and the jackal to the east sounded louder. "It's working. He's coming in." Then four more howled.

"You got enough ammo? We're surrounded," I said, only half joking. In a foreign land where jackals could be joined by leopards or even a lion, the security offered by the back of an open truck felt insufficient.

But our jackals gave no indication that anything bigger was sneaking our way, so when they sounded close enough, Mike flicked on his powerful spotlight, illuminating a set of yellow eyes about one hundred-fifty yards out. A second pair glowed weakly in the background. Alas, I missed with the unfamiliar rifle, but Mike had proved his point. We could call jackals at night.

That discovery certainly didn't surprise me. Americans have been luring coyotes, fox, bobcats, raccoons, and even black bears by starlight for decades. The graveyard shift has never approached the popularity of daylight calling simply because we are biologically built for diurnal work. Our cone-rich eyes see better in daylight, we feel more comfortable in daylight, and—because of our normal sleep-wake rhythms—we function better in daylight. But portable spotlights, night scopes, and illuminated reticles on regular scopes now promise a bright future in night work. Hunters who practice nocturnal calling enjoy impressive success. And, yes, they really do call their customers within easy rifle shot of trucks, in North America as well as Africa.

This simplifies the whole enterprise—if you don't mind the esthetics of hunting out of a vehicle. It hasn't the romance or

A few supplies for a successful night hunt include a 400,000 candle power spotlight, a powerful SureFire M4 Devastator flashlight, Streamlight headlamp with green filter, Burnham Brothers electronic Compucaller III, Woods Wise Red Dawg Coyote howler and Mini Three mouth calls, and a variety of ammunition.

woodsmanship of hiking, tracking, and stealth, but it saves time and puts fur on the stretcher. Instead of stumbling around in the dark, tripping on rocks, walking into barbed wire fences, and sitting on cacti, you merely cruise by the seat of your pants into a suitable pasture or field— the kind of place a hungry predator would hunt mice and rabbits. Then you either climb in the back or sit at the open windows with your lights and guns ready. Stick your call out and blow or fire up the electronic player. Heck, you can even run the CD or MP3 files through your truck stereo.

During a full moon on snow or short, yellow grass, you can often see game well enough to shoot to one hundred yards, sometimes as far as two hundred yards. Fox and bobcat will usually trot closer than that before hesitating. Gray fox will practically run right into the wheels. Coyote response varies from equally gullible to extremely cautious, depending on how much of this night calling they've experienced before.

If you don't wish to wait for a full moon to hunt, fire up the spotlights. A normal white, yellow, or blue light will eventually spook predators, which is why Mike kept his off until we judged the jackals were close enough to hit. Their response was typical. They stared at the light for a few seconds, then looked away and began shying away. Additional calling did not bring them closer. When they stared at the light, their eyes made a good target. When they looked away, it was more difficult aligning sights clearly on their hides, which blended all too well with surrounding grass and brush. One fix for this is to use a red light. For some reason this doesn't alarm predators nearly as much as white light, so they'll come closer. Some say it's because they can't "see" red. Okay, but they can see light. It might look yellow to them. It might even look dimmer than white light (as it does to us). But I don't believe they are unable to detect the electromagnetic energy of red light. Regardless, if red lights minimally alarm them, I'm going to use red lights. The trade-off with red is that it doesn't illuminate nearly as well as white, so you need your subjects closer and/or you need to start with a much more powerful light.

Rob Lancellotti and I shot with extremely powerful red lights during a West Texas hunt with outfitter Steve Jones of Backcountry Hunts a few years ago. Steve and his crew had two 4-wheel drive trucks rigged with high seats in back and twin red spotlights swiveling off each side. The driver/guide would stop at a likely spot, fire up an electronic caller, and sweep the landscape with the light, watching for red eye shine. And finding it. At one of our very first stops we picked up two glowing orbs approaching from the south. I found them in my Z6 scope and put the illuminated red center dot on them. "I think it's a bobcat," I whispered to Rob.

He agreed. The critter was trotting ever closer and, even though it looked plenty big enough through the scope at 10X, I let it continue its approach. Close is always better. And bobcats are notorious for tolerating both man-scent and night lights. But eventually they balk, and this one did at about seventy-five yards. Estimating this distance was difficult in the dark, but I didn't want to drop my aim in order to use a range finder. Rob and I should have arranged this before we'd even started. One hunter shoots, the other ranges. At the next setup, rotate jobs.

A 400,000 candle power spotlight run via truck battery can light up the night, but a red filter would make it less objectionable to incoming predators.

But on this occasion I had to wing it, which wasn't too challenging. Given the trajectory of a 50-grain Accutip-V .223 bullet fired from an R-15, anything from ten yards and two hundred was a dead-on hold. So I held for the cat's neck, clicked the R-15s "send" button, and breathed relief when the cat collapsed. It was a big, big tom and a great start to a wild, disorienting night of cruising, calling, and shooting under the mysterious stare of Orion, Ursus Major, and all the other famous constellations of the night.

By 3 AM, dizzy and groggy, we gave it up, having learned that swift fox and gray fox are equally unafraid of big trucks and red lights. But we never even saw a coyote. Whether that was due to scarcity or their experience, I don't know. The next night we hunted another region one hundred-fifty miles away with similar results. Fox, bobcats, and even a ringtailed cat showed up—but no coyotes.

This doesn't mean coyotes can't be taken at night. They can, and quite readily. According to dedicated night hunters, song dogs are no more shy of red lights than are fox or bobcat. But they may be smarter about trucks sitting in the open. For best results on coyotes—or any other predators, I imagine—you are advised to call while out of sight of your rig. Treat a nocturnal setup much as you would one in daylight. Ease into position, wear camo, and call upwind. Predators certainly see much better at night than you or I, but probably not as well as they do in daylight. Either that or they just feel extra secure in the dark because they are not as spooky. Rancher friends and I have spotlighted them from a truck and even cruised along with them as they hunted grass fields at night. They certainly knew we were there, but they calmed down when about one hundred-fifty to two hundred yards away, and largely ignored us if we stayed three hundred yards or farther. Of course, at that range it was becoming difficult to see them clearly.

Gear for Night Hunting

A shotgun makes it easier to hit anything at night—if it's close enough. But too often critters aren't close enough. They have a maddening habit of hanging up just outside shotgun range. Fortunately, a rifle with the right sight works perfectly during nocturnal hunts. A traditional scope will suffice if your spotlight is bright enough. Shine your truck headlights on a target one hundred yards away some night and see how easily you can center standard black reticles on it. Move to two hundred yards and notice how dim the target becomes. With distance and deteriorating light, black reticles become increasingly difficult and eventually impossible to use. Two-stage reticles with fat crosshairs that step down or taper toward thin in the middle, help, but illuminated reticles help even more. Either the center of the reticle or just a tiny dot in the middle glows red, yellow, or green. This makes it easy to see your aiming point, but it doesn't do anything to brighten the target. That is done strictly by ambient light (moon) or spotlight. Still, if you can discern the outline of your quarry, you can put the lighted aiming point on it and score.

Most illuminated reticles get their rosy glow from a battery. Trijicon scopes use a tritium element that glows, and Bushnell has a model that works by phosphorescence. You shine a flashlight into the scope for a few seconds to charge the reticle, which then glows green for an hour or two.

An excessively bright reticle will overpower dim targets. Instead of seeing a bright dot on a rather dim fox, you'll see an overly bright dot on nothing but blackness. When buying a lighted reticle, test it in full darkness, not in a bright store, with your eyes adjusted to the dark. Ideally the reticle illumination should be adjustable from barely glowing to so intense that you can clearly see it in daylight. This bright level is effective against black animals in full daylight. Intermediate levels work perfectly at dawn and dusk when you think you don't need anything but a standard reticle. I once worked with a custom 6mm Remington topped with a Trijicon scope on a Nevada coyote adventure. Cory Lundberg was calling with Eddie Stevenson covering the left side, I the right. Cloudy. An hour before sunset. When a big male coyote popped over a ridge, I could hardly see him against the camouflaging gray sage. Gray light, gray coyote, gray vegetation. Tough. Neither Cory nor Eddie saw him at all until we walked out to pick him up after my shot. What impressed me was how easily and confidently I was able to center that glowing yellow aiming point on the big dog's chest. I could have accomplished the shot with a standard reticle, but the illumination was a real confidence boost.

When hunting with any illuminated reticle, test and properly set the brightness level. As the hunt progresses, keep tweaking the brightness, preferably just before you start each calling session. And turn off all other lights like bright dash lights and headlights so your eyes remain fully dilated.

Obviously you have to turn the scope's illumination off and on. This raises the specter of forgetting to turn it off, earning yourself the dreaded dead battery. Some scopes include a sensory switch that turns the device off after feeling no motion for a certain amount of time. Some turn the unit on automatically via mercury switch when the rifle is held horizontally, off when positioned vertically. Blazer and Zeiss have cooperated to make a magnetic switch that fires up the Zeiss reticle only when the cocking switch on a Blaser R8 is pushed forward. Uncock the rifle and the light goes off. The system is both foolproof and extremely safe. Study such light control options before purchasing any illuminated reticle scope.

Another option for better night aiming is a laser sight, the kind that projects a green or red dot on the target. These have surprisingly long range. I tried a Crimson Trace lasergrip sight on my Kimber 45 ACP Pro Carry and easily targeted a boulder at eighty-five yards in the pitch of night. But, again, I needed ambient light (in this case a SureFire, high-intensity LED flashlight) to illuminate the rock. The tiny red laser dot isn't bright enough to tell you what it's reflecting from, but seeing that red dot on target sure boosts your confidence.

Finally, there are the various night scopes; the military "image intensification" type that actually gathers starlight, runs it through a photocathode tube, and converts it to electrons. These electrons, along with battery energy and special chemicals, stimulate thousands of additional electrons (this is the light enhancing part), that are pushed through a phosphor screen and turned back into photons which you see as the bright, green image in the scope's eyepiece. Basically, Generation 1 scopes (roughly $300 to $800) require an infrared illuminator to add light (predators can't see it, but humans with other infrared detecting devices can). Gen 1 scopes have low image quality, small field of view, limited range (seventy-five yards), fairly poor low light performance, and a short life span (1,500 hours). Gen 2 scopes are a huge step up in image quality and performance, range to two hundred yards, run for about 5,000 hours, don't need the infrared illuminator boost, and sell in the $1,100 to $3,000 range. Gen 3 scopes are that much better than Gen 2, range slightly past three hundred yards, and run more than 10,000 hours, but they'll set you back $3,500 to as much as $9,000.

Magnifications are not high on any of these, say 2X to 6X, and the units are bulky, weighing 30 to 59 ounces. Plan on doing a lot of serious night hunting before buying one of these.

Hey Buddy, Got a Light?

If you're going to hunt under the dark of a new moon (which, weirdly, means no moon glow at all), you'll need a light. Headlights are unacceptable because they too often spook the game and ruin your night vision. Turn headlights off, dim dashboard lights, and navigate by starlight or red spotlight.

A spotlight charged by the truck battery through a power outlet (cigarette lighter, etc.) can throw out as many as one million candle power units of light. Is that a lot? Yes. One-tenth that will suffice, although 200,000 candle power is a better compromise. You'll see eyes farther out with the highest powers, but they aren't essential.

Aiming these lights can be a challenge unless one "hunter" is dedicated to it while the other shoots. If you must aim both light and gun, figure out some way to accomplish both simultaneously. Texans, the kings of night hunting, rig up swiveling chairs with gun rest brackets. They clamp spotlights to those brackets. As you spin the chair, the light swings with it. All you need to do with your hands is run the rifle.

Another option is to mount a light to your rifle or scope. Clamps and flash-lights on a barrel will change its point of impact, but as long as this is consistent, no harm. Just check your zero with the accouterments aboard. Clamping the light to the scope is much less likely to change where bullets go, but will unbalance the gun. You can get used to this. Many scope-mount lights weigh a pound or less. They are most easily ignited via a switch taped to your gun's stock near your fore-

hand. Brightness levels of these small lights vary, but most aren't as bright as you'll wish they were. Many are rated for effective distance, and those ratings are usually generous by twice the real world effective range. It's frustratingly frustrating to vaguely see a coyote in your small light yet

A variety of modern flashlights aid in night calling. Some are bright enough to illuminate targets as far as two hundred-fifty yards away. Red filters reduce range drastically.

not be able to clearly line up your sights. So figure a light rated to one hundred yards will suffice at fifty. Chances are you'll upgrade to a 200,000 candle power "real" spotlight eventually. White gun lights reach a lot farther than red ones.

When buying, consider power sources. You probably don't want to carry a car battery into the brush for remote setups. And you probably don't want to be buying new alkaline or lithium D-cells for a big light you run for hours on end. Consider rechargeable units. Tactical lights geared for the military can provide bright output in small packages, but they can't be operated long before batteries die. I've used some of SureFire's biggest LED flashlights effectively to two hundred-fifty yards, and some of their smaller units are useable to one hundred yards thanks to both their intensity and focused beam. Again, this is white light. After you add a red filter, brightness drops dramatically. Still, lights like this are an effective option, especially when mounted to a scope and flicked on only when you're ready to shoot. Most predators will stop and stare at a bright, white light for a few seconds before leaving.

How To Light Up Their World

The most effective way to wield the spotlight is to cast its center just over ground level, back and forth or in a circle. The edge light is softer than the center and less likely to alarm game, yet bright enough to cause eye shine. Eye's shine, by the way, is due to the tapetum lucidum, a layer of reflective cells on the retina. These are what enable nocturnal animals to see so well in dim light. Nothing can see in absolute darkness because there is no electromagnetic energy to be detected. And no predator's eyes can shine of their own accord, regardless what you read in novels or see in movies. They only reflect. And the red light in the outer edge of a spotlight's beam is sufficient for this at four hundred yards, sometimes six hundred yards.

When you pick up those twin orbs, keep the lower fringe of light on them as the animal approaches. This prevents it from clearly seeing you and your truck. Watch the critter through your scope or binocular, striving to clearly identify it. You don't want to shoot a farmer's dog, housecat, or cow. We were calling on a big African ranch one night when my PH, Dirk deBod instructed me to shoot at a big brown hyena. All I could see were two glowing eyes a long way out, but Dirk insisted, so I launched one—and missed. This was a good thing because the dreaded hyena raced right in for protection. It was the ranch dog. Sometimes it's good to miss.

With your target clearly identified and in range, you may center it in the light or just shoot with the edge illumination. Often you'll have just the eyes as a clear

Check potential lights for spotlighting to see both how bright they are and how far they reach.

target, so you'll be taking head shots, which aren't necessarily easy to make. Getting a precise laser rangefinder reading can help. Lasers, of course, work beautifully at night. If the animal is close enough to align your sights on its shoulder, this would be a better bet for a sure hit.

Night hunting is otherworldly at first. You can easily become disoriented. And you'll see some unusual sights like foxes sitting calmly just off the trail, watching you drive by. Or badgers chasing cottontails, owls swooping across fields, and deer sleeping right in the open. The most romantic night hunt of all could be calling wolves by moonlight. You hear stories like this out of the Great White North, so I suppose they're true—whether Jack London wrote them or not. The bold hunter snowshoes out to a snow-covered lake and sends a territorial challenge howl into the Arctic night. He then waits as the resident pack of wolves races in from the surrounding tundra to rip him apart. Before they do, he finds the alpha male in his sights and drops him. Then, if all goes according to plan, he takes down one more before the pack races out of sight, or converges to rip him apart.

Don't Break The Law

Before trying a night hunt, know your state regulations. Some states permit night hunting for predators, but not with artificial lights. Some require you have permission from a private landowner. Some don't allow night hunting at all. Some don't even allow shining lights across fields. But where legal, a nocturnal predator hunt can turn hum drum into hot action. Night hunting might be the best way to draw coyotes out of the woodwork in Eastern and Midwestern forests where they are particularly shy. But it has to be legal first.

15

That Warm, Fuzzy Feeling

Handling Fur

The pelts of predators you shoot can be converted into cash and coats, rugs, or wall decor. They are an abundant natural resource. Unfortunately, their value fluctuates wildly with the whims of fashion. Pelts that fetched $100 thirty-five years ago might bring but $20 on today's market. This could change in the matter of a single year, however. Meanwhile, rest assured you can make a few dollars by properly caring for your predator pelts.

Good fur care begins with the harvest. Don't hunt animals too early or too late in the season. In the north, furs prime by early November, peak in mid-December, and begin losing quality by February. In the high mountains, October pelts can be pretty prime. In the South, you may have to wait until December before furs have any value, and they'll never be as good as lush, northern hides. Hey, if you want to survive thirty degrees below zero, you grow a heck of a coat.

For highest quality furs, shoot a bullet that doesn't tear hides. See Chapter 5 for details. When you bag an animal, you have the option of skinning it immediately or waiting until the end of the hunt to skin everything at once. Warm carcasses skin more easily than cold. If you don't skin in the field, take care to keep animals clean and as blood-free as possible. Plug wound channels with paper towels, and lay animals hole-side up while transporting. In freezing temperatures, pelts can be stored on the carcass for weeks. Some fur buyers will buy raw carcasses. You won't get as much for these as for a finished pelt, but you won't have to work as hard either. Check the Yellow Pages for fur buyers, or ask your local fish and game department officer.

Skinning is a rather simple chore easier done than explained. Just diving in and doing it—while following a few basic directions— is the best way to learn. First, cut through the hide around the rear leg "ankles." Don't cut so deep as to sever tendons. Next, stick the point of your knife beneath the hide and slide it toward the junction of the tail and anus. On a coyote, this line follows the junction of the dark upper hair and pale belly hair. Cut around the anus, leaving it with the carcass. Slice up the underside of the tail for a few inches.

At this point, you'll need to hire a partner to hold the back legs—or tie them securely to an overhanging branch or two-by-four—because you're about to

Skinning coyotes in the field reduces weight and makes long hiking hunts easier.

indulge in some hefty pulling. With the carcass anchored, work the hide down around the hind legs and the base of the tail, slicing tissue and pulling. When several inches of tailbone are exposed, wrap two fingers tightly around it, your other hand around the base of the tail/rump, and pull the bone out of the hide/ hair portion of the tail. It will zip right out, but it takes some muscle power to get it started. With the bone out, slit the tail all the way to its tip to aid drying later.

With the tail free, continue pulling the hide down off the carcass like a sock off a foot. You may need to slice a bit of tissue here and there. Things will grind to a halt at the front legs. Here you must work the hide away from the upper legs, pushing with your fingers to punch through the front of them. Once you've managed this—and it takes persistence and some sweat—it's easy to finish pulling the hide down to each lower foot, one at a time. At the joint, cut clear around to free the hide and pull the lower leg through. It'll be a tight fit. Be careful that bobcat claws don't slice the skin as you pull. Now pull until you see the bases of the ears bulging. Cut low and close to the skull to free the ears. Nip and slice tissue to release the hide until you see the eyes. Cut beneath the lids, tight against the orbital ridge, to avoid slicing through the thin hide here. Take your time. It's not as complicated as it first looks. Continue pulling the hide down the nose. You'll need to cut the lips free around the jaw. Cut deep enough so you don't slice through the skin. When you get to the nose, cut it back far enough that the cartilage remains with the skin. That's it.

Now turn the hide fur side out and comb or brush free all burs. A dog brush works pretty well. For best quality, wash the entire hide in cold water—lots of rinse

Comb through the hide with a dog brush to remove all burs.

cycles. This takes out the blood and makes the entire fur lighter and brighter.

Most predators (raccoons and bears excepted) have very little fat clinging to their hides, but turn the skin inside out and trim away any fat and muscle clinging to it. There's usually a clump at the base of each front leg and often some on the belly. You'll essentially shave this away. The best tool for this is a fleshing knife with the hide pulled over a four-by-four post rounded at the tip and edges and set at a forty-five-degree angle, but you can get by with a skinning knife or a small pocket knife and the hide laid flat on a table or board. It just takes more time that way. Be careful not to cut through the hide. Work with the broad side of the blade almost flat to the hide. Trim excess fat and flesh from the base of the ears and from the tail, too. Muscle tissue will dry, but oily fat will seep, turn rancid, and ruin a pelt. Wipe off excess fat with paper towels.

With the hide cleaned and fleshed, you're ready to dry it. Pull it over a commercial wire or board stretcher fur side in for three to twelve hours to let the skin dry. While the skin is still pliable enough to work, turn the hide fur side out, and place it back over the stretcher, looping the nose over the apex and centering the entire pelt. Do not actually stretch the hide. Just pull it firmly down and tack the lower legs or hook them into the claws provided on wire stretchers. You can slide a thin wedge rod between the board and

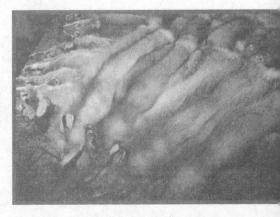

Regional auctions may be the best place to get the highest prices for your pelts.

175

the back and belly of the pelt to aid air circulation. Dry all but raccoon pelts fur side out. When finished, a pelt should crackle like a dry grocery bag and retain its form with the stretcher removed.

When you get your furs stretched, take a few pictures. Not many Americans can brag about their fur harvest anymore.

Off to the Sale

A local fur buyer is the most convenient outlet for the casual fur seller. Small buyers will usually take carcasses and make a profit by skinning them or hiring it done. If you sell finished furs, you'll get a higher price, but not as high as if you sold them at an auction. Regional auctions are usually sponsored by trappers who join together in order to attract several buyers. As a result, you get nearly top dollar for your furs, but may have to pay a commission. Ask your state fish and game agency for information on fur buyers in your area. Check the Web, too. Some big fur houses buy through the mail, but of course, you won't be present to counter their offers or question their grading of your pelts.

Other possible buyers include taxidermists, artists, tourist gift shops (tanned pelts), and modern mountain men who attend annual rendezvous or summer camps in traditional nineteenth-century garb. Search the Web and you'll find many places to sell not only furs but also claws, skulls, and teeth. If you're really ambitious, you can probably even collect and sell urine from your animals.

In recent years, with prices low, trappers and predator hunters have been collecting skins, getting them tanned, and having tailors and local seamstresses sew them into jackets, stoles, and coats. In this manner, it's possible to get a stunning

Author with eleven of thirteen coyotes taken in Kansas and Colorado in one week.

coat for well under store prices. And how about a fur quilt for the bed? An even less expensive option is to have a few pelts tanned as trophies to hang in your den. They lend a wonderful ambience to a trophy room and can always be sold or converted into clothing.

TAKE PRECAUTIONS TO STAY DISEASE-FREE

Like thousands of hunters and trappers, I've handled hundreds of furbearers without ill effect, but it is possible to contract bubonic plague from fleas, maybe a weird fungus or who knows what from body fluids. To be safe, don rubber kitchen gloves, plastic surgical gloves, or painting gloves from the hardware store when skinning. Place skins or whole animals in plastic bags with a handful of flea powder, and the pests should be history by the time you get to the skinning shed.

Wise hunters handle predators with gloves in the field as well as back home when skinning furbearers.

16

Lessons Learned

Stories of Success and Disaster

You can read all you want, watch videos, listen to tapes, get good advice from experts and friends, but sometimes you just have to make your own mistakes. Then you remember. What follows are lessons friends and I have been taught by various critters over the years. Read and learn from them, but then get out and attend your own school of hard knocks. It the most fun you'll ever have in class.

Too Much Cover

I sat against a knobby trunk in a quiet cottonwood grove surrounded by knee-high gumweed stems and low hills no more than three hundred yards away. I'd be able to see any approaching coyote against the sky and have plenty of time to line it up for the shot. Yeah, right. A pair of pointy ears and a black nose bouncing past at less than thirty yards were my first indication I had company. I couldn't see through the gumweed stems for a clear shot. The lanky dog hit my scent line and disappeared. No shots fired. **Lesson:** Never set up in ground cover you can't see over or down into— at least not when you're holding a rifle. Use a shotgun in heavy cover, or make sure you have clear shooting all around, especially close. Don't assume you can take your game in a few open patches. They may sneak or blast through too quickly for you to react.

A Challenge Answered

From the hillside, I could see across miles of Texas brush with plenty of openings in which to stop a cat or coyote. Gary was into his third calling series when a dark coyote came on the run from the northwest. It was charging so fast that it was entering the last opening before I could bring the rifle to bear, but there was still plenty of room to stop it. I barked. It threw its head up, raised its hackles, turned toward me, and started a stiff-legged bounce that said, "You're on my turf, pup!" I barked again. It came even faster. A few more bounds, and it'd be in the brush below me, out of sight. The only other opening between us was under my boots. I put the reticle on its chest and fired just as it hit the first lacy branches.

Always set up with some type of cover that will help mask your movement.

Lesson: Don't assume you can stop a coyote anywhere, anytime. The old, bold ones sometimes take your bark challenge and run it back at you. Try a sharp, crisp "Hey you!" if your imitation bark only adds fuel to its engine.

Backdoor Surprise

Terry Clarkson thought he had a South Dakota coyote on a string, but suddenly it stopped in the dusk and started barking. Terry recognized the alarm bark and knew more calling would be futile. So he left his cap on a weed and bellied out of sight—sneaked along a draw behind a ridge and crawled to the top. Mr. Coyote was still sitting there, watching Terry's old position and barking warnings to all his cousins. Terry flipped

Coyotes know what their neighbors are saying. Do you? Learn to interpret coyote yips and howls and you'll know when to use them, when to shut up.

179

down his bipod legs, laid the cross hairs just over the tattletale's back, and took him cleanly at slightly over four hundred yards.

Lesson: Learn and heed the cries of the coyote. When you know one has grown suspicious, see if you can't somehow stalk within range.

Yankee Ingenuity

Gordy Krahn and I had just shot a coyote when we saw a second one running in from our right. At the rate it was going it would soon be out of sight behind

Be ready to move quickly should changing conditions, such as wind, mess up your original stand.

a bump in the slope on which we sat. Then it could climb unseen and catch our scent. To prevent that, I threw a stone down the hill, hoping the coyote would think it had been dislodged by whatever was killing the "rabbit." The bouncing rock grabbed its attention. It started barking. "I'm going for that big rock," I said, pointing my chin toward a spot from which I'd probably get a clear view of what lay below. I did. Our invited guest was running back and forth at the base of the hill like a carnival target, leaping off his front feet and tossing his head up to bark before spinning around and running back. I rested the rifle over the boulder, swung with the carnival target and barked. Target stopped. Carnival over.

Lesson: Don't just sit there—do something. When the best laid plans of mice and men go astray, innovate. Interpret what is happening and decide what to do to improve your odds.

Eyes Front and Center

After Tom's third calling series without a response, I figured nothing would show. Coyotes on the ranch where we were hunting usually came quick and hard. But I knew better than to stand before Tom whistled his signal. It never came. Instead, he started squeaking. That meant he had a customer and was maneuvering him for a perfect shot. Only he didn't shoot—just kept squeaking. Man, I wanted to turn around and see what he was working on, but I knew better than that, too. Still, I strained my eyes as far as I could to either side. Nothing. Finally he shot. Again, from long experience, I knew enough to sit still and watch. A missed dog or its partner could run right by, or perhaps another dog could be called in. But Tom didn't launch into his usual hurt-coyote yipes. There was silence for several seconds. Then another shot. What the heck was going on? After a few more seconds I heard footsteps.

"Why didn't you shoot that one?" Tom asked as he walked up behind me.

"Which one?"

"This one that was standing right in front of you."

"Where?"

"By that yucca bush." Tom walked fifty yards to the bush, bent over, and started whooping as if he'd struck gold. Then he hoisted a big tom bobcat. "I kept waiting for you to shoot, but finally figured you couldn't see him. I missed the first shot and didn't even budge him."

Tom Berger admires his bobcat called in while hunting coyotes.

Lesson: Don't get so fixated on what you think should happen that you fail to notice what is happening. I was so busy watching the far and middle distance for running coyotes that I never noticed the cat slipping in quietly right in front of me.

Repeat Customers

"Should have come along," Brad said, punctuating the obvious with the thud of a bright red fox hitting the porch.

"You're kidding. You got another one?"

"I told you I would. Just like last time." Brad Deffenbaugh was referring to the success he'd had bringing fox up to a low bench above a prairie creek where two fence lines met, dividing a pasture and a grain field. And he did it every year. Same place, same time. As a trapper, he knew red fox were creatures of habit, so he became one, too.

Lesson: Remember calling stands that worked in the past and try them again, watching for patterns such as crop rotation, winds, and time of year. Good habitat is sought and recognized by predators. Remove one, and another will move in to take its place.

Close Enough to Pet

Tom Berger couldn't believe a coyote wasn't responding to his calls. The habitat looked good, so he gave it a few more minutes than usual. Nothing turned up, but his sixth sense told him to slowly turn and look left. There was a bobcat hungrily creeping up on him. To prevent frightening the kitty, Tom, a left-handed shooter, minimized his body contortions by merely poking the barrel at the cat and pulling the trigger with the action still in his lap. I asked him later why he risked an unaimed shot. "Because the bobcat wasn't more than two feet from the end of the barrel!"

Raining cats and dogs? Bobcats share habitat with coyotes and foxes, so be ready for anything.

Lesson: Expect the unexpected with bobcats on the menu. They are predictably unpredictable. Also, move slowly, and they'll probably only watch instead of run. Quick, sharp motions are more likely to spook them.

Record Day

As long as I'm telling Tom Berger stories, I might as well tell you about his record-setting day that almost didn't happen. After a summer move to a new job in a distant part of the state, Tom returned to his old stomping grounds in early November to enter the sportman's club's annual coyote calling contest. Unfortunately, his former contest partner didn't know Tom was planning to make the hunt, so he teamed up with someone else.

"Well, is there any rule says I can't hunt alone?" Tom asked the judges.

"No, but you won't have much of a chance competing against two-man teams." Tom didn't care. He just wanted to hunt. He worked two ranches between 7 AM and 5 PM, making some twenty stands. "I wasn't going far

Neither sleet nor snow will keep a dedicated predator hunter from his appointed rounds. Why stay in bed when you can have an adventure like this?

182

between them," he explained. "It was a perfect day, just a light breeze out of the northwest, and sunny." And when it was over, Tom won the contest with eleven coyotes. "I called in thirteen, but missed two," he said. We all should have such troubles.

Lesson: Go. Partner or no partner, good weather or bad, roll out of bed and go. You never know when you'll hit that magic day.

Hot Dogs, Anyone?

We were four miles from camp when we heard Sota and Boo barking, which was out of character for them. Sota, a scrawny English setter, usually stayed in the tent while we hunted. Boo was chained to her kennel box to prevent her from following us. Springers are not the world's best elk hunters.

The snow around camp was covered with coyote tracks when we got back. "That's what they were barking at. Probably smelled our food. Trying to get in and steal some. Good dogs. You defended the manor." Both dogs and I were accustomed to coyotes around our rural Idaho home, so I wasn't concerned. The pair had backed down and chased off plenty of them.

The daytime barking and the ring of coyote tracks continued for the duration of our elk hunt. On the morning we were packing to leave, I let Sota run free. She set to barking a familiar tune. I dug my .280 Improved Strata Stainless rifle from its case and tiptoed toward the barking. A huge coyote stood twenty feet in front of my dog, smiling and drooling over the prospect of a setter supper. A 150-grain X-Bullet ended his dinner plans. His canines were worn to stumps, and he must have weighed forty pounds. He was the oldest and biggest coyote I've even taken. And Sota was glad I did.

Lesson: Don't let a predator eat your dog.

Look Before You Leave

Tom had been playing every tune on his electronic caller he knew for thirty minutes in an effort to pull something furry from what looked like excellent cover in front of us. We'd set up in a few trees before a small pasture at sunset for our last call of the day. The heavy bedding cover lay just one hundred-fifty yards beyond the short grass, far enough to give us time to aim at any critter that broke from the cover. But none did. Tom played the usual cottontail screams, then tried flicker, jackrabbit, coyote howls, and even a few hog calls. These were enough to elicit some howls from the far side of the cover, so we thought surely a coyote would lope in. When one didn't and it appeared we'd leave empty-handed, I raised my compact Swarovski EL 32mm binocular and carefully scanned the distant cover.

And there it was. Mr. Coyote standing between a couple of small cedars with a concealing patch of grass in front. He was staring, curious, but not approaching any closer. I fished out my Bushnell rangefinder and punched up the numbers. Three hundred-seventy yards. Yikes. That meant the 95-grain Ballistic Silvertip in my .243 Win Mossberg bolt-action would drop about seven inches, based on my zero distance. The coyote was facing me. Not much of a target. I raised the center reticle just over its ears, nestled the fore-end into the shooting sticks, wriggled my back tight against the tree trunk, and locked my elbows in my knees. Exhale, increase the trigger pressure . . . Bang. I came out of recoil in time to see a tail flipping in the grass.

Lesson: It often pays to check carefully before giving up.

Too Excited

Veterans are supposed to be cool, calm, and collected.

Yeah, right.

I was hiking up a grassy draw with Rob Lancelotti in the beautiful desert mountains of extreme southwest Texas. We were shooting the then-new Remington R-15 rifles in .223 Rem, dressed neatly in Mossy Oak Brush camouflage and topped with big, 3-18x50mm Z6 Swarovski scopes. Fortunately we had the powers turned down to 5X because when we climbed out of a dry creek channel to set up on the bank, we spotted a coyote already hunting its way down a side-draw right toward us.

"There's one less than eighty yards away!" I whispered. "Get ready." Rob spread his bipod and nestled behind his rifle. I did the same. And then Rob hit just three short but quiet blasts on his mouth call. El Coyote popped right up. Inside of thirty yards. Can't miss range, and we each had five shots at our disposal without even the need to remove our fingers from the triggers.

We needed nearly all those rounds. I choked under pressure and jerked the trigger, pulling my shot low. Rob and I then proceeded to pour lead through those rifles as if they were designed for that. Roughly the ninth bullet downrange finally hit something other than dirt.

Lesson: Don't get excited. It's only a coyote. Yeah, right. Listen, when my heart no longer leaps at the site of a predator coming at me, I'm hanging up my calls. Laugh at your misses. They mean you're still having fun out there.

17

The Buddy System

Partner Tactics to Take More Game

After your calls, firearm, and ammo, a savvy partner could be your best tool for taking more game: another set of eyes and ears to spot sneaky cats or surprise-attack foxes and another shooter to take care of business when you're out of position. How about someone to help with skinning, share gas expenses, and help dig the truck out of a drift? There are plenty of great reasons to partner up. If you do, study your options, discuss them, and lay out a game plan before beginning your hunts. Over time, you'll fine-tune your system until the pair of you function as smoothly as the bow and stern of a canoe.

Get Your Backs Up

One of the most successful and common buddy tactics is to sit back-to-back in open country. This provides 360 degrees of coverage and backrests for both shooters, an adjunct to accuracy as long as you agree on a signal to indicate when you're about to shoot. My partners and I speak softly but clearly if predators are beyond one hundred yards and switch to shoulder nudges if we suspect they're

A seasoned hunting partner is often the best tactic for taking more game.

close enough to hear (one nudge could be an involuntary twitch, so the signal is two in a row).

Here's how a typical calling session progresses once one of us sees a customer:

"Got one. Southwest, four hundred yards. Oops. We've got a double. I'll tell you when to spin around." The coyotes disappear into a draw. "Okay!" Tom turns and sets up his shooting sticks to help me cover the southwest. By long-standing agreement, we both know the person who shoots first will take the closest animal or the one on his side if both are close. Establishing this order ahead of time allows both shooters to get their sights on the appropriate animal. Since we take turns shooting first and often forget the schedule, we clear that up before we begin a calling sequence and again as the action heats up, just to be sure. "Your turn, right?" I ask.

"Yes." Short and sweet. None of this "After you, dear Alphonse" politeness that often results in everyone passing up the best shot. By moving quickly, we are both settled into solid shooting positions when our visitors emerge from the draw, still loping in. The first is one hundred yards closer than the second, so I put my cross hairs on the far one and follow it in, ready to shoot at my first good opportunity after I hear Tom's shot. It is important that I concentrate on my animal and not attempt to watch Tom's. It's his responsibility, and I must trust him to handle it. My dog stops 150 yards out and stares in our direction. From this behavior, I assume it is a subordinate animal, probably younger than the close dog. I keep the cross hairs on its chest, wishing I could take the shot, telling myself to wait for the explosion of Tom's rifle. A second later it pops. My target spins to run straight away—a relatively easy shot. I hold the sight on its rump and flatten it.

Tom flashes me a quick grin, puts his call to his mouth and ki-yii-yipes like a frightened pup. We both resume our watch, but when nothing shows after five minutes, we rise to collect our trophies, ending a most successful little hunt. Onward to the next stand.

Any thinking hunter might ask, "Why not shoot the far coyote first since the close one will be easier to hit as it runs?" Here's my reasoning: A coyote in the hand is worth one in the

The back-to-back buddy system allows both hunters to cover more ground. Be certain both shooters know who is going to shoot first.

bush. The first shooter takes the closest dog because that's our surest chance to get at least one. If he were forced to take the farthest target, the near one could run us over or detect us and split before the far one even offers a decent standing shot. Also, there's a good chance a distant dog will remain standing after hearing a shot, stop upon hearing a wounded coyote call, or even return to such a call. A predator close to a shooter is more likely to see him recoil or reload. That animal will probably split for good.

Not all hunters subscribe to my theory. If you feel more comfortable trying for the distant animal first, go for it. Just be certain the shooters know their roles.

Near and Far

A productive variant within the back-to-back system is for one shooter to pack a rifle, the other a scatter-gun. When possible, the rifle hunter shoots first at any standing targets beyond shotgun range, and the partner cleans up the close-in runners. If a single animal approaches, the rifle hunter can shoot first and the shotgunner can bat cleanup, or the shotgunner can simply take all the close runners. Lots of options here. Just be sure each of you understands who bats first.

Separate but Equal

A useful alternative to sitting back-to-back is sitting apart to better cover approach avenues. This often means sitting forty to eighty yards apart on opposite sides of a ridge or hill in order to look over different draws or valleys. In these cases the hunters take their best shots when they're presented. What must be agreed upon before the calling begins is who will call. The caller then determines when the session ends. Here's how a typical setup would work:

Brad sits against a rusty, abandoned plow on the side of a hill overlooking a brushy draw. I slink over to the south side and sit against a juniper sapling just large enough to provide back support. We've agreed that I will call. I sit for a couple of minutes just in case Brad has decided to shift positions slightly or has forgotten to chamber a round. I double-check my chamber and the position of my shooting sticks, swinging my rifle in an arc and up and down to determine how much area I can conveniently cover. Then I move the sticks and swing through the area I think least likely to bring a customer. Satisfied, I return sticks and rifle to cover the original direction and start my call, softly. By my fourth series I am beginning to doubt, but I give it one more loud, twenty-second blast, then wait another three minutes. When nothing shows, I turn my head slowly, scanning the entire area. I can't see Brad because of the hill, so I whistle. He returns two whistles, our all-clear signal, and we quietly leave the area.

At our next stand, it's Brad's turn to call, but I double-check. "You're calling this stand, right?"

"Yup." It's always good to double-check to make sure you're on the same page. Nothing makes two hunters feel more foolish than sitting for half an hour waiting for the other guy to quit calling and blow the all-clear signal only to discover no one has been calling. Depending on wind speed and the lay of the land, it's often impossible to hear your partner calling. Winds are calm this time, though, and I hear Brad clearly. After only his first series, he sees a red fox slinking in cautiously. I have no idea it's in the area until I hear Brad switch from rabbit screams to a squeaker. Over the next minute he entices the fox closer, then shoots. I remain sitting, but scan the landscape for any sign of fleeing animals. A predator shot at and missed sometimes runs right into the arms of the noncalling partner—or at least into the noncaller's shooting lane. This time nothing shows, and Brad resumes calling. Since the fox responded so quickly, chances are good that a more distant predator hasn't even heard the calls. After Brad's fourth series with a clear, high-pitched cottontail cry, I spy a second fox trotting over the horizon. It drops into my draw and bounds over the grass, obviously confident. If it continues on a line to Brad's call, it will disappear into the bottom of the weedy draw, at which point it could slink along out of sight and possibly catch Brad's scent. If it plows straight through the cover, it will step into the clear less than thirty yards away for an easy shot. Even though it is now more than one hundred yards away, I determine that my best option is to try to shoot it before it reaches the cover, so I give a blast with my own call. The fox stops, I settle the cross hairs on its chest, and punch my lucky lotto ticket of the week. I hear Brad start the hurt-pup call, but after just two series, he whistles at me, I whistle back, and we retrieve our respective animals.

When partners sit far apart, announcing the conclusion of the stand becomes a critical interaction. The caller should decide when to quit, but usually won't know if his silent partner has anything approaching. If the caller simply stands and walks over, it ruins the game. Thus it is important that the caller proceed cautiously, first waiting three to five minutes after the last call to give any approaching game time to get within range. During this wait, the caller also listens for any calls from the partner, who may begin calling at any time in order to finish pulling in an interested shopper. If nothing is heard from the silent partner, the caller whistles once to signal quitting time. If the partner hears and agrees, he or she whistles twice to agree or once to say "No, stay for a while"—either because an animal has come into view or the partner has a hunch something may show.

I've tried using a no-whistle response to indicate a desire to stay. While this eliminates any chance that a predator will spook, it gives no indication that the initial querying whistle was even heard, and that gets confusing. A single whistle response often alerts predators, but it doesn't usually spook them, and it proves that the initial query was heard.

What if it's so windy neither hunter can hear the other's whistle? Then we switch to common-sense mode. The caller decides when to quit, scans all around slowly, and cautiously walks over to his partner, whistling when close enough to be heard. Sometimes my calling partner Kevin Howard carries a pair of Motorola Talk About radios. Whistle signals through the radios work every time. Just keep the volume turned low. Cell phones on vibrate work nicely, too.

Careful planning with a partner can increase your fun and harvest.

When hunting apart, make absolutely certain you know where your partner is sitting and vice versa. Don't change positions without signaling each other. The potential for a "mistaken game" shooting accident is too high. I prefer to sit completely hidden from my partner by solid ground. Where this isn't possible, our rule is that neither shoots into the area of coverage of the other—as if we're sitting back-to-back. Be careful. I can't overemphasize the inherent danger in this situation. You're expecting a furtive, naturally camouflaged animal to approach. Don't assume a vague shape or similarly colored flicker of motion is that animal. Be positively positive about identification before you shoot. I know of two conservation officers—both of whom taught hunter safety education classes—who changed positions in the fog while calling coyotes. When one saw the other's brown cap shift behind a bush where it wasn't supposed to be, he shot his partner in the head and back with buckshot. The man survived with permanent impairment. No predator is worth that.

The Downwind Partner

In places where cover enables responding predators to circle unseen and get your wind, try posting the noncaller one hundred to two hundred yards downwind from the caller in a location that provides a good view. Again, be careful which direction you shoot. Know where your partner is, and never shoot in that direction. A real danger in this scenario comes when a coyote walks between two shooters. Both must wait until the animal is well beyond any angle that could send a deflected shot toward the other. Ideally, use shotguns or highly frangible bullets in these situations to minimize ricochets.

Communicating over these distances is best arranged through simple hand signals or two-way radios. A raised cap, for instance, can signal "Quit."

Partners are not essential to successful calling. In fact, a second person can double your chances for screwing up if you don't thoroughly and carefully plan your strategies and fulfill your obligations. Do that, however, and you may double your pleasure, fun and harvest.

NOTES